I0114399

INTRODUCTION TO INTEGRAL PSYCHOLOGY:
INTEGRAL PSYCHOLOGY OF PERSONALITY DEVELOPMENT

Author

Dr. Chandrakant P. Patel, Ph. D.

(Specialisation in Integral Education and Integral Psychology)

The Mother's Study and Guidance Center
34215 Mimosa Terrace, Fremont, CA 94555, USA
Email: chandrakantpatel1@yahoo.com

First Edition: It consists of Revised Chapters 1, 4, 5 and 6 of the Study of the Psychological Foundation of the "Free Progress System" as Evolved in Sri Aurobindo International Centre of Education: 1986

Copyright © 2017 by Dr. Chandrakant P. Patel, Ph.D.

Extracts from Sri Aurobindo Ashram publications included in this book are copyrighted by Sri Aurobindo Ashram, Puducherry, 600 002, India.

Significance given by The Mother to the flower, Nelumbo nucifera, on the front cover:
    Avatar - the Supreme Manifested in a Body upon Earth
    The pink lotus is the flower of Sri Aurobindo.

ISBN: 979-8-9881859-0-1

Library of Congress Control Number: 2023906860

Published by: The Mother's Study and Guidance Center
34215 Mimosa Terrace, Fremont, CA 94555, USA
Email: chandrakantpatel1@yahoo.com

"The object sought after (by integral psychology) is not an individual achievement of divine realisation for the sake of the individual, but something to be gained for the earth-consciousness here, a cosmic, not solely a supra-cosmic achievement. The thing to be gained also is the bringing in of a Power of Consciousness (the supramental) not yet organised or active directly in earth nature, even in the spiritual life, but yet to be organised and made directly active."

– Sri Aurobindo; *Sri Aurobindo on Himself: SABCL Vol. 26; p.109*

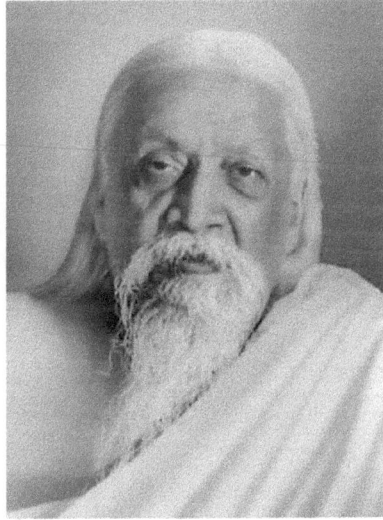

Offered at the feet of Sri Aurobindo and The Mother:

The Creator of Integral Yoga

AUTHOR: Patel Chandrakant P.; 34215 Mimosa Terrace, Fremont, CA 94555, USA; Email: chandrakantpatel1@yahoo.com.

Birth: Oct. 30, 1933

Study in Academy: Certificate in Intermediate Science (Mumbai University, India); Secondary Teaching Certificate (Government of Gujarat, India); B. A. Degree: Major Subjects: Eastern & Western Philosophy and Scientific Psychology & Indian Yogic Psychology (Gujarat University, Ahmedabad, the State of Gujarat, India); M.A. Degree: Scientific & Indian Yogic Psychology (Gujarat University, Ahmedabad, the State of Gujarat, India; Ph.D.: Integral Psychology & Integral Education (Saurashtra University, Rajkot, the Gujarat State, India).

Work in Academy: Primary, Secondary and Higher Secondary School Teacher for 9 years; State College Lecturer and University Post-Graduate Teacher, Integral Psychologist, Integral Psychotherapist and Integral Educationist, Worked in academy for 38 years.

Publications: Gujarati: *Tarkashashtrani Ruprekha* (**1970**), *Sukhi Jivan Mate Manovignan* (**1973**), *Sangnalaxi Adhunik Tarkashashtra* (1973), *Sri Arvind Ane Aryasamaj* (1973), *Samajlaxi Manovignan* (**1975**), *Balmanovignan* (**1982**), *Shikshan Mateni Mukta Pragati Paddhati* (**1985**), **English:** *Study of the Psychological Foundation of the 'Free Progress System' as evolved in Sri Aurobindo International Centre of Education* (**1986,** Ph. D. research report), **Gujarati:** *Samanya Manovignan*/General Psychology (**1991**). *Samajlaxi Manovignan* (**1995,** Graduate level); **English:** *Tics and Suicidal Proneness Treated with Integral Psychology* (**1999,** Research Report), *Studies in Integral Psychology, Integral Education and Integration of the Nation and the World* (1999), Ragging Activity at an Indian Institute of Technology and Action against it by Parent and His Son (1999); **Gujarati:** Sri Aravind ane Sri Matajina Samagratalakshi Manovignan Prakashman Abhyaso (1999), *Sri Sundaramna Porbandarmana Pravachano ane Chandrakant Patelne Patro* (1999); *Manav Vikas Chakra: Samajik Vikasnun Manovignan* (**2019,** translation of Sri Aurobindo's Book Human Cycle: The Psychology of Social Development); **Research Papers**: 20.

Unpublished Writings: Gujarati: Shaikshanik Nibandho: Collected Essays on Education (**1958-1959**), *Vaiyaktic Samayojananun Manovignan: Vyakhyan Nondho*: Psychology of Personal Adjustment: Lecture Notes (**1985**), *Samajik Vikas Chakra (Abridged) & Work Book for Human Cycle & English to Gujarati Dictionary of Terms in Human Cycle* (March 1974 — March 2000), Several Research Papers Submitted to and or Presented in National and International Conferences (**2000-2012**).

Life Member: World Union, Pondicherry; Sri Aurobindo Society, Pondicherry, India; Indian Science Congress Association, Kolkata, India; Vishva Sanskrit Pratisthanam, Varanasi, India; The Mother's Study and Guidance Centre (Center), Fremont, USA and Bangalore, India; Gujarat Gurukul Sabha, Gurukul Supa; Gujarati Sahitya Parishad, Ahmedabad, Gujarat, India; Common Cause, New Delhi, India; NBT Book Club, New Delhi, India; All Indian Psychological Association, New Delhi; Gujarat Psychology Association, Vallabh Vidyanagar, Gujarat, India; Indian Academy of Applied Psychology, Chennai, India; **Member:** Association of Transpersonal Psychology, Palo Alto, California, USA.

Activities: South Asian Unity and World Unity and Global Peace, Spiritualisation of himself and the Society and Study and Promotion of Integral Psycho-philosophy in Academic world.

WORDS OF THE MOTHER AND SRI AUROBINDO THAT A READER AND SADHAK OF INTEGRAL PSYCHOLOGY SHOULD REMEMBER

"To the Students, Young and Old

"THERE are, in the history of the earth, moments of transition when things that have existed for thousands of years must give way to those that are about to manifest. A special concentration of the world consciousness, one might almost say, an intensification of its effort, occurs at such times, varying according to the kind of progress to be made, the quality of the transformation to be realised. We are at precisely such a turning-point in the world's history. Just as Nature has already created upon earth a mental being, man, so too there is now a concentrated activity in this mentality to bring forth a supramental consciousness and individuality."[1]

THE MOTHER

***   ***   ***

"For the sadhaka of the integral Yoga it is necessary to remember that no written Shastra, however great its authority or however large its spirit, can be more than a partial expression of the eternal Knowledge. He will use, but never bind himself even by the greatest Scripture. Where the Scripture is profound, wide, catholic, it may exercise upon him an influence for the highest good and of incalculable importance. It may be associated in his experience with his awakening to crowning verities and his realisation of the highest

---

[1] The Mother; *On Education CWM Vol. 12 (travel size)* (Publisher: Madanlal Himmatsingka on behalf of All India Books, Pondicherry, 605002, India, 1984); p. 70

experiences. His Yoga may be governed for a long time by one Scripture or by several successively, — if it is in the line of the great Hindu tradition, by the Gita, for example, the Upanishads, the Veda. Or it may be a good part of his development to include in its material a richly varied experience of the truths of many Scriptures and make the future opulent with all that is best in the past. But in the end he must take his station, or better still, if he can, always and from the beginning he must live in his own soul beyond the limitations of the word that he uses. The Gita itself thus declares that the Yogin in his progress must pass beyond the written Truth, — *śabdabrahmātivartate* — beyond all that he has heard and all that he has yet to hear, — *śrotavyasya śrutasya ca*. For he is not the sadhaka of a book or of many books; he is a sadhaka of the Infinite."[2]

SRI AUROBINDO

---

[2] Sri Aurobindo; *The Synthesis of Yoga I-II; CWSA Vol. 23-24* (Publisher: Sri Aurobindo Ashram Publication Department, Sri Aurobindo Ashram, Pondicherry, 605002, India, 1999); p. 55

PREFACE

Yoga = applied psychology: Yoga is in fact applied psychology. For, the Science of Yoga (योगशास्त्र) is theoretical and practical knowledge of the development of consciousness and human personality. Nowadays, many kinds of yoga are practiced all over the world. Integral yoga is one of them and the most comprehensive. It is a science of evolutionary development. Sri Aurobindo and The Mother have jointly found and established it. It is an entirely new yoga, a new applied psychology. One of its objective is to develop current human personality into supramental personality and realise the next stage of evolution on earth.

The text of this book starts with describing the nature of integral psychology. Then, follows the description of creation of the universe and evolution of man on earth. Next, it describes the structure and nature of human consciousness and personality in the context of terrestrial evolution. After that are noted goals and methods of perfection of human personality. Application of integral psychology in Business is suggested by presenting a plan of application of it in hotel business.

The description and discussion of integral psychology is more conceptual and less descriptive. Author wants to add operational definitions of concepts by adding human behaviours and activities that illustrate their meanings. It is necessary to do so, for the language of integral psychology is in certain aspects different from the languages of other kinds of current and old psychology. It is also imperative for making the text easier for beginner students. More explanatory elaborations will be included in the second edition. It will be profitable if the readers refer Dictionaries of Integral Yoga.

Thanks are due to my son Kant and my daughter-in-law Falguni for helping me in certain editorial tasks. I have to thank Sri H. P. Rama for encouraging me to develop a shorter and easier text of integral psychology from my previous longer one. I am grateful to Copyright Sections of Sri Aurobindo Ashram and Sri Aurobindo Society to allow

ix

me to include writings of their publications. I have referred to some other writings that prove validity of integral psychology; I am to thank them also. And I bow, in reverence, to The Mother and Sri Aurobindo, whose Grace constantly guides my intellect and my efforts of sadhana.

If students and teachers of the Department of Integral Studies as well as other readers of this book would send their comments and suggestions to the author, it will be a great help to him in the work of not only the present revision but also in the writing of advance level text of integral psychology, which he has already commenced. (March 12, 2017)

Chandrakant P. Patel (The Mother's Study and Guidance Center)
34215 Mimosa Terrace, Fremont, CA 94555, USA
Email: chandrakantpatel1@yahoo.com

To the Instructor:

The Mother's writing is easier to read and understand. Sri Aurobindo's writing is pretty difficult. So, it would be more helpful for understanding difficult concepts of integral yoga and integral psychology, if her books and Collected Works of The Mother are referred to often. Dictionaries or Glossaries of Terms in Sri Aurobindo's Writing are also much helpful in the study of integral yoga and integral psychology. The author of this book has tried to mention references of The Mother's books also, so as to provide ready reference to readers. Author would like to request the instructor to establish live contact with him.

Students may be assigned to do projects, to do exercises, to write summaries of some part of the text, to give and participate in seminars on chosen topics in class. To select topics for such work, the workbook at the end of the chapter may be referred to.

Students may be encouraged to maintain a private personal journal of personal experience received due to practice of integral psychology they study for self-development. That will help each student to self-observe, to self-progress and create his personal dynamic *Shastra* of integral Living and psychology.

To the Students:

Survey Q 3R: An Effective Method of Study

A student should choose the highest and widest aim of study: To understand, to remember and to practice it not only for passing the examination but for eternity. If one reads only for the test, one's mind will concentrate only on the subject-matter that is considered important for passing the test, and thus motivated it will tend to forget the thing read after the test has passed. While if one reads with an aspiration for permanent retention and for continuous practice in life, the mind is motivated to hold, apply and increase the knowledge continuously and feel the joy of growing.

One may follow the psychological method, "the Survey Q3R Method of Study", suggested below:

Use the *Survey Q3R Method of study*:

SURVEY:

1. Survey the whole book:

Read [1] four cover pages and [2] the introductory and prefatory pages (forward, preface, Index of Chapters, the lists of figures, tables, appendices and any other matter that is there), [3] main headings and/or sub-headings of all the chapters if they are not in the main Index and

2. Survey the first chapter: Read title-head and section-heads of the chapter. Then read the text of the chapter fast from beginning to end without stopping and waiting to understand anything you do not understand.

QUESTIONS:

Read questions at the end of each chapter.

3R: Read, Recite and Review:

READ, remembering your aim of study, the first topic of the chapter very carefully to understand it completely as much as possible. Refer dictionary for meaning of the words.

RECITE: If topic is lengthy, stop periodically and try to recall what you have read and thus recite. After reaching the end of the topic, recite the whole topic. You may list main points of the topic read and check with text if any main point is missing. Read all topics of a chapter in this manner. When you have completed the chapter recall in mind all main ideas in the chapter and ascertain if any is missed.

REVIEW: At the end of the study of the chapter, answer briefly the questions given at the end of the chapter silently to yourself. All chapters are to be read in this manner. Review the whole text before you appear at the final test. Only main points may be recalled in mind or noted down on paper. While reviewing the portions whose details do not appear in the mind may be read. Do not bother if you feel certain portions to be too difficult to understand and grasp. A few reviews during the semester of the learned portions may be good.

IN MEMORY OF

Norman C. Dowsett (1908-1984)

In 1942 he met Sri Aurobindo and The Mother in Pondicherry, and three years later became a permanent member of their Ashram. He participated in the free progress education at the Sri Aurobindo International Centre of Education, where he taught for 25 years and later, in 1970, he started this type of education in the newly founded international township of Auroville. In 1971, he took the directorship of the Department of Educational Research and Development of the Sri Aurobindo Society in Pondicherry. With a multinational team he pursued his Research in Education, based on Sri Aurobindo's psycho-philosophy, until his passing away in June 1984. He was a prolific writer and a poet.

Also IN MEMORY OF

Prof. Haribhai G. Desai (1925-1985)

Prof. Desai, a U.G.C. national lecturer, a reformist and an author of 15 books and 25 research papers four of which fetched state level awards, had his bachelor's and master's degrees in education from the Gujarat University with first rank to his credit and Ph.D. degree in psychology from the University of New Mexico, U.S.A. He taught at school level for nine years and then at University level in the Department of Education. He was the Acting Vice-Chancellor of the University twice and had worked as resource person for numerous workshops, etc. at State and all-India level.

Also IN MEMORY OF

Dr. Indra Sen (1903-1994)

Dr. Indra Sen taught psychology and philosophy in the Delhi University from 1928 to 1944. During this period, from 1931 to 1933, he studied The Psychology of C. G. Jung at the University of Freiburg and was awarded a Ph.D. degree by the University. He also attended lectures of Martin Heidegger and taught Indian Philosophy and Sanskrit at the University of Konigsberg, Germany. He is the first person to investigate a case of incarnation, which was known as "Shanti Devi" case. The study report stands even today as a significant scientific document. In 1939 he came into contact with Sri Aurobindo and The Mother and devoted himself to the study and sadhana of integral yoga under them. He joined Sri Aurobindo Ashram in 1945 and taught integral psychology at Sri Aurobindo International Centre of Education. He is the first person to coin the word integral psychology, and the first author of Integral Psychology. He authored the book "Integral psychology". It is the first comprehensive book on General Integral Psychology. Thus, he is the originator of Auromere Integral Psychology. A rational psychologist Dr. H. C. Ganguli, Professor of Psychology, University of Delhi, appreciates the book with the words: "Dr. Indra Sen's book is the first serious and systematic attempt by an Indian psychologist to expound the thoughts of Sri Aurobindo in the language of psychology. Many of us (Psychologists) are beholden to him for this. He is prolific writer of integral psychology and Integral Education, Integral Philosophy and integral Yoga." A few of his books on Psychology are (i) Sri Aurobindo on Yoga (Hind Kitabs, Paper Back, Delhi (ii) The Integral Man, Mysore University, (iii) The Urge for Wholeness, Presidential Address, Psychology Section, Indian Science Congress, 1946, "Sri Arvindka Jeevan Darshan, Sasta Sahitya Mandal, Delhi".

CONTENT

INDEX OF PICTURES

INDEX OF BOXES

INDEX OF TABLES

INDEX OF FIGURES

INDEX OF APPENDICES AT
THE END OF EACH CHAPTER

ABBREVIATIONS USED

AU	=	Auro University, Surat, India
CWM Vol. 2	=	The Mother, *Words of Long Ago,* (Pondicherry: Sri Aurobindo Ashram, 1978)
CWM Vol. 3	=	The Mother, *Questions and Answers 1929-1931,* (Pondicherry: Sri Aurobindo Ashram, 1977)
CWM Vol. 4	=	The Mother, *Questions and Answers 1950-1951,* (Pondicherry: Sri Aurobindo Ashram, 1972)
CWM Vol. 5	=	The Mother, *Questions and Answers 1953,* (Pondicherry: Sri Aurobindo Ashram, 1976)
CWM Vol. 6	=	The Mother, *Questions and Answers 1954,* (Pondicherry: Sri Aurobindo Ashram, 1979)
CWM Vol. 7	=	The Mother, *Questions and Answers 1955,* (Pondicherry: Sri Aurobindo Ashram, 1979)
CWM Vol. 8	=	The Mother, *Questions and Answers 1956,* (Pondicherry: Sri Aurobindo Ashram, 1977)
CWM Vol. 9	=	The Mother, *Questions and Answers 1957-1958,* (Pondicherry: Sri Aurobindo Ashram, 1977)
CWM Vol. 10	=	The Mother, *On Thoughts and Aphorisms,* (Pondicherry: Sri Aurobindo Ashram, 1977)
CWM Vol. 11	=	The Mother, *Notes on the Way,* (Pondicherry: Sri Aurobindo Ashram, 1980)
CWM Vol. 12	=	The Mother, *On Education,* (Pondicherry: Sri Aurobindo Ashram, 1978)
CWM Vol. 13	=	The Mother, *Words of the Mather - I,* (Pondicherry: Sri Aurobindo Ashram, 1980)
CWM Vol. 14	=	The Mother, *Words of the Mother - II,* (Pondicherry: Sri Aurobindo Ashram, 1980)

CWM Vol. 15   =   The Mother, *Words of the Mother - III,* (Pondicherry: Sri Aurobindo Ashram, 1980)

CWSA   =   COLLECTED WORKS OF SRI AUROBINDO

CWSA Vol. 19   =   Sri Aurobindo; *Essays on the Gita* (Sri Aurobindo Ashram, Pondicherry, 605002, India, 1997)

D.E.R.A.D   =   Department of Educational Research and Development, Sri Aurobindo Society, Pondicherry, 605002, India

IP   =   Integral Psychology

ISOL   =   Integral Science of Living

ITIP   =   Introduction to Integral Psychology

ITP   =   Introduction to Psychology

N.C.E.R.T   =   National Council of Educational Research and Training, New Delhi

PATEL   =   Patel C. P.; *Psychological Foundation of the "Free Progress System" as Evolved in Sri Aurobindo International Centre of Education* (Publisher: Sri Aurobindo Study Circle (Bokhira-Porbandar), Bokhira, Gujarat, 360579, India, 1986)

SABCL Vol   =   Sri Aurobindo Birth Centenary Library, Popular Edition, Volume

SABCL Vol. 3   =   Sri Aurobindo, *The Harmony of Virtue,* (Pondicherry: Sri Aurobindo Ashram, 1972)

SABCL Vol. 5   =   Sri Aurobindo, *Collected Poems,* (Pondicherry: Sri Aurobindo Ashram, 1972)

SABCL Vol. 8   =   Sri Aurobindo, *The Translations,* (Pondicherry: Sri Aurobindo Ashram, 1972)

SABCL Vol. 9   =   Sri Aurobindo, *The Future Poetry,* (Pondicherry: Sri Aurobindo Ashram, 1972)

SABCL Vol.10   =   Sri Aurobindo, *The Secret of the Veda,* (Pondicherry: Sri Aurobindo Ashram, 1971)

SABCL Vol. 12 = Sri Aurobindo, *The Upanishads,* (Pondicherry: Sri Aurobindo Ashram, 1972)

SABCL Vol. 13 = Sri Aurobindo, *Essays on the Gita,* (Pondicherry: Sri Aurobindo Ashram, 1970

SABCL Vol. 15 = Sri Aurobindo, *Social and Political Thought,* (Pondicherry: Sri Aurobindo Ashram, 1971)

SABCL Vol. 16 = Sri Aurobindo, *The Supramental Manifestation,* (Pondicherry: Sri Aurobindo Ashram, 1971)

SABCL Vol. 17 = Sri Aurobindo, *The Hour of God,* (Pondicherry: Sri Aurobindo Ashram, 1972)

SABCL Vol. 18 = Sri Aurobindo, *The Life Divine Book I Part I & Book II Part I,* (Pondicherry: Sri Aurobindo Ashram, 1970)

SABCL Vol. 19 = Sri Aurobindo, *The Life Divine Book II Part II,* (Pondicherry: Sri Aurobindo Ashram, 1970)

SABCL Vol. 20 = Sri Aurobindo, *The Synthesis of Yoga Part I & II,* (Pondicherry: Sri Aurobindo Ashram, 1971)

SABCL Vol. 21 = Sri Aurobindo, *The Synthesis of Yoga Part III & IV,* (Pondicherry: Sri Aurobindo Ashram, 1971)

SABCL Vol. 22 = Sri Aurobindo, *Letters on Yoga Part I,* (Pondicherry: Sri Aurobindo Ashram, 1970)

SABCL Vol. 23 = Sri Aurobindo, *Letters on Yoga Part II & III,* (Pondicherry: Sri Aurobindo Ashram, 1970)

SABCL Vol. 24 = Sri Aurobindo, *Letters on Yoga Part IV,* (Pondicherry: Sri Aurobindo Ashram, 1970)

SABCL Vol. 25 = Sri Aurobindo, *The Mother,* (Pondicherry: Sri Aurobindo Ashram, 1972)

SABCL Vol. 26 = Sri Aurobindo, *On Himself,* (Pondicherry: Sri Aurobindo Ashram, 1972)

SABCL Vol. 27 = Sri Aurobindo, *Supplement,* (Pondicherry: Sri Aurobindo Ashram, 1972)

SABCL Vol. 28 = Sri Aurobindo, *Savitri Part I* (Pondicherry: Sri Aurobindo Ashram, 1970)

SABCL Vol. 29 = Sri Aurobindo, *Savitri Part II & III,* (Pondicherry: Sri Aurobindo Ashram, 1970)

SABDA = Sri Aurobindo Books Distribution Agency, Pondicherry, 605002, India

S.A.I.C.E = Sri Aurobindo International Centre of Education, Pondicherry, 605002, India

RECOMMENDED REFERENCE BOOKS

1. Indra Sen; *Integral Psychology* (Publisher: Sri Aurobindo International Centre of Education, Pondicherry, India, 1986); pp. xvi+381

   The author is the first person to coin the word integral psychology and to conceive the idea of deriving theory and praxis of it from Sri Aurobindo and The Mother's writings; Prof. Indra Sen, in that sense, is the founder of integral psychology. It is a seminal and model and first published book on Integral Psychology in the format of Rational Psychology. If students of integral psychology identify the seeds of numerous applications of integral psychology and develop them, all fields of life would be completely explained and both the traditional psychology and the Integral Psychology would be enriched.

2. Tulsidas Chatterjee, *Sri Aurobindo's Integral Yoga* (Publisher: Tulsidas Chatterjee, 22, Bajeshibpur Road, Howrah-2, West Bengal, Available with The Secretary, Sri Aurobindo Ashram, Pondicherry, 600 002, India; 1970), pp. 365

   This treatise of integral psychology presents the findings of integral yoga given by Sri Aurobindo and The Mother in a pristine and summary form. The book presents a comprehensive theory and practice (blended into each other) of integral psychology (yoga).

3. Acharya K. D.; *Guide to Sri Aurobindo's Philosophy* (Publisher: Divya Jivan Sahitya Prakashan, Pondicherry, 605 002, India); pp.222

   It is a unique dictionary of terms of integral yoga (psycho-philosophy) in which meanings of terms are given in words of Sri Aurobindo and The Mother and terms are so arranged in serial order that the dictionary presents a statement of real comprehensive integral psychology.

4. Patel Chandrakant P.; *Study of the Psychological Foundation of the "Free Progress System" as evolved in Sri Aurobindo International Centre of Education;* (Publisher: Sri Aurobindo Study Circle-(Bokhira), Gujarat, 360579, India, Publisher's new address: The Mother's Study and Guidance Centre (Center), 34215 Mimosa Terrace, Fremont, CA 94555, USA, Edition of 1986; Distributor: SABDA, Sri Aurobindo Ashram, Pondicherry, 605002)

    It is the first Ph. D. level study of integral psychology done under the guidance of Dr. Indra Sen, Prof. of psychology, Sri Aurobindo International Centre of education, Sri Aurobindo Ashram, Pondicherry, 605002, India and Prof. Norman Dowsett, Director of the Department of Educational Research and Development, Sri Aurobindo Society, Pondicherry, 605 002, India, and Dr. H. G. Desai, The Head of the Department of Education, Saurashtra University, Rajkot, Gujarat, India. The study was recognised as an innovative educational research by the National Council of Education, Research and Training, The Government of India, New Delhi, India. The study used multi-research methods and includes a specially constructed Questionnaire for measuring development in the personality of the students exposed to the system of integral education under experiment in the SAICE (Sri Aurobindo International Centre of Education). Researchers may view it.

5. Jyoti and Prem Sobel; *The Hierarchy of Minds: The Mind Levels* (Publisher: Sri Aurobindo Ashram, Pondicherry, 605 002, India, 1984); pp. 174

    It is a compilation of writings of Sri Aurobindo on five minds of man and corresponding five minds of universe. It can be extremely useful to scholar and students of psychology and also to students studying this course.

6. Purani A. B.; આર્યમાનસશાસ્ત્ર યાને ચિત્તંત્રની રૂપરેખા: *Arya Manasshastra Yane Cittantranii Rooprekha* (Publisher: Mulajibhai Tri. Talati, Pathic Prakashan Mandir, Umreth, Gujarat, India, August 1967)

> Sri A. B. Purani, was a very close disciple and a sadhak practicing integral yoga under the guidance of Sri Aurobindo and The Mother. He is a versatile student of Eastern and Western thought and authority on Sri Aurobindo and The Mother and he has lucidly discussed two opposite standpoints of psychology.

7. Dalal A. S. (Ed.); *A Greater Psychology* (Publisher: Sri Aurobindo Ashram, Puducherry, 605 002, India, 2008); pp. 325-335

> A very good book on Integral Psychology. It provides an introduction to the Psychological Thought of Sri Aurobindo.

8. Dalal A. S. (Ed.); *Sri Aurobindo and the Future Psychology* (Publisher: Sri Aurobindo Ashram, Puducherry, 605 002, India, 2008); Supplement to a Greater Psychology.

> A very good book on Integral Psychology. History and limitations of Scientific Psychology is also discussed.

RECOMMENDED ORIGINAL SOURCE LITERATURE FOR LIFE LONG CONTINUOUS LEARNING: SRI AUROBINDO AND THE MOTHER'S WRITINGS

1. Georges Van Vrekhem (Editor); *The Mother's Vision* (Publisher: Sri Aurobindo Ashram, Pondicherry, 605002, India)

   It is a good compilation from Sri Auromere's writings on integral psychology and would be very useful to the students of this course.

2. Sri Aurobindo Birth Centenary Library Vol. 1-30 (Publisher: Sri Aurobindo Ashram, Pondicherry, 605002, India)

   Note: The Last Index Volume would help to locate relevant matter on integral psychology in the Collected Works of Sri Aurobindo Vol. 1-36 (Publisher: Sri Aurobindo Ashram, Pondicherry, 605002, India).

3. Collected Works of The Mother Vol. 1-17 (Publisher: Sri Aurobindo Ashram, Pondicherry, 605002, India)

   Note: Each of the volumes has subject index at the end and in the beginning, index of chapters' titles and sub-titles. Both indexes are much useful for locating reference for any subject of integral psychology.

CHAPTER I

TO GROW INTO A SUPRAMENTAL DIVINE BEING IS THE REAL BUSINESS OF MAN

Since the beginning of human life on earth, various disciplines have been used for developing human being and his personality and consciousness. They are either social, ethical, religious, psychological or spiritual or some combinations of these disciplines. They have been useful and are still useful. The yogic, psychological and spiritual disciplines are more comprehensive, more effective, surer and more endurable than other developmental disciplines. But the latest yogic psychology called integral psychology is the most far-reaching and the most effective and truly holistic psychology (पूर्ण चित्तशास्त्र/मनोविज्ञान); it ensures the mundane (पार्थिव), psychic-spiritual (आत्मिक-आध्यात्मिक) and supramental (अतिमानसिक) perfection of the nature and soul (प्रकृति व अन्तरात्मा) of individual, society and even cosmos.

Mind, with its highest logical capacity and scientific findings, confidently hoped to create a heavenly life on the earth. Instead, it has brought fruits of mechanical life, inhumanness, alienation, anxiety, pollution, strife and constantly impending threat of total annihilation of mankind and its civilization by nuclear world war. America dropped two nuclear bombs on the cities of Hiroshima and Nagasaki of Japan in 1946. Those bombs burned to death millions of man, animal, vegetation and made large areas of earth barren in a fraction of a moment. Seeing this unprecedented catastrophic results, nuclear governments vow not to repeat the mistake and are promoting the ideal of non-proliferation of nuclear arms and ban on the use of nuclear arms in war. And yet they wouldn't desire to destroy the stockpile of nuclear arms and cease to produce more lethal nuclear arms and increase the stockpile. Survival instinct of mind is not victorious over the killer instinct. This is a glaring

1

example of failure and duplicity of mind of reason. Mind has thus proved itself inadequate for solving the problems of humanity.

The knowledge of science and scientific psychology has been applied to better the life of man and society, and life has considerably profited from this endeavour no doubt, but at the same time reaped poisonous fruits of serious psychological and social problems and aberrations also. Research studies in industrial and business management made with spiritual approach[3] infer that corporate big business guided by science, scientific psychology and profit-centered economy has created serious problems in human life. It has dehumanized man. CEOs and top administrators in business offices have been found to have more mental breakdowns than people labouring at lower hierarchy. Psychologists and social scientists say that industrial age has created a negative culture of stress, depression, suicide, divorce, assault, aggressive and angry behaviour, disease, rape, sexual aberrations, etc. The scientific psychology is knowledge created by mind and it has not been able to provide joyful, peaceful, harmonious and loveful life, which it had promised. Isn't there a way that can lead humanity out from this dark alley? Our ancient fathers knew the way and today Sri Aurobindo and The Mother has created the integral yogic knowledge that can illumine the darkness enveloping human life. Integral psychology is derived from integral yoga.

---

[3] Ramakrishna Mission, Rajkot (Organiser); "*Two-Day Workshop (1-2 July, 1995) on Indian Ethos for Management*", Themes: *Spiritual Approach for Strength, Harmony and Success, New Leaders – Rajarshis and Holistic Way for Excellence and Productivity in Global Competition* (Sri Ramakrishna Ashram, Dr. Yagnik Road, Rajkot, Gujarat, 360 001, India; 1995); [The book "*Indian Ethos for Management*" from the same publisher (pp.164) contains Vedantic Holistic Spiritual Psychology given by Swami Vivekananda, a mighty resurgent force of India; this book indicates a solution of the human problems created by corporate large Industries]; **A few other books that describe application of Yogic/Spiritual psychology in business management:** Malik Pravir; *India's Contribution to Management: A Vision* (Publisher: Sri Aurobindo Institute of Research in Social Sciences, Sri Aurobindo Society, Pondicherry, 605 002, India; 2000); pp. 162+09; Gupta G. P. (Ed.); *Management by Consciousness* (Publisher: Sri Aurobindo Institute of Research in Social Sciences, Sri Aurobindo Society, Pondicherry, 605 002, India; 2009); pp. 202

Mind, according to Sri Aurobindo and The Mother's integral psychology, is not the last summit of consciousness available to man. There is a latent inner and higher consciousness of man which he can realise and make dynamic in his life. There is also a still higher consciousness, the supramental consciousness, into which he can evolve. It is by rising into the supramental consciousness and organizing life with its light and power that man shall have enduring solutions to his problems, individual and collective. Man will realise then the ever cherished ancient dream of a golden age on earth. So, to evolve a nucleus of community life which moves by the supramental consciousness Sri Aurobindo established his Ashram at Pondicherry in 1926 with the Mother as its spiritual head. The Mother, after Sri Aurobindo left his material sheath, continued his work and created in addition an international city near Pondicherry for the same purpose. People inspired by these two projects and integral yoga have organised organisations to achieve the same objective of evolution. It seems, Yoga-Shakti has moved out of seclusion in forest dwelling to work in the entire field of earth. The sensitive ears hear the tinkling footfalls of the Supramental God nearing the earth.

This being the prospectus of integral yoga and integral psychology academies should teach and students, who are future managers of social life, should learn courses on integral psychology and integral science of living.

In this small treatise on integral psychology, an attempt has been made to present a statement of integral psychology of personal development. Chapter two explains the nature of the science of integral psychology and limitations of other psychologies. The third chapter explains creation of the universe and earth and advent of human being on earth. The fourth one briefly describes two interacting factors of heredity and environment that develop human personality. Chapter five dwells on the planes and parts of consciousness of human being and the cardinal method of their development. Chapters six through thirteen delve into various details of each of these planes and parts of consciousness along with techniques for perfection. Chapter fourteen presents the process and goals of personality development and chapter fifteen explains the principles of development. Chapter sixteen briefly describes the perfection of the triple being. Chapter seventeen notes the applications of integral psychology in hotel business, and chapter eighteen presents a summary of findings and the conclusion.

Suggestions for Further Reading

Swami Jitatmananda; *Indian Ethos for Management* (Publisher: Sri Ramakrishna Ashram, Dr. Yagnik Road, Rajkot, Gujarat, 360 001, India; 1995); pp. 164

WORKBOOK: QUESTIONS FOR PREVIEW AND REVIEW

Essay Type Questions

1. Why do management students need to learn Integral Psychology and Integral Science of living?

Short Answer Type Questions:

1. What type of development of personality integral psychology ensures? Give answer in a short paragraph.

Exercise

1. Create a list of benevolent and adverse effects of large corporate business on individual and the society and create a list of practices that enhance benevolent effects and diminish or eliminate adverse effects.

CHAPTER II

DEFINITION AND NATURE (SCOPE, METHOD AND PURPOSE) OF INTEGRAL PSYCHOLOGY

I. DEFINITIONS OF INTEGRAL PSYCHOLOGY

II. THE SOURCE LITERATURE OF INTEGRAL PSYCHOLOGY

1. Sri Aurobindo's Writings Documented in Sri Aurobindo Birth Centenary Library
   (i) Primary Source Literature
   (ii) Secondary Source Literature
2. The Mother's Writings
3. The Vastness of Psychological Writing of Sri Aurobindo and The Mother is Amazing.
4. Sri Aurobindo and The Mother's Knowledge is a Dynamic Force for Developing One's Personality and Knowledge and for developing Different Branches of Integral Psychology.
5. Integral Psychology can be called Sri Auromere's Psychology.

III. SRI AUROMERE'S PSYCHOLOGY IS INTEGRAL IN NATURE

1. Its Field of Study is Integral.
2. Aim of Integral Psychology is Integral.
3. Method of Integral Psychology is Integral:
   (i) Super-Rational Method: Method of Direct Knowledge, Metaphysical Method
   (ii) Rational Scientific Method

IV. OTHER CHARACTERISTICS OF INTEGRAL PSYCHOLOGY

1. It is a Compound of Science and Metaphysical Knowledge.
2. It is an Evolutionary Psychology.

5

3. It is a Truly Yogic Psychology.
4. It is an Experimental Psychology.
5. Sri Auromere's Integral Psychology can be called a Global Psychology.
6. Continuous Study and Practice of Integral Yoga or Psychology is Necessary for Self-perfection.
7. A Learner and Practitioner of Integral Psychology must Approach the Supramental Wisdom Given by Sri Aurobindo and The Mother with Open Mind.
8. The Term psychology is in Fact Applicable to Integral Psychology only, not to the scientific psychology.
9. It is a Fast Developing Psychology.
10. Conscious and Constant Reliance on The Mother's force is a must for Realising Transformation of nature (*Prakriti*).

V. INTEGRAL PSYCHOLOGY COMPARED TO SCIENTIFIC PSYCHOLOGY AND OTHER YOGIC PSYCHOLOGY

1. Scientific Psychology is Becoming More Complete.
2. Sri Aurobindo and The Mother's Remarks on Psychoanalysis
3. The Mother's Remark on the Study of Scientific Psychology
4. Integral Psychology and Old Yoga and Indian Psychology

Pictures:
(2.1) Neurosurgeon Dr. Eben Alexander, M. D
(2.2) Sri Aurobindo
(2.3) Sri Krishna
(2.4) The Mother as she was when infantryman John actually met her in 1966
(2.5) The heaven Lady (The Mother) as infantryman John saw her on the battlefield of World War II in 1944
(2.6) "Great Sir": Sri Aurobindo as seen by infantryman John on the battlefield of World War II in 1944

Sri Aurobindo and The Mother's (Sri Auromere's) integral psychology, like their integral yoga from which it is derived, is a developmental psychology based on yogic experiences experienced during performance of integral yoga by them and by their disciples living in Sri Aurobindo Ashram, Pondicherry, India, and in Auroville, Tamil Nadu, India and living elsewhere. The aim of integral yoga is to manifest the supramental consciousness in subtle physical atmosphere of earth and develop man into superman and the mental society of today into a supramental-society and thus prepare ground for the descent of a new supramental species of man on earth. Naturally, integral psychology must have the same aim. The author of this book, is unable to perceive difference in aim, method and field of integral yoga and integral psychology; they seem synonymous to him; and so he has used in narrations and discussions of the subject both names, integral psychology and integral yoga for each other. Reader should bear this thing in mind while reading this book.

If a reader has never read literature on integral yoga and integral psychology, he will come across concepts and statements mentioned without their descriptive meaning given; he will have to refer to other chapters, where they are described in detail. Cross references noted and the index will help him to do so.

I. DEFINITIONS OF INTEGRAL PSYCHOLOGY

1. "I mean by Yogic psychology an examination of the nature and movements of consciousness as they are revealed to us by the processes and results of Yoga."[4] [**Sri Aurobindo**]

Obviously, this definition is applicable to all kinds of yoga and all kinds of psychological knowledge based on them, such as *Ashtang*

---

[4] Sri Aurobindo; "Psychology, the Science of Consciousness", *Bulletin of Sri Aurobindo International Centre of Education*, XXX, 2 (April, 1978); (Publisher: Sri Aurobindo Ashram, Pondicherry, 605 002, India); p. 4

Yoga (*अष्टांग योग*) and *Psychology of Ashtang Yoga, Yoga of Gita and Psychology of Gita, Sankhya Yoga (सांख्य योग) and Psychology of Sankhya Yoga and so on.* Sri Aurobindo's this definition of Yoga suggests the following specific definition of Integral Psychology.

2. Integral Yogic psychology (or integral psychology) is an examination of the nature and movements of consciousness as they are revealed to us by the processes and results of Integral Yoga, or say by the practice of the integral yogic psychology.

3. The psychology that aims at possessing the fullness of God is *Purna* (पूर्ण) Psychology (Integral Psychology).

This definition is based on Sri Aurobindo's statement quoted below:

> "By yoga we can rise out of falsehood into truth, out of weakness into force, out of pain and grief into bliss, out of bondage into freedom, out of death into immortality, out of darkness into light, out of confusion into purity, out of Maya into God. All other utilisation of Yoga is for special and fragmentary advantages not always worth pursuing. Only that which aims at possessing the fullness of God is *Purna* (पूर्ण) Yoga; the *sadhak* of the Divine Perfection (दिव्य पूर्णता) is the *Purna* (पूर्ण) Yogin."[5].

It means integral yoga aims at evolving lower triple physical-vital-mental consciousness of human being gradually through spiritual and supramental consciousness into the Supreme Divine Consciousness; *Details of this evolutionary aim are described in chapter III under the captions devolution and evolution.*

---

[5] Sri Aurobindo; SABCL Vol. 17; p. 61 [Sri Aurobindo's early writings on Integral Yoga and Psychology and evolution are in this volume from p.7-76 and are interesting.]

4. "Psychology is the science of consciousness and its states and operations in Nature (प्रकृति) and, if that can be glimpsed or experienced, its states and operations beyond what we know as Nature (प्रकृति)."[6] **[Sri Aurobindo]**

5. Systematic record of the experiences experienced during performance of integral yoga is called integral psychology. **[Chandrakant P. Patel]**

6. Integral psychology is the study of man and the society in the universe. **[Chandrakant P. Patel]**

7. Integral psychology is the study of all planes and parts of the human consciousness in the context of all planes and parts of the social consciousness, universal consciousness and the transcendental consciousness. **[Chandrakant P. Patel]**

8. Integral psychology is the study of involution of transcendental consciousness into inconscient and evolution of that involved transcendental consciousness towards that transcendental consciousness. **[Chandrakant P. Patel]**

9. Integral psychology is the study of man as a transitional being on earth in the context of involution and evolution. **[Chandrakant P. Patel]**

10. "This (Integral) Yoga is not a cut out system. It is a growth by experience."[7] **[Sri Aurobindo]**

---

[6] Sri Aurobindo; SABCL Vol. 17: p. 21; *Glossary of Terms in Sri Aurobindo's Writings* (Pondicherry: Sri Aurobindo Ashram, 1978); p. 124

[7] Purani A. B. Ed.; Evening Talks with Sri Aurobindo (Publisher: Sri Aurobindo Ashram Publication Department, Sri Aurobindo Ashram, Puducherry, 605002 India, Fourth Edition, 2007); p. 159

Knowledge of integral yoga given by The Mother and Sri Aurobindo is like a profound very vast ocean. Human intellect, as Ambubhai Purani used to say, can feast upon it for millennium and enrich the human culture and civilisation. List of their documents on integral yoga noted in the next section II will show the vastness of the knowledge. Thesis in this book attempts only to sketch a description of fundamental outlines of Integral psychology and has concentrated largely on the personal development of the individual being and consciousness.

II. THE SOURCE LITERATURE OF INTEGRAL PSYCHOLOGY

1. SRI AUROBINDO'S WRITINGS DOCUMENTED IN SRI AUROBINDO BIRTH CENTENARY LIBRARY

Sri Aurobindo's writings on integral yoga and integral psychology can be classified into two types: one, the primary source literature (**pages 7,741**) and second, the secondary source literature (**pages 2,722**). **So, the total** comes to **pages 10,463**, *a staggering number.*

(i) Primary Source Literature on integral yoga and integral psychology: Sri Aurobindo's original yogic evolutionary psychology can be found in the below-listed **13 volumes** of "Sri Aurobindo Birth Centenary Library" published during 1970-1972. Total number of **pages** of these volumes come to **about 7,741**. Integral psychology has to be derived from these writings on integral yoga.

1) SABCL Vol. 3: *The Harmony of Virtue*: It contains Sri Aurobindo's early prose writings. They cover a period of 20 years from 1890-1910 prior to his withdrawal to Pondicherry. These writings are on Yoga an evolution, Yogic Psychology, A Profound Spiritual Psychology of learning, Education and

Human Development, Psychology of literary writing, Ancient Indian Psychology of Aesthesis, of Hindu Drama and a Biography of Bankim, as Sri Aurobindo says, "The creator and king of Bengali Prose".

2) SABCL Vol. 9: *The Future Poetry:* It discusses poetic aesthesis of mental as well as overmental (spiritual level) aesthesis.

3) SABCL Vol. 14: *The Foundation of Indian Culture*: It contains integral psychology of Indian Culture, Integral Psychology of Indian Civilization and Society, Integral Social Psychology, Integral Political Psychology, Integral Aesthetic Psychology of Architecture, Sculpture, and Painting.

4) SABCL Vol. 15: It includes two books. *Human Cycle (Psychology of social development)* which contains integral social psychology, and *Ideal of Human Unity*, which contains integral psychology of national and international life.

5) SABCL Vol. 16: *The Supramental Manifestation*: it provides information on the supramental manifestation upon earth and some other psychological matters.

6) SABCL Vol. 17: The Hour of God

7) SABCL Vol. 18-19: The Life Divine: it presents integral psychology in philosophical language.

8) SABCL Vol. 20-21: Synthesis of Yoga

9) SABCL Vol. 22, 23 & 24: Letters on Yoga: comprises 1775 pages of Sri Aurobindo's letters to his disciples on the subjects of different types of yoga, integral yoga, difficulties of the sadhana of the integral yoga, experiences in yoga, and the triple transformation: Psychic, spiritual and supramental, transformation of mind, vital, physical and the subconscient and the inconscient, and the hostile powers. They are letters so to say are letters of counselling and guidance and psychotherapy in the integral yoga.

10) SABCL Vol. 25: The Mother: It contains information about The Mother, The Divine Chit Shakti (Chit), the main dynamic guiding force for the practice of integral psychology.

11) SABCL Vol. 26: On Himself: It contains autobiographical information on Sri Aurobindo, The Supramental Divine Being (Sat), that supports and works through the Divine Shakti.

12) SABCL Vol. 27: Supplement: It contains supplementary literature on integral psychology.

13) SABCL Vol. 28-29: Savitri: It is an Epic Poem, an overmental creative poetry, and presents integral psychology in a poetic and story-telling style.

(ii) Secondary Source Literature on integral yoga and integral psychology: The below-listed 8 volumes of "Sri Aurobindo Birth Centenary Library" published during 1970-1972 can be considered the *Secondary Source Literature on integral yoga and integral psychology.* **Number of pages** of this *Secondary* literature are **about 2,722.**

1) SABCL Vol. 1: Bande Mataram: Writings in this volume are on the political philosophy and psychology, especially on philosophy and psychology of Indian political activities from 1890 to 1908.

2) SABCL Vol. 2: Karmayogin: Writings in this volume are on the political philosophy and psychology, especially on philosophy and psychology of Indian political activities from 1909 - 1910.

3) SABCL Vol. 4: Writings in Bengali: Major part of these writings is on ancient Indian psychology and philosophy.

4) SABCL Vol. 5: Collected Poems: There are in this volume many poetry of psychological and philosophical import.

5) SABCL Vol. 10: The Secret of the Veda: In this volume Sri Aurobindo has explained the Vedic psychology.

6) SABCL Vol. 11: Hymns to the Mystic Fire: In this volume, Sri Aurobindo has explained the Vedic psychology.

7) SABCL Vol. 12: The Upanishads: In this volume, Sri Aurobindo has explained the Upanishadic psychology.

8) SABCL Vol. 13: Essays on The Gita: In this volume, Sri Aurobindo has explained the psychology of the Gita.

Volumes 10, 11 and 12 contain fresh and original interpretation of pre-historic Vedic supramental knowledge of consciousness by the supramental wisdom of Sri Aurobindo. Vedic Categories of Consciousness seem to be similar to but are not exactly the same as what Sri Aurobindo and The Mother arrived at finally. **So it is a big error to assume** that their knowledge has developed gradually from past Indian Spiritual Knowledge and so one should first study past scriptures Veda, Upanishad and Bhagavad Gita and then study them if one wants to understand them with ease, for a direct approach to them is a difficult proposal.

Vedic knowledge is supramental knowledge and Gita's knowledge is overmental spiritual knowledge given by Sri Krishna to Sri Aurobindo, when he was interned in a solitary cell in the Alipore Jail; Sri Aurobindo had reveled this fact in his Uttarpara speech, which he had delivered in the public conference organised by Hindu Sabha at Uttarpara (Bengal, India) for honouring him after his release from the Alipore Jail[8]. This knowledge is spiritual (over-mental) wisdom, as Sri Krishna was a spiritual Avatar[9]. Hence, the secondary source needs to be studied in the light of Sri Auromere's Psychology found in the primary source.

---

[8] Sri Aurobindo; *"Uttarpara Speech"* in SABCL Vol. 2; pp. 1-10

[9] SABCL Vol. 22; p. 405

2. THE MOTHER'S WRITINGS

The **Mother's literature**[10] (*total pages 7,099+*) contains theoretical and practical knowledge about almost all sorts of developmental issues of individual, personal, social as well as of universal life and of the consciousness. She has given unfailing remedies for all problems. Her words of advice contain a superb dynamic force for evolving one's being into a spiritual and supramental being. She is also a super psychologist of the modern era and a world-redeeming psychologist. She also needs to be recognised as a supreme psychologist possessing fundamental effective and dynamic knowledge of consciousness of matter, animal, man, Devas, Asuras, invisible benevolent and hostile beings and the universe.

3. THE VASTNESS OF PSYCHOLOGICAL WRITINGS BY SRI AUROBINDO AND THE MOTHER IS AMAZING

When we add **10,463** pages of the psychological literature given by Sri Aurobindo to *7,099* pages of the psychological literature given by The Mother, the sum comes to pages *17,562.*

This calculation is made on the basis of "Sri Aurobindo Birth Centenary Library (SABCL) published during 1970 – 1972 and which consists of 30 volumes and on the basis of the 17 volumes of the Collected Works of The Mother (CWM). The other writings of Sri Aurobindo found later on were added in the contents of the SABCL and this new enlarged version of the SABCL is now, at the time of the celebration of Sri Aurobindo's 125th anniversary, published and named "Complete Works of Sri Aurobindo (CWSA)", which consists of 36 volumes. There is a great amount of writing of The Mother that is not

---

[10] CWM Vol. 1-17 and Her other books containing her talks and comments on Sri Aurobindo's writings, Her letters containing integral psychological guidance to numerous disciples, her letters to managers and leaders of the Sri Aurobindo Ashram that contains integral organisational and management psychology, her book on spiritual meaning of flowers and other writings constitute an unbelievably large mass of words containing dynamic supramental wisdom-force.

included in the CWM. **So, in fact, there are more than 17,562 pages of their knowledge on the integral yoga and integral psychology**. So one can assert that **they must be identified as twin (two-in-one) modern unsurpassed super-psychologists**, twin because they are absolutely one in their inner consciousness and The Mother is executive Shakti of Sri Aurobindo. It means The Mother's Knowledge and Sri Aurobindo's Knowledge is identical. So, Sri Aurobindo's integral yoga and integral psychology means Sri Aurobindo and The Mother's integral yoga and integral psychology, or we can say Auromere's integral yoga and integral psychology.

4. SRI AUROBINDO AND THE MOTHER'S WRITING IS A DYNAMIC FORCE FOR DEVELOPING ONE'S PERSONALITY AND ONE'S KNOWLEDGE AND DIFFERENT BRANCHES OF INTEGRAL PSYCHOLOGY

This vast literature offers a possibility for developing various branches of integral psychology by synthesizing current and past psychological knowledge with the knowledge of integral yoga and integral psychology: such as Integral Psychology of Personal Development, Integral Psychology of Social Development, Integral Psychology of War and Peace, Integral Psychology of Political Development, Integral Psychology of Business, Integral Psychology of Management, Integral Psychology of Child Development, Integral Psychology of Family Life, Integral Psychology of World Union, Integral Psychology of Sexual Behaviour, Integral Psychology of Education, Integral Psychology of Human Relation, Integral Clinical Psychology, Integral Psycho-therapy, Integral Psychoanalysis and so on. Several books on different branches of integral psychology are already published in different countries and are available with SABDA, Sri Aurobindo Ashram, Pondicherry, 605002, India. Intellectuals all over the world have found a great psychology and a great Purna Yoga in their writings; also many simple minds all over the world have started to practice their integral yoga and integral psychology; these are some of the proofs of the greatness of their teaching and their personality.

They have provided practical psychological knowledge on all problems of existence. Study of their psychological literature makes us see Sri Aurobindo and The Mother (Sri Auromere) as modern Shiva-Parvati sitting on the Himalaya of Wisdom in a supra-majestic posture and facilitating the flow of supramental Knowledge-Ganga on the Earth so that by taking a deep dip in it, the individual and the society may emancipate their triple consciousness/nature (mental-vital-physical complex) into the supramental consciousness and realise the long-cherished Golden Age on The Earth. Verily Sri Aurobindo and The Mother are two biune super-psychologist of today.

An aspirant of personal development can find an effective advice and guidance from their literature and personality for developing higher consciousness and personality, if he is sincere and ready to persevere till he achieves his goal.

5. INTEGRAL PSYCHOLOGY CAN BE CALLED SRI AUROMERE'S PSYCHOLOGY

Sri Aurobindo's and The Mother's rational, experimental and experiential findings are results of the process of the Integral Yoga performed jointly by them. Integral yoga is joint creation of Sri Aurobindo and The Mother, says Vrekhem, Georges Van.[11] It is not possible to derive two separate statements of psychology from writings of either of them; one can derive the same integral psychology from writings of either of them. **So, Integral Psychology derived from integral yoga must be called Sri Aurobindo and The Mother's or *Sri Auromere's Integral Psychology.***

---

[11] Vrekhem, Georges Van; *The Mother; The Divine Shakti* (Rupa & Co, 7/16, Ansari Road, Daryaganj, New Delhi, 110002, India); p. 5

III. SRI AUROMERE'S PSYCHOLOGY IS INTEGRAL IN NATURE

Field, aim and method of integral psychology are integral and so it is called the integral psychology:

1. ITS FIELD OF STUDY IS INTEGRAL[12]

(i) **Field of Integral Psychology is Consciousness and it examines all Grades of the Consciousness:** Consciousness is (i) power of awareness of self, things and forces and (ii) is or has dynamic and creative energy and it has many grades.

The supramental mind of our ancient vedic Seers (ऋषि) had seen that the Consciousness (चित) aspect of the One Eternal Infinite सच्चिदानद (*Sat-Chit-Anand*: Existence-Consciousness-Bliss), has created the Creation (सृष्टि:). This fact has been confirmed and validated later on by many persons and spiritual *shastras.* Sri Krishna says in the Gita, "ऊर्ध्वमूलमधः शाखमश्वत्थं प्राहुरव्ययम्"[13]: "... with its original source above (in the Eternal), its branches stretching below, the Ashwattha is said to be eternal and imperishable (translation by Anilbaran Roy)[14]"; and a footnote by Anilbaran: "Here is a description of cosmic existence in the Vedantic image of the Ashwattha tree."[15] Sri Aurobindo, the modern supramental mind, describing Gita's view on the reality of our world, writes,

---

[12] SABCL, Vol. 22, pp. 234-77; SABCL, Vol. 20, pp. 170-72; SABCL, Vol. 18, p. 194; Purani, A.B., "Some questions of Psychology and Yoga", *Mother India*, XIII, 10 (Dec. 1961), p. 97; Pandit Madhav, "Sri Arbind Ane Temanun Tattvagnan", *Sri Arbind Karmadhara*, VIII, 1 (March 1978), pp. 4-6; Jugal Kishore Mukherjee, "The Destiny of the Body", *Mother India*, XVI, 10 & 11 (Dec. 1964), p. 33; and Tulsidas Chatterjee, *Sri Aurobindo's Integral Yoga* (Pondicherry: SABDA, Sri Aurobindo Ashram, 1970), p. 58

[13] Gita; Ch. 15, Verse 1

[14] Anilbaran Roy; The Gita (Sri Aurobindo Ashram, Pondicherry, 605002, India 1954); p. 236

[15] Ibid.

"All is self and soul and nature of the Godhead, all is Vasudeva. The world for the Gita is real, a creation of the Lord, a power of the Eternal, a manifestation from the Parabrahman, and even this lower nature of the triple Maya is a derivation from the supreme divine Nature."[16]

Thus the world is "a power of the Eternal", a shakti of the One Eternal Sachchidananda, a consciousness of the transcendental Consciousness, a consciousness of the supreme Divine (पुरूषोत्तम). Replying to a query of a disciple, Sri Aurobindo had written to him,

"Consciousness is a fundamental thing, the fundamental thing in existence – it is the energy, the motion, the movement of consciousness that creates the universe and all that is in it – not only the macrocosm but the microcosm is nothing but consciousness arranging itself. For instance, when consciousness in its movement or rather in certain stress of movement forgets itself in the action it becomes an apparently "unconscious" energy; when it forgets itself in the form it becomes the electron, the atom, the material object. "[17]

Consciousness is the fundamental thing in and behind man's personality and actions. The predominant consciousness of man determines his type of personality and behaviour. A man, who has strong mental consciousness, is generally a sober and calm *satvic* personality and if someone abuses and insults him, he will not shout at him, will not abuse and insult him but will quietly ignore him or peacefully tell him to learn to speak gentle and civilised speech, will tell him to establish mental and soul control over his impulsive unrestrained aggressive behaviours against others. If that other person succeeds in realising a civil moderate peaceful mental consciousness and put a rein on his unruly vital consciousness and ultimately establish a peaceful

---

[16] SABCL Vol. 13; p. 426
[17] SABCL Vol. 22; p. 236

civil vital that obeys mental civility, he will cease to be an angry personality, will stop directing abusive and aggressive behaviours against others. He will be judged to have a *satvic* personality and not a *rajasic* one. A man having a predominant physical consciousness will be slow in action and lazy in action and so a lazy personality, a *tamasic* personality. Thus, personality is seen as dependent on the consciousness of a person. Personality and behaviour pattern of a person is nothing but expressed form of his/her consciousness.

Let us ponder over another illustration: one day 78 year old Mr. Pinto comes to the dining table for lunch. He notices that a dish of salad is absent. He knows salad is fibrous and is prescribed by his doctor as a helping remedy for his extremely slowed down bowel movement; his daughter-in-law, Sheela, who manages the kitchen and meals knew that the salad is a medicine for her father-in-law, Pinto. But she had somehow forgotten to prepare the dish. Pinto requested her to prepare a dish of salad. Now, Sheela was washing plates and finishing that work she had to leave for her office soon. She thinks that she will be late if she waits for preparing the dish. Her mind gets frustrated, gets agitated and loses calm consciousness and she suddenly blurts out, "Don't you see, I am busy, I have to leave soon, I am not your servant, you do not have to go to office, why don't you prepare the salad yourself." Her unusual disturbed mental consciousness makes her to forget her usual calm and civil soft behaviour and to display sudden rude behavior and personality. The aged senior Pinto was taken aback, but quietly he admonishes her, "I know you are not my servant, but you have forgotten that you are my daughter-in-law and according to Indian tradition, which you always advocate, it is your duty to take care of me and serve me and be kind to me". She feels the civil truth in the kind words of her father-in-law, make herself calm down, quickly prepares and serves the dish, finishes the washing and leaves for office with a calm mind. Here, Pinto's behaviour and personality is cool, because his consciousness is always cool. It is not prone to react angrily; it is prone to display calm action only. Next day, he suffers a heavy loss because the prices of the stocks he had purchased becomes extremely low in the stock market.

He is under high tension and the episode with the daughter-in law is repeated when on dining table. He loses his usual calm consciousness and blurts out angry words to admonish Sheela for the negligence of her duty. And the battle issues. It is clear Pinto's and Sheela's existent states of consciousness determined their momentary behaviours and personality. This means that the existent consciousness is fundamental to the existent personality and behaviour; surface personality and behaviour are phenomenal expression of underlying behind-the-scene consciousness and so psychology must understand and deal with them in reference of the underlying originator consciousness.

As we have seen in the first two paragraphs of this section, the consciousness aspect of the Sachchidananda is known in Indian spiritual science as the *Adya Shakti* (आद्या शक्ति) – the Supreme Mother. She has created all things as different forms of her own stuff within its own Eternal Infinite Consciousness. Everything created is thus a form of the consciousness, so all can be described and rendered into terms of consciousness. We can speak of the universe as the universal consciousness, of the matter as the material consciousness, of the mind as the mental consciousness, of the animal as the animal consciousness and so on. In this sense, the subject matter of integral psychology is the consciousness: the transcendental consciousness, the universal consciousness and the individual human consciousness. Integral psychology generally uses the language of consciousness and so it is the psychology of consciousness.

Sri Aurobindo has described and explained to a disciple in detail the fundamentalness of consciousness, planes and parts of consciousness and relationship of consciousness with personality in the following letter.

"Consciousness is not, to my experience, a phenomenon dependent on the reactions of personality to the forces of Nature and amounting to no more than a seeing or interpretation of these reactions. If that were so, then when the personality becomes silent and immobile and gives no reactions, as there would be no seeing or interpretative action, there would therefore be no consciousness. That contradicts some of the fundamental experiences of yoga, e.g., a silent and immobile consciousness infinitely spread out, not dependent on the personality but impersonal and universal, not seeing and interpreting contacts but motionlessly self-aware, not dependent on the reactions, but persistent in itself even when no reactions take place. The subjective personality itself is only a formation of consciousness which is a power inherent, not in the activity of the temporary manifested personality, but in the being, the Self or Purusha.

"Consciousness is a reality inherent in existence. It is there even when it is not active on the surface, but silent and immobile; it is there even when it is invisible on the surface, not reacting on outward things or sensible to them, but withdrawn and either active or inactive within; it is there even when it seems to us to be quite absent and the being to our view unconscious and inanimate.

"Consciousness is not only power of awareness of self and things; it is or has also a dynamic and creative energy. It can determine its own reactions or abstain from reactions; it can not only answer to forces, but create or put out from itself forces. Consciousness is Chit but also Chit Shakti.

"Consciousness is usually identified with mind, but **mental consciousness is only the human range** which no more exhausts all the possible ranges of consciousness than human sight exhausts all the gradations of colour or human hearing all the gradations of sound – for there is much above or below that is to man invisible and inaudible. So there are ranges of consciousness above and below the human range, with which the normal human has no contact and they seem to it unconscious, – supramental or overmental and submental ranges.

"When Yajnavalkya says there is no consciousness in the Brahman state, he is speaking of consciousness as the human being knows it. The Brahman state is that of a supreme existence supremely aware of itself, *svayaṁprakāśa*,—it is Sachchidananda, Existence-Consciousness-Bliss. Even if it be spoken of as beyond that, *parātparam*, it does not mean that it is a state of Non-existence or Non-consciousness, but beyond even the highest spiritual substratum (the "foundation above" in the luminous paradox of the Rig Veda) of cosmic existence and consciousness. As it is evident from the description of Chinese Tao and the Buddhist Shunya that that is a Nothingness in which all is, so with the negation of consciousness here. Superconscient and subconscient are only relative terms; as we rise into the superconscient we see that it is a consciousness greater than the highest we yet have and therefore in our normal state inaccessible to us and, if we can go down into the subconscient, we find there a consciousness other than our own at its lowest mental limit and therefore ordinarily inaccessible to us. The Inconscient itself is only an involved state of consciousness which like the *Tao or Shunya*, though in a different way, contains all things suppressed within it so that under a pressure from above or within all can evolve out of it —"an inert Soul with a somnambulist Force".

"The gradations of consciousness are universal states not dependent on the outlook of the subjective personality; rather the outlook of the subjective personality is determined by the grade of consciousness in which it is organised according to its typal nature or its evolutionary stage.

"It will be evident that by consciousness is meant something which is essentially the same throughout but variable in status, condition and operation, in which in some grades or conditions the activities we call consciousness can exist either in a suppressed or an unorganised or a differently organised state; while in other states some other activities may manifest which in us are suppressed, unorganised or latent or else are less perfectly manifested, less intensive, extended and powerful than in those higher grades above our highest mental limit."[18]

---

[18] SABCL Vol. 22; pp. 233-235 [*Bold letters are ours.*]

Sri Aurobindo has here described his **"In the Life Experience"** of God, consciousness, soul and relation between them.

Now, Studies of **near death experiences (NDEs)** have found truthfulness in super-normal phenomena of consciousness, which were known long before to Vedic yogis and Indian yogas and Indian psychology. They say now that consciousness, soul, Cosmic Soul, gods, goddesses and the God are real and do exist. An agnostic and materialist academic Neurosurgeon Dr. Eben Alexander of America (www.ebenalexander.com) was for a week in coma. Due to bacterial meningitis his cortex was totally out of function. During coma his consciousness travelled to other higher world and met Angels (devas) and Asuras and numerous beings and the personal God and personal creatrix consciousness and what Vedic integral psychology calls the Sachchidananda. He had many incredible experiences. After suddenly and miraculously coming out of coma, he wrote a book *"Proof of Heaven: a Neurosurgeon's Journey into the Afterlife"*. In this book, he has narrated beautifully Near Death Experiences he had during his out of the body journey to other world. Given the medical fact that his

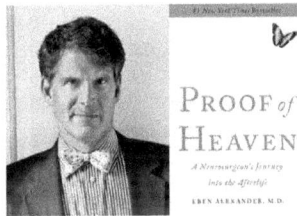

Picture 2.1 Neurosurgeon Dr. Eben Alexander, M.D.

brain was not at all functioning, neurological or neuroscientific explanation is out of place for his experiences of supraphysical realities. They can be explained in terms of higher order supraphysical consciousness only, which is known to Indian psychology since Vedic times. A few of his experiences and their implications for psychology are noted below:

1. He knew that he was part of the Divine (p.76). [In integral psychology, this is called the experience of *Sayujya Mukti* – सायुज्य मुक्ति & *salokya Mukti* – सालोक्य मुक्ति; *Sita's father king Janak had achieved sadharmya mukti* – साधर्म्य मुक्ति]

2. He had entered the Supraphysical Universe:

(i) Because he had lost completely his mortal identity, he was granted full access to the true cosmic being that he is and all persons are (p. 78). [Experience of Universal Soul – विश्वात्मा].

(ii) In the supra-physical universe, he discovered that "to know and think of something is all one needs in order to move towards it (p. 70)". Whenever he was in the dark inconscient and no sooner did he long for the higher world, he was there. Thinking and action are one thing not two in that higher world. Particular knowledge and the particular action are always simultaneous. This must be the level of supramental consciousness and world identified by integral psychology and which is the goal of integral psychology.

(iii) He saw many universes: He was in darkness – like submerged in mud yet able to see through it. Here he says, "I wasn't human nor even animal; I was something before, and below all that, I was simply a lone point of awareness in a time-less red-brown sea" (pp. 29-32). [This is inconscient universe of integral psychology. *See chapter III of this book: Creation of the Universe and the Earth and Evolution of the Human Being.*] From this dark murky world he shoots up to a world of white-gold light; where he met a super-conscient girl whose look was of Divine Love, a Love beyond all human loves. She spoke to him without using any words and gave him three messages pp. 38-41). *[The girl must be an emanation or a form of the Supreme Mother in that subtle universe]*

(iv) He saw good and evil beings in the universes. *[Sri Aurobindo has described in details all these subtle supra-physical*

worlds and beings in them in second book of his epic poem Savitri: The
Book of the Traveller of the Worlds[19].]

3. He heard the sound of Om (ओम); Om spoke to him; he
experienced it as God. (pp. 46-47; 85; 104; 157; 160). He further says,
"But–again, paradoxically — Om is "human" as well — even more
human than you and I are. Om understands and sympathizes with our
human situations more profoundly and personally than we can even
imagine because Om knows what we have forgotten, and understands
the terrible burden it is to live with amnesia of the Divine for even a
moment (pp. 85-86)."

4. What I discovered out beyond is the indescribable immensity
and complexity of the universe, and that consciousness is the basis of
all that exists (p. 154).

5. He sees universe as Womb (p. 47). [Bhrahmand – ब्रह्मांड]

6. He had met dead Forefathers. [Pitru – पितृ] He says, "Today,
I believe that true health can be achieved only when we realize that God
and the soul are real and that death is not the end of personal existence
but only a transition (4th Cover-page)."[20]

So, Dr. Eben who had no knowledge of Indian Scriptural
Psychology or Ayurveda or integral psychology proves through his
experiences that the truths given in Vedic and integral psychology are
true.

Numerous persons are known to have "In-Life Experiences" of
Devas (gods) and God and wisdom given by God. The author would
like to cite two examples of In-Life Experiences; One of Ramanujan and
the other of Sri Aurobindo.

---

[19] SABCL Vol. 28; pp.95-304; CWSA Vol.33; pp. 94-304

[20] Eben Alexander, M. D.; *Proof of Heaven: a Neurosurgeon's Journey into the Afterlife*
(Simon & Schuster Paperbacks, A Division of Simon & Schuster, Inc. 1230 Avenue of
the Americas, New York, NY, 10020, USA, 2012)

Internationally acclaimed *Vibhuti* (विभूति) of Mathematics and a Fellow of Royal Society of Trinity College, Cambridge University, Srinivas Ramanujan of India, on whom an English producer has created a Movie, "Man who knew Infinity", was asked by his mentor Prof. Hardy and the committee of mathematicians of Trinity College, Cambridge University, how he could find his original theorems and formulas. He had replied to them that his mind has not derived them from previous mathematical knowledge, he had received them intuitively from God. And all had to accept the power of intuition and the God, for his theorems though not explicable to mind were found true. Ramanujan's findings changed the old mathematical theory. His formula of infinity and other formulas are now used for space research and black holes.

Overmental Avatar Sri Krishna had appeared to supramental Avatar Sri Aurobindo in Alipore Jail and explained to him the meaning of Gita and Hindu Dharma and assigned to him the work he has to do for Sanatan Dharma, nation and the World. Regarding teaching of Gita, Sri Aurobindo had reported in his famous Uttarpara Speech:

"It seemed to me that He spoke to me again and said, "The bonds you had not strength to break, I have broken for you, because it is not my will nor was it ever my intention that that should continue. I have another thing for you to do and it is for that I have brought you here, to teach you what you could not learn for yourself and to train you for my work." Then He placed the Gita in my hands. His strength entered into me and I was able to do the *sadhana* of the Gita. I was not only to understand intellectually but to realise what Sri Krishna demanded of Arjuna and what He demands of those who aspire to do His work, to be free from repulsion and desire, to do work for Him without the demand for fruit, to renounce self-will and become a passive and faithful instrument in His hands, to have an equal heart for high and low, friend and opponent, success and failure, yet not to do His work negligently."

Picture 2.2 Sri Aurobindo in Alipore Jail

(ii) *Integral psychology studies all aspects of the Original Supreme Divine Consciousness*: It studies not only the Sachchidananda (the Divine), which is above all creation and out of creation, but also his

Picture 2.3 Sri Krishna

different divine emanations (*svarupa*) put forth on all the lower (physical-vital-mental) and superior (overmental and supramental) planes of consciousness. Sri Aurobindo has asserted this fact in the words that follow:

> "The Divine is everywhere on all the planes of consciousness seen by us in different ways and aspects

of His being. But there is a Supreme which is above all these planes and ways and aspects and from which they come.

** ** **

"The Divine can be and is everywhere, masked or half-manifest or beginning to be manifest, in all the planes of consciousness; in the Supramental it begins to be manifest without disguise or veil in its own *svarupa.*"[21]

(iii) *Integral psychology examines complete process of evolution*: Integral psychology studies the devolution of the Supreme Divine Consciousness into the inconsciousness forming on the way of devolution the universal planes of the supramental, overmental, mental, vital, and subtle physical in descending order and the gradual evolution of that devolved Supreme Consciousness in the forms of universal material, vital, mental, overmental and supramental planes of consciousness and beings in ascending order of consciousness. Traditional rational psychology does study the phenomena of evolution but it studies only the evolution of forms, it does not study the evolution as well as devolution of the consciousness. So, it is not completely evolutionary psychology; while integral psychology is the complete and real evolutionary psychology. (*See Ch. III*)

(iv) *It is Integral for it studies man in the universe: It is Integral for it studies complete man with reference to his complete hereditary inner environment and complete outer environment:* it describes inner soul (psychic being) of man and society, Oversoul (Jivatman) of man and society and also physical-vital-mental-overmental-supramental consciousness/nature (*Prakriti*) of man and

---

[21] SABCL Vol. 22; p. 249

society: it studies *atman* and *prakriti* both. It examines mental, psychic, spiritual and supramental perfection of human being and society also.

It studies all the gradations of consciousness of man and society: the inconscient, the subconscient, the conscient triple nature consisting of the mental, vital and physical consciousness, the subliminal triple nature consisting of the inner mental, vital and physical, the spiritual overmental consciousness, the supramental consciousness and the ultimate Divine consciousness.

It studies all the twelve types of environments and four types of heredity of man: genetic, atavistic, pre-birth and heritage from sub-human origins of life. (*See Ch. III*)

It examines mutual relation between all levels of individual, social and universal consciousness, for they are inextricably connected with each other. Referring to the mutually collaborative relationship between individual being and the universal consciousness for the sake of their evolution, Sri Aurobindo[22] writes, "The universe and the individual are necessary to each other in their ascent. Always indeed they exist for each other and profit by each other." For Sri Aurobindo's complete statement of this relationship (*Refer to the Appendix 3.4 in Ch. III*).

While studying the individual consciousness it does not restrict itself to the subconscient and the conscient level of consciousness only, as the western Psychology does, but it also includes in its study of man the psychological dynamic forces of inconscient, the subconscient, the conscient, the subliminal, the psychic, the spiritual, the supramental and the Divine Consciousness. Thus integral psychology studies totality of consciousness and behaviour, while scientific psychology studies some parts of consciousness and behaviour. The field of integral psychology is integral while that of the scientific psychology is partial.

---

[22] SABCL Vol. 18; p. 45

2. AIM OF INTEGRAL PSYCHOLOGY IS INTEGRAL

Its aim is more wide, high and comprehensive than other Yogic psychology. Sri Aurobindo says, "It (integral yoga) aims not at a departure out of the world and life into Heaven and Nirvana, but at a change of life and existence, not as something subordinate or incidental but as a distinct and central object"[23]. While the old Yogas and spiritual disciplines were other-worldly and their aim was not to perfect nature (*Prakriti*) but to realise the Soul and depart to other worlds leaving this world as imperfect as it is. But unlike them integral yoga aims at "an individual achievement of divine realisation for the sake of the individual ...[24] and also aims at its ultimate complete generalisation".[25] Its aim is to divinise the humanity also. Sri Aurobindo had clarified on November 7, 1946 that, "... the very principle of my Yoga is not only to realise the Divine and attain to a complete spiritual consciousness, but also to take all life and all world activity into the scope of this spiritual consciousness and action and to base life on the Spirit and give it a spiritual meaning."[26]

It means the aim of the integral Yoga and its derivative the integral psychology is to achieve perfect mundane development of physical-vital-mental triple nature of the individual and the humanity (the nations and the world), to change their triple nature by raising it to psychic and spiritual level and ultimately transform it into the divine supramental nature and accomplish the next stage of evolution of life on earth. Or, as Patel says, its goal is to usher the individual and the society into a new age of love, peace, knowledge, vigour, beauty, harmony and unity, the golden age for which the enlightened part of humanity is yearning so much today.[27] In other words, its aim is to transform man, the transitional being, into the supramental being, the society into the

---

[23] SABCL Vol. 26; p. 109

[24] Ibid.

[25] SABCL Vol. 20; p. 44

[26] CWSA Vol. 36; p. 65

[27] Patel C. P.; Preface p. ix

supramental society and the earth's environmental universal consciousness into the supramental consciousness: Its aim is to realise the next stage of evolution, the stage of supramental consciousness and life. (*See Ch. IV Section I: The Environmental Universe and the Human Individual and the Divine.*)

Explaining the meaning of transformation, Sri Aurobindo wrote in his letter dated October 5, 1935,

> "By transformation I do not mean some change of nature – I do not mean, for instance, sainthood or ethical perfection or Yogic Siddhis (like the Tantric's) or a transcendental (*cinmaya*) body. I use transformation in special sense, a change of consciousness radical and complete and of a certain specific kind which is so conceived as to bring about a strong and assured step forward in the spiritual evolution of the being of a greater and higher kind and of a larger sweep and completeness than what took place when a mentalised being first appeared in a vital and material animal world."[28]

Defining the newness of the aim and method of integral yoga he wrote in the same letter,

> "It is new as compared with the old Yogas:

> "(1) Because it aims not at a departure out of world and life into Heaven or a Nirvana, but at a change of life and existence, not as something subordinate or incidental, but as a distinct and central object. If there is a descent in other Yogas, yet it is only an incident on the way or resulting from the ascent — the ascent is the real thing. Here the ascent is indispensable, but what is decisive, what is finally aimed at is the resulting descent. It is the descent of the new consciousness attained by the ascent that is the stamp and seal of the sadhana. Even Tantra

---

[28] SABCL Vol. 26, 106-107; CWSA Vol.29, p. 398

and Vaishnavism end in the release from life; here the object is the divine fulfilment of life.

"(2) Because the object sought after is not an individual achievement of divine realisation for the sole sake of the individual, but something to be gained for the earth-consciousness here, a cosmic, not solely a supra-cosmic achievement. The thing to be gained also is the bringing in of a Power of consciousness (the supramental) not yet organised or active directly in earth-nature, even in the spiritual life, but yet to be organised and made directly active."

"(3) Because a method has been preconised for achieving this purpose which is as total and integral as the aim set before it, viz. the total and integral change of the consciousness and nature, taking up old methods but only as a part action and passing on to others that are distinctive. I have not found this method (as a whole) or anything like it in its totality proposed or realised in the old Yogas. If I had I should not have wasted my time in hewing out a road and in thirty years of search and inner creation when I could have hastened home safely to my goal in an easy canter over paths already blazed out, laid down, perfectly mapped, macadamised, made secure and public. Our Yoga is not a retreading of old walks, but a spiritual adventure."[29]

Viewing this transformational aim of the integral psychology, Jobst Mühling[30], a Western scholar of Sri Aurobindo and The Mother and a psychologist, has observed in his essay *"The Future of Psychology"* that the modern Western psychology betrays man if he seeks its help to change his nature, for it aims at only mundane perfection of mental-vital-physical consciousness and behaviour and

---

[29] SABCL Vol.26, p. 109; CWSA Vol. 29, Letters on Yoga II, pp. 400-401

[30] Jobst Mühling, "The Future of Psychology", *Mother India, XII,* 3 (April, 1960), pp. 20-26, XII, 4 (May, 1960), pp. 14-18 and XII, 5 (June, 1960), pp. 26-32

because it doesn't possess the Psychic-spiritual method, which can only transform and evolve the human being, the society and the humanity into the supramental nature. But, integral psychology possesses this knowledge and method and it is not satisfied with achieving the efficient man only, but the supramental man, the next evolutionary species after man. (*See last para. of the section V-2.*)

3. METHOD OF INTEGRAL PSYCHOLOGY IS INTEGRAL

As noted above, its method is "as total and as integral as the aim set before it."[31] Sri Aurobindo took up "the essence and many processes of the Old Yogas,"[32] and synthesised them into an integral method of yoga, which was first described by him in *The Synthesis of Yoga*[33] and later in the revised form in guiding letters[34] to disciples. Moreover, Sri Aurobindo and The Mother wouldn't deny to use any technique and method recommended by other eastern and western psychological disciplines, if they are helpful to a seeker of change of consciousness. In this sense, its method is all inclusive and yet each has to find his own personalized method and technique for oneself. This characteristic of the method is fully illustrated in Sri Aurobindo's words quoted below,

> "For the sadhaka of the integral Yoga it is necessary to remember that no written Shastra, however great its authority or however large its spirit, can be more than a partial expression of the eternal Knowledge. He will use, but never bind himself even by the greatest Scripture. Where the Scripture is profound, wide, catholic, it may exercise upon him an influence for the highest good and of incalculable importance. It may be associated in his experience with his awakening to crowning

---

[31] Ibid., p. 109

[32] Ibid., p. 108; SABCL, Vol. 20, pp. 36-44

[33] SABCL, Vol. 20 and 21

[34] SABCL, Vol. 22, pp. 39-136; SABCL, Vol. 23, pp. 503-886; SABCL, Vol. 24; SABCL, Vol. 25 and SABCL, Vol. 26, pp. 95-220

verities and his realisation of the highest experiences. His Yoga may be governed for a long time by one Scripture or by several successively, — if it is in the line of the great Hindu tradition, by the Gita, for example, the Upanishads, the Veda. Or it may be a good part of his development to include in its material a richly varied experience of the truths of many Scriptures and make the future opulent with all that is best in the past. But in the end he must take his station, or better still, if he can, always and from the beginning he must live in his own soul beyond the limitations of the word that he uses. The Gita itself thus declares that the Yogin in his progress must pass beyond the written Truth, — *śabdabrahmātivartate* — beyond all that he has heard and all that he has yet to hear, — *śrotavyasya śrutasya ca.* For he is not the sadhaka of a book or of many books; he is a sadhaka of the Infinite."[35]

Aspiration in the heart for change of consciousness and surrender to The Mother, the eternal infinite Shakti, are the only two prime principles a seeker of integral yoga and integral psychology has to follow and proceed evolving personal method, *Shastra,* all along the way. In this context, it can be said that the supra-rational method and the rational method described below are the two kinds of methods employed by integral yoga and integral psychology.

*(i) **Super-Rational Method:** Method of Direct Cognition (or, Method of Direct Knowledge/ Method of Knowledge by Identity/ Metaphysical Method) is the primary and main method of integral psychology. In other words, Psychic-spiritual introspection and observation of individual, social, universal and transcendental fields of consciousness is the main method of integral psychology.*

Integral psychology employs a wider form of introspection. Ordinary introspection used by scientific psychology is merely mental

---

[35] CWSA Vol. 23-24; p.55

introspection, while integral psychology uses for the study of consciousness and behaviour introspection with not only the mind, but also with the inner mental-vital-physical consciousness, inmost psychic consciousness and upper spiritual consciousness. This is called Integral Introspection or yogic introspection. For example, the behaviour of anger is viewed from inner psychic centre and from above spiritual vision also along with mental perception.

Our rational mind can know only the mental range of consciousness in two manners. Ordinary mind can visualise or feel certain things, forces and movements in mental region of consciousness directly, even though they are not channelised through the senses. But it cannot know whatever is beyond the mental range. Psychic mind and spiritual mind – (Higher mind, intuitive mind, illumined mind and overmind are levels of spiritual mind in ascending order on evolutionary scale) – and mind of light and supramental consciousness can cognize things in the regions of consciousness beyond mind. For example, if one has realised the spiritual consciousness, one can spiritually and silently intervene in the movements of the individual and world forces, without using outer physical means of action. They have not to use the channel of the sense-mind to know. These higher faculties of perception and knowledge can directly identify with the object and know it from within without the use of the senses, rational mind and physical instruments.

People, who have realised the spiritual consciousness, possess power of pre-vision. If they choose they can act from distance on anything. Time and space is no barrier for them. Sri Aurobindo and The Mother had realised the spiritual and supramental Consciousness and they had the power of pre-vision (direct knowledge) and capacity to act silently and spiritually upon individual and world forces for the needed change in them without moving any organs of action (direct action). Numerous incidences that vouch for both of their abilities as well as for efficacy of spiritual force have been documented and some are still in oral circulation waiting for documentation. Here, first are mentioned orally circulated two incidences followed by documented ones.

Once, The Mother pre-visioned that an earthquake is to occur in the region of San Francisco and the city is to go under the sea. To avert the impending catastrophe, She sent one of her chosen disciples to the city to organise group meditation to invoke the Divine Grace for changing the course of nature's movement and save people. Her instructions were followed up and the impending danger did not materialise.

The second one is about catastrophic health problem of one of her attendant. One day The Mother directly saw that her attendant lady had cancer. The Mother advised that she should go to a hospital. The lady had no idea of having cancer. So, she wondered why she was being sent to a hospital at Mumbai from Pondicherry for a surgery. But, being obedient and as she had faith in The Mother she went. The doctor after studying her body conditions decided that to operate was contra-indicated, as she may die during the operation. The Mother was informed. The Mother talked to the doctor on phone, "Operate her, and do not worry". Operation was performed and it was successful. The doctor was so astonished that with his apron on dashed to the Ashram at Pondicherry to pay respect to The Mother. She told him, "I needed your body to operate her; in fact I had performed the operation using your body". Hundreds of Anecdotes and case histories of such direct cognition and connation are documented. Even some of her disciples had once in a while demonstrated such capacities. Sri Ramakrishna Paramhans is the best example of these faculties of direct knowledge: He was illiterate, yet could know and speak high spiritual truths. How can it be explained? Ability of receiving direct knowledge is the only explanation for such extra-mental and extra-sensory cognition and connation. Now, follows the recorded incidences.

The following incidence narrated by Narayan Prasad illustrates that The Mother had pre-vision of India's independence:

"In 1914 The Mother had pre-visioned India's independence and had told of it to Sri Aurobindo. ...

"In 1927 one day sadhak A asked her, "How is India likely to get freedom?"

"The Mother replied, "Hear! The British did not conquer India. You yourself handed over the country to the British. In the same manner the British will themselves hand over the country to you. And they will do in a hurry as if a ship were waiting to take them away.

"A asked when this would happen?

"The Mother replied, "When a Japanese warship will come to the Indian Ocean, India will get freedom."

"The Mother said this to A in 1927 – all of it was fulfilled to the letter in 1947."[36]

Sri Aurobindo and The Mother[37] had used their supra-rational spiritual consciousness powers to help the Allied powers to win the World War II and to defeat the Axis powers, for the victory of Hitler would have set back the evolution and stopped the descent of the supramental evolutionary force on earth. He was working against the social evolution under the guidance of one of the four prime Asuras, the Lord of Falsehood who is also called the Lord of Nations, while the victory of the Allied powers would keep the present achievement of evolution safe and keep the road of evolution open.

---

[36] Narayan Prasad; *Life in Sri Aurobindo Ashram* (Publisher: Sri Aurobindo Karmi Sangha Trust, Matrimandir, Sri Aurobindo Sarani, P. O. Habra-Prafullanagar, North 24 Parganas, West Bengal, 743268, India, 2010); p.302

[37] CWSA Vol. 35, pp. 219-221, CWSA Vol. 36; 65-66, 453-468; Narayan Prasad; Ibid.; pp.281-302; Anil Puri; " Sri Aurobindo and the Second Great War" in *Mother India, Vol. LXVII No. 6,* June 2014); pp. 477-495

Disclosing his intervention in the affair of the World War II, Sri Aurobindo had declared referring in third person to himself on 7 November 1946,

"In his retirement Sri Aurobindo kept a close watch on all that was happening in the world and in India and actively intervened whenever necessary, but solely with a spiritual force and silent spiritual action; for it is part of the experience of those who have advanced far in Yoga that besides the ordinary forces and activities of the mind and life and body in Matter, there are other forces and powers that can act and do act from behind and from above; there is also **a spiritual dynamic power** which can be possessed by those who are advanced in the spiritual consciousness, though all do not care to possess or, possessing, to use it, and this power is greater than any other and more effective. It was this force which, as soon as he had attained to it, he used, **at first only in a limited field of personal work, but afterwards in a constant action upon the world forces.** He had no reason to be dissatisfied with the results or to feel the necessity of any other kind of action. ... When it appeared as if Hitler would crush all the forces opposed to him and Nazism dominate the world, he began to intervene. ... Inwardly, he put his spiritual force behind the Allies from the moment of Dunkirk when everybody was expecting the immediate fall of England and the definite triumph of Hitler, and he had the satisfaction of seeing the rush of German victory almost immediately arrested and the tide of war begin to turn in the opposite direction. This he did, because he saw that behind Hitler and Nazism were dark Asuric forces and that their success would mean the enslavement of mankind to the tyranny of evil, and a set-back to the course of evolution and especially to the spiritual evolution of mankind: it would lead also to the enslavement not only of Europe but of Asia, and in it India, an enslavement far more terrible than any this country had ever endured, and the undoing of all the work that had been done for her liberation. ... He had not, for various reasons, intervened with his spiritual force against the Japanese aggression until it became evident that Japan intended to attack and even invade and conquer India. ... had the satisfaction of seeing the tide of Japanese victory, which had till then swept everything before it, changed immediately into a tide of rapid, crushing and finally immense and overwhelming defeat.

(Written 7 November 1946; revised and published 1948)"[38]

The Mother had said in her Playground Class on *March 8, 1951* about the being that possessed and "guided" Hitler:

"Hitler was in contact with a being whom he considered to be the Supreme: that being would come and give him advice and tell him all that he had to do. Hitler would withdraw into solitude and wait long enough to come into contact with his 'guide' and receive inspirations from him which he would afterwards carry out very faithfully. That being whom Hitler took for the Supreme was quite simply an Asura, the one called in occultism 'the Lord of Falsehood', and he proclaimed himself to be 'the Lord of Nations'. He had a resplendent appearance and could pull the wool over anyone's eyes, except one who truly had occult knowledge and could thus see what was there, behind the appearance. He could have deluded anyone, he was so splendid. He generally appeared to Hitler wearing a breast-plate and a silver helmet (with a sort of flame coming out of his head), and there was around him an atmosphere of dazzling light, so dazzling that Hitler could hardly look at him. He would tell him all that he had to do – he would play with him as with a monkey or a mouse. He had set his mind on making Hitler do all possible kinds of folly... until the day when he would come a cropper, which is what

---

[38] CWSA Vol. 36; pp. 65-66

happened. But there are many cases like that one, on a smaller scale, naturally. Hitler was a very good medium, he had great mediumistic capacities, but he lacked intelligence and discernment. That being could tell him anything and he would swallow it all. That's what prodded him on little by little. And that being would do that as a pastime, he didn't take life seriously. For those beings, people are very small things with which they play as a cat plays with a mouse, until the day when they eat them up."[39]

Talking to Satprem about a silent spiritual intervention in The World War II, The Mother had said on November 5, 1961,

"For instance, during the last war I spent all my nights hovering above Paris (not integrally, but a part of myself) so that nothing would happen to the city. Later it came out that several people had seen what seemed to be a great white Force with an indistinct form hovering above Paris so that it wouldn't be destroyed.

**

"Throughout the war Sri Aurobindo and I were in such a CONSTANT tension that it completely interrupted the yoga. And that is why the war started in the first place – to stop the Work. At that time there was an extraordinary descent of the Supermind; it was coming like that *(massive gesture),* a descent! Exactly in '39. Then the war broke out and stopped everything cold. For had we personally continued [the work of transformation] we were not sure of having enough time to finish it before 'the other one' crushed the earth to a pulp,

---

[39] Satprem; The Mother's Agenda Vol. 6: Conversation dated January 12, 1965; pp. 16-17; and CWM Vol. 4; pp. 185-186

setting the whole Affair back... centuries. The FIRST thing to be done was stop the action of the Lord of Nations."[40]

Later on, on January 12, 1965 during a conversation with Satprem referring to this talk The Mother had revealed how she took appearance of the Lord of Nations and misguided Hitler to attack Russia. She had told:

"I knew that being very well (for other reasons... the story would be too long to tell), and once, I knew he was going to visit Hitler – I went before he did: I took his appearance, it was very easy. Then I said to Hitler, "Go and attack Russia." I don't exactly remember the words or the details, but the fact was that I told him, "Go... In order to have the supreme victory, go and attack Russia." That was the end of Hitler. He believed it and did it – two days later, we got the news of the attack. And then, the next day, that is, when I came back from Hitler, I met that being and told him, "I've done your job!" Naturally enough, he was furious!

"But all the same, in that consciousness, there is with that being (the Lord of Falsehood, one of the first four Emanations), there is despite everything a very deep relationship, of course. He said to me, "I know, I know I will be defeated eventually, but before my end comes I will wreak as much destruction on earth as I can."

"Then, as I told you, the next day, the news of the attack came, and that was really the end of Hitler.

As for Sri Aurobindo... (You know that there is a place in Russia where they were defeated – Stalingrad, on February 2, 1943), Sri Aurobindo had foreseen the defeat

---

[40] Satprem; The Mother's Agenda Vol. 2: Conversation dated November 5, 1961; pp. 374-375

and had worked the night before, and that's how it happened – we knew ALL THE DETAILS.

"We never told this, of course, but it was perfectly precise.

"But I knew that being, I had already seen him in Japan – he called himself "the Lord of Nations." And he really was a form of the Asura of Falsehood, that is, of Truth which became Falsehood: the first Emanation of Truth, who became Falsehood.

"And he hasn't been destroyed yet."[41]

In the above quote, we read that The Asura, Lord of Falsehood, had promised to The Mother, "I know, I know I will be defeated eventually, but before my end comes I will wreak as much destruction on earth as I can." Describing the mega-destruction caused by him, Anil Puri notes,

"The war officially ended on 15th August 1945 (on Sri Aurobindo's birthday) with the surrender of Japan, after it had ended in Europe a couple of months earlier. The total loss of human life was in excess of 50 million. An estimate 6 Million Jews, including 1 million children and 2 million women, were killed in the notorious Nazi concentration camps. About 80,000 men, women and children were instantly vaporized in a few seconds when the first atomic bomb was dropped on Hiroshima. As the Mother has mentioned above the Asura cares little about human life."[42]

---

[41] Satprem; The Mother's Agenda Vol. 6: Conversation dated January 12, 1965; pp. 17-18 [*Bold letters are ours.*]

[42] Anil Puri; " Sri Aurobindo and the Second Great War" in *Mother India, Vol. LXVII No. 6,* June 2014); p. 493

Maggi Lidchi Grassi has written the true story with a novelistic approach of experiences of Irish American Infantryman John Kelly with Sri Aurobindo and The Mother on the battlefield of World War II.[43] In the last paragraph of her book she has noted John Kelly's Army Unit Regiment Number: 70th Infantry Division, 276th Infantry Regiment, "Easy Company", of American Army fighting German Army in World War II. Two beings of Light, as John Kelly would say, used to appear to him, instruct him, lead him and protect him on the battlefield of World War II. Following the instruction of these two beings, once he even happened to save his battalion miraculously from an attack by the enemy. He had named these two beings as "Great Sir" and "the Heaven Lady". He had no knowledge whatsoever of Sri Aurobindo and The Mother at that time. After the war he came to know that they were subtle physical appearances of Sri Aurobindo and The Mother. Describing his touching meet with The Mother, Maggi writes:

> "He first met The Mother on his birthday shortly after his arrival in February 1966. The Mother was nearing ninety and John was at last kneeling at his Heaven Lady's feet. For a longtime she gazed lovingly at John and then she nodded slowly. After a while he too very slowly nodded. Neither uttered a word.

> "She gave him his flowers; he groped his way out of the room with tears running down his cheeks."[44]

---

[43] Maggi Lidchi Grassi; Great Sir and the Heaven Lady (A Writers Workshop Greenbird Book, 1993)

[44] Ibid.; p. 241

Picture 2.4 The Mother as she was when infantryman John actually met her in 1966

Picture 2.5 The Heaven Lady (The Mother) as infantryman John saw her on the battlefield of World War II in 1944

Picture 2.6 "Great Sir": Sri Aurobindo as seen by infantryman John on the battlefield of World War II in 1944

Maggi's another book *The Light that Shone into the Dark Abyss* is about the battle of occult forces in World War II and was published by Sri Aurobindo Ashram Press. She has given in this book the true story of a Rumanian detainee who had experiences with Sri Aurobindo in the concentration camp. Describing one of her conversation with The Mother she writes in this book:

> "The Mother told the author (Maggi) how Sri Aurobindo used to tell her of the words that he would put into the mouth of Churchill before the famous broadcasts, and certain passages were spoken by Churchill word for word. I have not found any written references to this in the texts written

on Sri Aurobindo but his secretary Nirodbaran had heard of this and Dyumanbhai, [then] managing Trustee of the Ashram, has confirmed it. He told me that certain passages in Churchill speeches often were repetitions of words already spoken in Pondicherry. Anubahen Purani tells me that her father A. B. Purani, one of the few people who saw Sri Aurobindo every day, told her the same thing."[45]

Narayan Prasad has also noted that

"With the War taking the definite turn on the fall of Dunkirk ... Sri Aurobindo also concentrated himself all the more on struggle. From that time he wanted to listen directly the war news and more especially speeches of Churchill ... It would be interesting to note that the epoch making speeches of Churchill, of President Roosevelt and of General de Gaulle started from this time, and Sri Aurobindo and The Mother listened to them. ... The Mother and Sri Aurobindo willed the return to power, for the fourth term, of President Roosevelt, because he was the only man of strong determination and will power, just the man needed for the hour."[46]

This Method of Direct Knowledge and Action is the true method to know the Reality and real things and act accordingly in the material as well as supra-physical worlds is vouchsafed by the Near Death Experiences (NDE) that American Neurosurgeon Dr. Eben had during his Coma. *(Refer above III-1. Its Field of Study is Integral: (i) Field of Integral Psychology is Consciousness and it examines all Grades of the Consciousness.)*

---

[45] Anil Puri; " Sri Aurobindo and the Second Great War" in *Mother India, Vol. LXVII No. 6,* June 2014); p. 489

[46] Narayan Prasad; *Life in Sri Aurobindo Ashram* (Publisher: Sri Aurobindo Karmi Sangha Trust, Matrimandir, Sri Aurobindo Sarani, P. O. Habra-Prafullanagar, North 24 Parganas, West Bengal, 743268, India, 2010); p. 299

(ii) Scientific Methods/ Rational Methods: Mental introspection and observation of individual, social, universal and transcendental consciousness is the adjunct secondary method of integral psychology:

Patel[47] argues and establishes that **introspection** is the original (*Adi*) and basic method of psychology, original because when Prof. Wilhelm Wundt began in 1879 the study of consciousness as a science of psychology separate from philosophy, he used the method of introspection to identify different factors of human consciousness, basic because it forms an integral indivisible part of all rational methods of psychology; for example, when emotions, feelings, and other human behaviours are studied with the method of experiment in the laboratory of experimental psychology, the introspective report of the subject is a must for obtaining complete data and correct inferences.

Scientific Methods (Rational Methods) are also used by integral psychology. Patel[48] is the first person to use rational methods to study the results of the application of the Auromere's integral psychology by Sri Aurobindo International Centre of Education in the school-classes: He had prepared and used a Licker Type of Scale and the methods of Questionnaire and interview to assess the mundane, psychic and spiritual development of personality of non-yogi students due to the impact of the application of integral psychology in the class-room teaching. His published study is the first Doctorate Level study of integral psychology and integral education. His study was considered innovative research by The National Council of Research and Training (NCERT), Government of India, New Delhi, India; the NCERT had granted generous financial aid for publication also. Patel has suggested

---

[47] Patel C. P.; *Samanya Manovignan - General Psychology* (Publisher: Chairman, University Book Production Board (Gujarat State), Ahmedabad, Gujarat, 380 006, India, 1991); p.59

[48] Patel C. P.; *Psychological Foundation of the "Free Progress System" as Evolved in Sri Aurobindo International Centre of Education* (Publisher: Sri Aurobindo Study Circle (Bokhira-Porbandar), Bokhira, Gujarat, 360579, India, 1986); pp. 187-210 and 241-270

20 areas of research in integral psychology, where rational method can be legitimately used.

IV. OTHER CHARACTERISTICS Of INTEGRAL PSYCHOLOGY

1. IT IS A COMPOUND OF SCIENCE AND METAPHYSICAL KNOWLEDGE

For, it admits both the empirical and abstract spiritual data and *findings*. It accepts higher mental (super-rational) data and would infer inferences from those data and even speculate also. It means integral psychology bases its knowledge also on the Logic of the Infinite, it is psycho-philosophy.

2. IT IS EVOLUTIONARY PSYCHOLOGY

It studies consciousness in terms of past and future stages of evolution and involution and aims at evolving human consciousness gradually into supramental consciousness of the next species, so it is evolutionary: Purpose of its yogic method is to help human beings to achieve union (yoga) with the divine. So, it is yogic also. The next paragraph elucidates this aspect of it in some detail.

3. IT IS TRULY A YOGIC PSYCHOLOGY

Its yogic developmental method helps man to unite, to achieve union – yoga – with the divine. It helps man not only to achieve mundane perfection of his nature but also to achieve psychic-spiritual and supramental divine perfection of his present natural personality. In other words, integral psychology helps human consciousness to rise up and ultimately achieve union (*yoga*) with the Divine nature: It aims at **Trans-Formation** of man into the supramental man and ordinary life into divine life. In this sense also, it is evolutionary. The transformation it aims at includes divinising the body also.

4. IT IS EXPERIMENTAL PSYCHOLOGY

The words of Sri Aurobindo quoted below explain experimental nature of integral psychology in clear terms:

"Yogic methods have something of the same relation to the customary psychological workings of man as has the scientific handling of the force of electricity or of steam to their normal operations in Nature. And they, too, like the operations of Science, are formed upon *a knowledge developed and confirmed by regular experiment, practical analysis and constant result*. All Rajayoga, for instance, depends on this perception and experience that our inner elements, combinations, functions, forces, can be separated or dissolved, can be new-combined and set to novel and formerly impossible workings or can be transformed and resolved into a new general synthesis by fixed internal processes. Hathayoga similarly depends on this perception and experience that the vital forces and functions to which our life is normally subjected and whose ordinary operations seem set and indispensable, can be mastered and the operations changed or suspended with results that would otherwise be impossible and that seem miraculous to those who have not seized the rationale of their process. And if in some other of its forms this character of Yoga is less apparent, because they are more intuitive and less mechanical, nearer, like the Yoga of Devotion, to a supernal ecstasy or, like the Yoga of Knowledge, to a supernal infinity of consciousness and being, yet they too start from the use of some principal faculty in us by ways and for ends not contemplated in its everyday spontaneous workings. All methods grouped under the common name of Yoga are special psychological processes founded on a fixed truth of Nature and developing, out of normal functions, powers and results which were always latent but which her ordinary movements do not easily or do not often manifest."[49]

Sri Aurobindo's integral yoga is experimental is absolutely clear from what he wrote on September 20, 1911 to a disciple:

> "My Yoga is proceeding with great rapidity, but I defer writing to you of the results until certain experiments in which I am now engaged, have yielded fruit sufficient to establish beyond dispute the theory and system of yoga which I have formed and which is giving great results not only to me, but to the young men who are with me. ... I expect these results within a month if all goes well."[50]

5. SRI AUROMERE'S INTEGRAL PSYCHOLOGY CAN BE CALLED A GLOBAL PSYCHOLOGY

Observing the all-inclusive approach of integral psychology, Patel C. P. remarks "Integral Psychology is global also, because it looks at, interprets and describes each part of consciousness with reference to the whole and the highest as well as in relation to other parts. While dwelling on a point Sri Aurobindo never loses sight of the whole field. Moreover, all the western and eastern psychologies can find their proper places in the globe of the integral psychology if interpreted in terms of it and then related to it. Sri Aurobindo[51] has made it clear that Freud's psycho-analytical psychology deals with the lower vital sub-conscient plane of human consciousness only; it studies vital sub-conscient plane of human being."[52] Integral psychology can reinterpret it in the context of the totality of consciousness and assimilate it in its own integral knowledge. (*Refer Section 7 below for more exposition*).

---

[49] SABCL Vol. 20; p.3

[50] CWSA Vol. 36; p. 284

[51] SABCL, Vol. 24, pp. 1605-8

[52] Patel C. P.; *Psychological Foundation of the "Free Progress System" as Evolved in Sri Aurobindo International Centre of Education* (Publisher: Sri Aurobindo Study Circle (Bokhira-Porbandar), Bokhira, Gujarat, 360579, India, 1986); pp.55-56

6. CONSTANT PRACTICE OF INTEGRAL YOGA/ PSYCHOLOGY BY A READER AND A SEEKER OF SELF-PERFECTION IS A MUST

As a seeker continues the practice of integral psychology he will be able to understand its principles better and better and he will be able to develop higher and higher consciousness for meanings of Sri Auromere's statements and words on integral psychology will reveal to him newer and newer imports and dynamic force behind them. Meanings of their statements understood by a student and practitioner are relative to or conditioned by the level of consciousness he has achieved due to intellectual study and active practice of integral psychology, i.e., integral yoga (Integral Karmayoga, Integral Yoga of Divine Love and Integral Yoga of Knowledge and Integral Yoga of self-perfection). Mere intellectual and casual study without intention for practicing whatever one understands is a useless and futile labour for developing higher personality and consciousness, which is the real purpose of integral psychology.

7. A LEARNER AND PRACTITIONER OF INTEGRAL PSYCHOLOGY MUST APPROACH SUPRAMENTAL WISDOM OF INTEGRAL PSYCHOLOGY WITH AN OPEN MIND

Reader should be free from the scientific bias that the experience or knowledge that does not satisfy mental logic is always an illusion or hallucination or just wishful imagination. One must be ready to accept Auromere's psychological statements received by the method of knowledge by identity as valid knowledge. If one sees that they contradict the knowledge of rational mental psychology, one must synthesise the lower rational knowledge with the higher order intuitional, spiritual and supramental knowledge. Thus, the measure of truth in the rational or other yogic and spiritual psychology can be properly understood and vindicated, and they may be assimilated into the integral psychology. Such synthetic approach will enrich the thought of integral psychology as well as of other kinds of psychology.

Assimilation means wisdom of all other psychologies should be interpreted in terms of Sri Auromere's Integral Psychology and then related to it and incorporated into it as an inseparable integral part of integral psychology.

In the section 5 above, pointing at the Global Nature of the integral psychology, it is noted that the sex motive and suppressed sex behaviour have been given undue primacy and importance by Freud for explaining human behaviours; he had no knowledge of driving force of sex and love operating at higher levels of consciousness than the level of the subconscient, where the suppressed sex resides; moreover, he had not identified driving force of other human motives. So, in his days unfortunately psychoanalysis created a culture of free and uncontrolled sex. Repressed sex behaviour resides in the province of sub-conscient lower vital consciousness of man and it has to be looked at and judged in the context of other motives of entire range of consciousness. He has exaggerated the role of sex in determination of human life. Integral psychology recognises sex as a legitimate motive of vital consciousness but it recognises role of other motives in determining the life of human being. For evolving the human personality and consciousness into higher stages of consciousness integral psychology would say: One has to be conscious of sex, accept it as a legitimate natural force, view its relative importance by considering it with reference to all other interacting needs and motives and allow it its proper play, not for perpetuating it exclusively, but for moderating its impulsive force and grossness by mental control and for changing it into a finer psychicised and spiritualised movement and ultimately transform it into a divine supramental love. For accomplishing this last ascension of human love a seeker has to call the Mother to make her divine Love, Anand and Beauty in the human vessel. The **whole theory and praxis of Freudian psychology can thus be corrected and synthesised with the wisdom of the** integral psychology.

8. THE TERM PSYCHOLOGY IN FACT IS APPLICABLE TO INTEGRAL PSYCHOLOGY ONLY, NOT TO THE SCIENTIFIC PSYCHOLOGY

As already mentioned before, Integral psychology studies psychic-spiritual consciousness also and in its reference considers man's triple physical-vital-mental consciousness. Moreover, the theory and practice of Integral Psychology is centered on the Psychic Consciousness. It employs psychic-spiritual sense and vision for the purification and change of the lower triple consciousness. So, the word psychology, which means science of psychic, is in fact applicable to it only and not to the scientific psychology, which avoids the study of soul (Psychic) and studies only the mind. Scientific psychology so in fact is mentology, the science of mind.

9. IT IS A FAST DEVELOPING PSYCHOLOGY

Sri Aurobindo Ashram at Pondicherry, which is created by the Mother, Sri Aurobindo International Centre of Education which aims at realising the aim in the educational field and in humanity, and many Integral Yoga Centres established in several countries are proof of its expansion of its practice in the society. Professor Dr. Indra Sen's pioneer publication *"Integral Psychology"*[53] the author's own published Ph.D. level study report[54] on integral psychology and integral educational psychology and free progress method of education that applies integral psychology in the field of education at the Sri Aurobindo International Centre of Education, Sri Aurobindo Ashram, Pondicherry, India, Publications of best sellers compilations and original works[55] on Sri Auromere's integral psychology by Dalal A. S.,

---

[53] Sen Indra; *Integral Psychology* (Publisher: Sri Aurobindo International Centre of Education, Sri Aurobindo Ashram, Pondicherry, India, 1986)

[54] Patel C. P.; *Psychological Foundation of the "Free Progress System" as Evolved in Sri Aurobindo International Centre of Education* (Publisher: Sri Aurobindo Study Circle (Bokhira-Porbandar), Bokhira, Gujarat, 360579, India, 1986); Preface p. vi

[55] Dalal A. S. ; *1. A greater psychology, 2. Sri Aurobindo and the Future Psychology* (Distributor: Sri Aurobindo Books Distribution Agency, Pondicherry, India

Prof. A. V. Sastri's book "The Psychology of Indian Nationalism"[56], Author's published report of successful cures achieved by him of chronic psychoneurotic diseases by applying the integral psychology[57], fruitful attempts to evolve an integral theory and practice of psychotherapy by Charles Maloney[58] and Brant Cortright[59] and of industrial management by Garry Jacob.[60] "The Academy of Future Man" conceived and proposed by Norman C. Dowsett[61] and establishment of "Sri Aurobindo Integral Teachers' Training College"[62] at New Delhi which imparts training in how to teach according to the free progress system of education and numerous spiritual organisations bearing the name of Sri Aurobindo and the Mother that have sprung up all over the world are some of the significant milestones on the road of progress of the evolving theory and practice of integral psychology.

10. CONSCIOUS AND CONSTANT RELIANCE ON THE MOTHER'S FORCE IS A MUST FOR ITS APPLICATION FOR THE TRANSFORMATION OF NATURE (*PRAKRITI*)

After a certain stage of personal development the existing science of integral psychology ceases to be fully valid and useful if used exclusively without conscious reliance on and the faith in The Mother's

---

[56] Sastri A. V.; *The Psychology of Indian Nationalism* (Dipti Publication, Sri Aurobindo Ashram, Pondicherry, 605002, India, 1968)

[57] Patel C. P.; *Tics and Suicidal Proneness Treated with Integral Psychology;* (Publisher: The Mother's Study and Guidance Center, 34215 Mimosa Terrace, Fremont, CA 94555, USA)

[58] Charles Maloney, "Evolutionary Psychology", *Mother India*, XXVII, 1-4 (Jan.-April, 1975), pp. 33-37, 138-41, 223-25 and 314-18

[59] Brant Cortright; *Integral Psychology: Yoga, Growth and Opening the Heart* (Publisher: State University of New York Press, Albany, NY, U. S. A.)

[60] Garry Jacob, "Consciousness Approach to Business Management", *Mother India*, XXVII, 1 to 8 (Jan. to Aug., 1976), pp. 54-56, 152-58, 229-30, 332-34, 440-42, 516-18, 701-4 and 778-79

[61] N. C. Dowsett, *Psychology for Future Education* (Pondicherry: Sri Aurobindo Society, 1977), pp. 207-4

[62] "Information Letter", *All India Magazine*, XI, 9 (April, 1982) , p. 37

force in the heart and above the head. After that stage one cannot advance further in his evolutionary development, if he does not depend primarily and entirely on The Mother's force[63, 64]. This being the inseparable aspect of the theory and practice of integral psychology, a psychological theory and psychological practice, that does not recognise Sri Aurobindo and The Mother's personal being and force, acting from even behind their words, as an integral and an important part of the practical discipline cannot be called integral psychology.

The differences between integral psychology and other kinds of psychology have been hinted at in the above discussion to highlight the unique spiritual aim and integrality of integral psychology. Below are briefly noted a few shortcomings of rational psychology and a movement in it to remove the errors and to make it more complete study of man.

V. INTEGRAL PSYCHOLOGY COMPARED TO SCIENTIFIC PSYCHOLOGY AND OTHER YOGIC PSYCHOLOGY

Sri Aurobindo's statements on the limitations of old yogas, Western psychology are so profound[65] and his exposition of ancient

---

[63]Patel C. P.; *Psychological Foundation of the "Free Progress System" as Evolved in Sri Aurobindo International Centre of Education* (Publisher: Sri Aurobindo Study Circle (Bokhira-Porbandar), Bokhira, Gujarat, 360579, India, 1986); pp. 75-76

[64] Patel C. P.; "The New World: Perceptible Sign of Its Arrival and Work on earth and preparation Needed for Entering into It" (Unpublished Paper Displayed at the AUM Conference, 2011, Lodi, CA, 95242, U. S. A.(June 30th to July 4th, 2011); p.3-4; Anand K. C.(Ed); *A NEW WORLD IS BORN: Words of The Mother, reprint of All India Magazine, November 2006* (Sri Aurobindo Society, Pondicherry, 605 002, India)

[65] SABCL Vol. 16, pp. 258-64; SABCL Vol. 12, pp. 192-99; SABCL Vol. 15, p.1; SABCL Vol. 27, p. 185; SABCL Vol. 22, pp. 220 and 321-24; SABCL Vol. 21, pp. 597-98; SABCL Vol. 24, pp. 1281, 1297-98, 1605-09; and, Sri Aurobindo,

Indian psychology and its shortcomings is so thorough, deep and true[66] that our mind would see in him an image of a keen, insightful and unmatched psychologist and an authentic student and critique of all varieties of psychology. For he had realised supramental consciousness that can know the Reality behind the surface Nature (*Prakriti*). The Mother also had realised the same supramental consciousness and vision and knowledge; her remarks are also profound and true[67]. For she was embodiment of the Transcendental Supreme Nature (*Para-Prakriti*). They had pre-visioned that the sincere desire of scientific psychology to know the truth of human nature will lead it to spiritualise and enlarge itself. That process is happening now.

1. SCIENTIFIC PSYCHOLOGY IS BECOMING MORE COMPLETE

In olden days study of self of man was done by philosophy. But Greek philosopher Goclenius Rudolf (1628) and his followers thought that to study the self of man a separate discipline of science is needed. So, they created a separate science to study the self of man and called it The Science of Psychology. Thus, the Western psychology has its root in the western philosophy. But with the passage of time, due to the stress on the importance of the empirical objective method of study, the subject-matter of psychology gradually changed from self to mind, from mind to consciousness, as expressed in behaviour, and then to behaviour observed as an outside object by a psychologist. Describing this gradual

---

"Psychology, the Science of Consciousness", *Bulletin of Sri Aurobindo International Centre of Education*, XXX, 2 (April, 1978), pp. 4-6.

[66] SABCL, Vol. 16, pp. 261-63; SABCL, Vol. 12; SABCL, Vol. 27, pp. 305-6 & 182-85; SABCL, Vol. 21, p. 521; SABCL, Vol. 20 and SABCL, Vol. 26, pp. 95-140.

[67] CWM Vol. 3: Travel Size Edition (1984): pp. 181-298; CWM Vol. 4, Travel Size, 1984: on Buddha & Buddhism; pp. 76-77, 79-80, 190, 194, 201, 203, 199, CWM Vol. 12, Travel Size 1984: on Hatha Yoga; p.285; On Psychology & Yoga; p. 246; on Science & Spirituality; p.246; on Buddha & Saint Vincent de Paul; pp.93-99; CWM Vol. 9, Travel Size, 1984: on Buddhism; pp. 8, 195-198; CWM Vol. 4, Travel Size, 1984: on Buddha; pp. 174, 213-214, 233-234, 257-258, 328, 382-383, 257-258, 299 ***(This list is incomplete)***

step by step downfall of psychology, Patel[68] observes that "psychology first lost its soul, then mind, then consciousness-behaviour and at the end some sorts of behaviour remained with it for study."

In recent times, professional psychologists found during the therapeutic and counselling work that the traditional knowledge of scientific psychology does not provide explanations and remedies for certain mental health problems. They turned to religious and spiritual disciplines to search out practical psychology to solve the impasse. They found several kinds of new religious and spiritual practical psychology, which have found applications in various fields of the society. For example, in a hospital of San Francisco of the State of California of the USA, group prayer was organised on almost daily basis in the rehabilitation quarter of a patient to help her body to accept and integrate the new foreign lever with itself as its own natural part. This programme of prayer was found successful. In the Washington Hospital of the city of Fremont of the State of California, a facility has been created for patients to learn and practise the spiritual knowledge of improving physical, vital and mental wellness. Credit goes to The Association of Transpersonal Psychology for creating a new correct and valid spiritual trend in the fields of medicine and psychology. It is a promise that scientific psychology will be a spiritual scientific psychology in future.

Now, due to the study and influence of Sri Auromere's integral psychology, a few American psychologists, choosing some aspects of soul and higher consciousness, have started to include self, higher self, and other levels of consciousness in their subject-matter and have started to give importance to the method of inner experience, the introspective method and the metaphysical method. But they haven't included in their study all the ranges of consciousness of the Divine Self and Nature. They accept soul (psychic being) of integral Yoga but their studies regarding soul are mostly in the context of therapeutic situations.

---

[68] Patel Chandrakant P.; *Samanya Manovignan* (Publisher: University Book Production Board, Gujarat Government, Ahmadabad, Gujarat, 380 006, India, 1991); p. 5

Their reported research works are rather patch-work. They have not arrived at a clear definition of their psychology and at a coherent statement of their theory. This is true for transpersonal psychology also. That is why Dalal A. S.[69] asserts that precise definition of transpersonal psychology yet remains to be formulated by its promoters.

So, the new spiritual psychology of the West is still imperfect psychology and needs to be perfected. It does not fulfill the expectation of William James,[70] who so eagerly expected somebody to come for changing and making perfect the earlier psychologies. Moreover, if it wants to be a perfect spiritual psychology it has to endorse and adopt the view of Prof. G. K. Dave[71] that **modern psychology can have its new birth as a perfect science of the whole man, if it turns to Sri Aurobindo and The Mother.** But that means they practice integral yoga.

In fact, Freud and Jung both had studied Indian spiritual teaching. A teacher, a physical educationist, from Germany, whom I, the author, had once met at Sri Aurobindo Ashram, Pondicherry, had told me, "Mr. Patel, do you know Freud had got the idea of the sub-conscious from the Indian spiritual literature that he had read". It seems also that Jung had got idea of "the centre" of person's consciousness from Eastern Spiritual Science. Evaluating analytical psychology of Jung in the light of Integral Yoga, Morwenna Donnelly[72] states that Jung had deep respect for psychological discernment of the East (China and

---

[69] Dalal A. S. ; *Sri Aurobindo and the Future Psychology* (Publisher: Sri Aurobindo International Centre of Education, Sri Aurobindo Ashram, Puducherry, 605 002, India, 2008); p.6

[70] James, William, Text-book of Psychology, cited by Purani Ambalal in *Chintanna Pushpo: Guchchha Bijo* (Umreth, Gujarat, India: Pathic Prakashan Mandir, 1964), p. 155

[71] G. K. Dave, "Need for an Integral Approach to Psychology" *M. P. Pandit 50th Birth Commemoration Volume*, Sastri, A. V., Editor, (Pondicherry: M. P. Pandit 50th Birth Day Commemoration Committee, 1968), p. 150

[72] Morwenna Donnelly; *"Some Reflections on the Analytical Psychology of C. J. Jung in the Light of Integral Yoga"*; in Sri Aurobindo Circle No. 6 (1950) (Publisher: Sri Aurobindo Circle, 32 Rampart Road, Fort, Bombay-1, India); pp.122-123

India) and he had considered that Richard Wilhelm's work in the field of Chinese studies and Anquetil du Perron's return from India to Europe with his translations of fifty Upanishads were the two events of the deepest importance. The East, Jung had said, is the cause of the spiritual change through which the West is passing these days. Jung asserts in his book *Modern Man in Search of Soul,* "... East and West cannot rend humanity into two different halves. **Psychic reality** exists in its original oneness, and awaits man's advance towards a level of consciousness where he no longer believes in the one part and denies the other, but recognises both as constituent elements of one psyche."[73] Psychology in the West has initiated return journey towards the psychic being (soul, अन्तरात्मा) from the time of Freud and Jung and now Transpersonal Psychology has included it in the subject matter of its study. But, the spiritual psychologists need to learn how scientific approach can be synthesised with the spiritual approach.

All kinds of the scientific psychology are in fact mentology, for they study only mental behaviour with the instrument of mind only; they describe and explain surface mental consciousness only; their field and methods and aims are in the ranges of mental level of consciousness. Dr. A. S. Dalal[74] surveys the structural, psychoanalytic, behavioristic, humanistic and the transpersonal psychology in his research essay titled *"Towards a Greater Psychology"* and finds that the structuralism scratched the surface of human personality with the tool of experiment and introspection, then psychoanalysis takes a step forward and sounds the depth of the human personality using increasingly the method of introspection, then the next psychology, the Maslow's humanistic psychology, concerns itself with the higher needs of human personality and aims at higher development of personality, the self-actualisation. The last transpersonal psychology scaling the heights of personality

---

[73] Ibid; p.124

[74] Dalal A. S. ; *Sri Aurobindo and the Future Psychology* (Publisher: Sri Aurobindo International Centre of Education, Sri Aurobindo Ashram, Puducherry, 605 002, India; 2007); p. 5

looks beyond the mind and behaviour, beyond introspection, measurement and analysis and beyond ego and self-actualisation and seeks to transcend the mental consciousness and personality. Dr. Dalal, a prominent integral psychologist and a sadhak of integral yoga, says at the end of his survey of the historical and qualitative ascension of the *mental psychology*:

> "The preceding panoramic survey of the developments in modern psychology shows that the young science has been, in the definition of its subject-matter, its methodology and in its objectives, steadily growing towards an increasingly and more comprehensive view of the human being and of human life."[75]

In the following comments on psychoanalysis of Sri Aurobindo it can be seen that Sri Aurobindo had envisioned this trend in the growth of the rational psychology.

2. SRI AUROBINDO AND THE MOTHER'S REMARKS ON PSYCHO-ANALYSIS

Commenting on Freud's psychoanalysis, Sri Aurobindo says,

> "I find it difficult to take these psycho-analysts at all seriously when they try to scrutinise spiritual experience by the flicker of their torch-lights, — yet perhaps one ought to, for **half-knowledge is a powerful thing and can be a great obstacle to the coming in front of the true Truth.** This new psychology looks to me very much like children learning some summary and not very adequate alphabet, exulting in putting their a-b-c-d of the subconscient and the mysterious underground super-ego together and imagining that their first book of obscure beginnings (c-a-t=cat, t-r-e-e=tree) is the very heart of the real knowledge. They look from down up and

---

[75] Dalal A. S. ; *Sri Aurobindo and the Future Psychology* (Publisher: Sri Aurobindo International Centre of Education, Sri Aurobindo Ashram, Puducherry, 605 002, India; 2007); p. 8

explain the higher lights by the lower obscurities; but the foundation of these things is above and not below, *'upari budhna eṣām'*. The superconscient, not the subconscient, is the true foundation of things. The significance of the lotus is not to be found by analysing the secrets of the mud from which it grows here; its secret is to be found in the heavenly archetype of the lotus that blooms forever in the Light above. **The self-chosen field of these psychologists is besides poor, dark and limited; you must know the whole before you can know the part and the highest before you can truly understand the lowest. That is the promise of the greater psychology awaiting its hour before which these poor gropings will disappear and come to nothing."**[76]

The Integral Psychology derived from the Integral yogic knowledge of Sri Aurobindo and The Mother is that greater psychology, influence of which has inspired a few psychologist to evolve Transpersonal and Humanistic Psychology by enlarging the method and scope and objective of the traditional psychology. This evolutionary movement of research in human consciousness, if pursued, must lead these two kinds of psychology to arrive at the synthetic view of the integral psychology.

The Mother explained the above remark of Sri Aurobindo in her Classes of April 6th & 13th, 1955 on Sri Aurobindo's book *Bases of Yoga Ch. 5*. The questions by students and answers – humorous and significantly enlightening – by The Mother are quoted below:

> "A student asks,
> *"What is this psychoanalysis of Freud, Sweet Mother?*
> "The Mother answers:

---

[76] SABCL Vol. 24; pp. 1608-1609 [*The bold letters are ours.*]

"Ah, my child, it is something that was in vogue, very much in vogue at the beginning of the century... no, in the middle of the century!

(*Mother turns to Pavitra*)[77] Do you know, Pavitra, when it was in fashion?

(Pavitra) At the beginning of the century.

At the beginning of the century, that's it. This is what Sri Aurobindo says: dangerous, useless, ignorant, superficial; and it was in fashion because people like these things, it corresponds precisely with all that is unhealthy in their nature. *You know how children love to waddle in the mud! Well, big people are no better than that.* There!"[78]

*** *** ***

What is "the heavenly archetype of the lotus?"

The answer given by The Mother is as follows:

"It means the primal idea of the lotus.

Each thing that is expressed physically was conceived somewhere before being realised materially.

There is an entire world which is the world of the fashioners, where all conceptions are made. And this world is very high, much higher than all the worlds of the mind; and from there these formations, these creations, these types which have been conceived by the fashioners come down and are expressed in physical realisations. And there is always a great

---

[77] Pavitra (P. B. Saint-Hillarie) was the first Director of "Sri Aurobindo International Centre of Education". Many adults, teachers, parents and members of the Ashram and even visitors of the Ashram also used to attend the classes. It reminds us of the classes conducted by ancient *Vedic Rishis*.

[78] CWM Vol. 7; p. 108

distance between the perfection of the idea and what is materialised. Very often the materialised things are like caricatures in comparison with the primal idea. This is what he calls the archetype. This takes place in worlds... not always the same ones, it depends on the things; but *for many things in the physical, the primal ideas, these archetypes, were in what Sri Aurobindo calls the* **Overmind.**

But there is a **still higher domain** *than this where the origins are still purer, and if one reaches this, attains this, one finds the absolutely pure types of what is manifested upon earth.* And then it is very interesting to compare, to see to what an extent earthly creation is a frightful distortion. And moreover, it is only when one can reach these regions and see the reality of things in their essence that one can work with knowledge to transform them here; otherwise on what can we take our stand to conceive a better world, more perfect, more beautiful than the existing one? It can't be on our imagination which is itself something very poor and very material. But **if one can enter that consciousness, rise right up to these higher worlds of creation, then with this in one's consciousness one can work at making material things take their real form."**[79]

In these words of The Mere is the true explanation of the incapacity of the reductionist materialistic psychology to help man to change his nature – the incapacity identified by Jobst Mühling. *For details of his views refer the last para of section III-2: Aim of Integral Psychology is integral.*

---

[79] CWM Vol. 7; pp. 122-123 [*The bold letters are ours.*]

3. THE MOTHER'S REMARK ON THE STUDY OF THE SCIENTIFIC PSYCHOLOGY

The Mother had told about the teaching of the subject of Psychology in Sri Aurobindo International Centre of Education that

"It seems to me that psychology without yoga is lifeless.

"The study of psychology must necessarily lead to yoga, at least to practical yoga if not theoretical. (23 December 1960)"[80]

This observation of The Mother on the study of scientific psychology signifies the necessity of practicing it in one's own life. Aim of scientific psychology is to help man improve his behaviours and personality using mental knowledge and will. For example, it suggests what discipline one should follow to control and sublimate anger and other negative emotions, to improve memory, to develop frustration tolerance, and so on. If a student consciously and willfully practices the discipline given by scientific psychology, he is already performing a sort of yoga and realising the change in himself; it would mean that psychology has led him to at least practical yoga of mental level perfection, and may be later on he may be led to the path of spiritual yoga. Thus for those who practice psychological knowledge, it is a living thing that creates new life. But if one does not care to practice it, then psychology may stuff his brain but wouldn't make an iota of change in his behaviour and personality; it would be a lifeless thing, a dead knowledge, for him and a burden on his intellect.

As it is mentioned in previous first section, psychology is on the way to become spiritual and yogic. In its quest for truth of inner nature of man and more effective knowledge for resolving problems of human behaviour it has started to study the subliminal consciousness of man

---

[80] CWM Vol. 12; p. 246

and created a branch of parapsychology. In Parapsychology Phenomena of subliminal consciousness is called extended consciousness phenomena, such as remote viewing, extrasensory perception, psychokinesis, clairvoyance, telepathy, and pre-cognition. Recently it has started to explore the soul factor as a determinant of human behaviour in the branch of transpersonal psychology and humanistic psychology. Both study near death experiences and explore the higher consciousness of man and higher supraphysical world. They are perhaps on the way to become integral yogic psychology.

4. INTEGRAL PSYCHOLOGY AND OLD YOGA AND INDIAN PSYCHOLOGY

Yoga of ancient Vedic and Upanishadic time did aim at supramental transformation of individual and society. But that effort was limited to special groups of individuals. While, as mentioned in the previous section III-1 Integral Yoga and integral psychology aims at transformation of individual and in addition of humanity also. Later old yogas, such as Ashtang Yoga (अष्टांग योग) and Psychology of Ashtang Yoga, Yoga of Gita and Psychology of Gita, Sankhya Yoga (सांख्य योग) and Psychology of Sankhya Yoga and so on are other worldly and their objective is spiritual change only and not supramental transformation and evolution.

SUMMARY

I-II. Aim, method and field of integral psychology and integral yoga are same, for integral psychology is derived from integral yoga. Sri Aurobindo and The Mother's writing occupy more than 17,562 pages. It is a rich source of knowledge for personal development and for development of various branches of psychology. Integral psychology can be called Sri Auromere's psychology.

III. Integral psychology examines all grades of consciousness from transcendental up to inconscient down, man with reference to all 4 types of his heredity and all 12 types of his universal environment and complete process of creation and evolution. Its aim is to realise mundane, psychic, spiritual and supramental change and transformation of all grades of consciousness of individual, society, nations and humanity and thus prepare conditions for the descent of the next supramental divine species of man and realise the Golden Age *(Suvarna yuga)* on earth. For study it uses supra-rational yogic metaphysical method of direct knowledge as well as all rational scientific methods that the scientific psychology employs. There are other features of it: it is evolutionary, yogic, experimental, global, fast developing, to be practiced by oneself for one's own development with the attitude of surrender to The Mother and with the spirit of adventure of hueing one's own path till the goal of transformation is reached. American neurosurgeon Dr. Eben's experiences in the comatose state, many other's NDEs and knowledge of Ramanujan and Sri Ramakrishna prove that the truths given in Vedic and integral psychology are true and knowledge of the scientific psychology is too limited and partially true.

IV. Integral psychology is compound of science and metaphysical knowledge. It is yogic for it is knowledge received by practicing integral yoga. It is experimental as the sadhak of integral psychology has to build knowledge and discipline of practice experimentally. Integral psychology can be intellectually best understood, if practiced in life. It is global because statements of all kinds of psychology can be interpreted in terms of its theory of hierarchical consciousness. If a seeker of self-perfection is not satisfied with mundane and spiritual perfection of personality and wants to achieve supramental transformation of personality and be a superman, entire reliance on The Mother's Force is a must. Integral psychology is science of man's psychic consciousness, so it is appropriate to call it "psychology". Scientific psychology is the study of the mental consciousness of man, so it is appropriate to call it "mentology." Ramifications of integral psychology in different branches are growing fast and Western scientific psychology has started to change and enlarge itself accepting the light from it, so it is a fast growing psychology.

V. Old yogic psychology aims at raising and enlarging human soul into universal and the Divine Spirit and not at divinising the nature of man, but integral psychology attempts at divinisation of soul and nature both. Integral psychology aims at mundane and psychic-spiritual change and supramental transformation of human consciousness and personality, while scientific psychology aims at only mundane change. "The self-chosen field of analytical psychology is poor, dark and limited" says Sri Aurobindo. Psychoanalysis "corresponds precisely with all that is unhealthy in nature. You know how children love to waddle in the mud. Well big people are no better than that." pronounces The Mother. She also says that psychology without yoga is lifeless.

Suggestions for Further Reading

1. Footnotes provide references for related subjects in Sri Aurobindo and The Mother's books. They are the best source for elaborate learning and practicing integral psychology. Moreover, by referring to Index Volume 30 of Sri Aurobindo Centenary Library and Indices of The Mother's Collected Works, one can find texts on a topic for further reading.

2. Sri Aurobindo; *The Integral Yoga: Sri Aurobindo's Teaching and Method* of *Practice: Selected Letters of Sri Aurobindo* (Publisher: Lotus Light Publication, P.O. Box 325, Twin Lakes, WI 53181, USA): "The Integral Yoga and Other Systems of Yoga and Philosophy", pp.22-42.

3. The Mother; The Mother's Vision: Selection from Questions and Answers Compiled by Georges Van Vrekhem (Sri Aurobindo Ashram, Pondicherry, 605002, India, 2005): Ch. 18 contains The Mother's talks on the nature of integral yoga.

4. Indra Sen; *Integral Psychology* (Publisher: Sri Aurobindo International Centre of Education, Pondicherry, India, 1998); The most authoritative and the pioneer textbook of General Integral Psychology. His way of original thinking and presentation of integral psychology is a model for all students of integral psychology. In this book, there is deep enlightening discussion on all the subjects of this chapter, such as definition, aim, field and nature of integral psychology, its comparison with other kinds of psychology, branches of integral psychology and consciousness. Dr. Indra Sen was a sadhak practicing integral yoga under the guidance of Sri Aurobindo and The Mother and had mastery over Western as well integral psychology inherent in integral yoga. Dr. Indra Sen was a student and teacher of scientific as well as integral psychology. So, he is very well able to interpret and upgrade scientific psychology and psychoanalysis in terms of integral psychology and synthesise it with integral psychology.

5. Purani A. B.; આર્યમાનસશાસ્ત્ર યાને ચિત્તંત્રની રૂપરેખા: *Arya Manasshastra Yane Cittantranii Rooprekha (*Publisher: Mulajibhai Tri. Talati, Pathic Prakashan Mandir, Umreth, Gujarat, India, August 1967); "The first chapter બે દૃષ્ટિબિંદુઓ, pp. 3-6"; Sri A. B. Purani was a very close disciple practicing integral yoga under the guidance of Sri Aurobindo and The Mother. He is a versatile student of Eastern and Western thought and authority on Sri Aurobindo and The Mother and two opposite standpoints of psychology are lucidly discussed in this book.

6. Dalal A. S. (Ed.); *A Greater Psychology* (Publisher: Sri Aurobindo Ashram, Puducherry, 605 002, 2008); "Consciousness, the Reality pp. 1-11"; "The Nature and Methodology of Yoga Psychology, pp. 303-314"; "States of Consciousness, 206-230"; "The Scientific Study of Consciousness, pp. 315-324"; "Consciousness: the Materialistic and the Mystical View, pp. 325-335

7. Dalal A. S. (Ed.); *Sri Aurobindo and the Future Psychology* (Publisher: Sri Aurobindo Ashram, Puducherry, 605 002, 2008);

Towards a Greater Psychology pp. 1-9"; "Sri Aurobindo and the Future Psychology pp. 384-394"

8. Miranda Vannucci; *Integral Yoga and Psychoanalysis* 2006 Edition (Publisher: www.grafichegiotto.it, Available with SABDA, Sri Aurobindo Ashram, Pondicherry, 605002, India): Author is a psychoanalyst in Italy and a sadhaka of Integral Yoga. She has upgraded the theory and practice of the Western Psychoanalysis in the light of integral yogic psychology and her own experiences received during active practice in health clinic in this report, and thus has synthesised it with and placed it in the Globe of integral psychology and enriched both.

9. Morwenna Donnelly; *"Some Reflections on the Analytical Psychology of C. J. Jung in the Light of Integral Yoga"; Sri Aurobindo Circle,No.1950,* (Publisher: Sri Aurobindo Circle, 32 Rampart Row, Fort, Bombay-1, India); pp. 121-145

10. Shree J. Patel; Ashtang Yoga and Integral Yoga – A Comparison (Publisher: Sunlit Path Trust, 139 St. John's Road, Colchester, Essex, CO4 4JH, UK): Chapter 3: Ashtang Yoga and Integral Yoga – A Comparison, pp. 59-74

WORKBOOK: QUESTIONS FOR PREVIEW AND REVIEW

I. DEFINITIONS OF INTEGRAL PSYCHOLOGY

Fill in the Gaps in the following

1. Psychology is science of _____. (Choose one correct word for filling the gap from this list: behaviour, mind, man, consciousness)
2. I mean by Yogic psychology an examination of _____ and _____of consciousness as they are revealed to us by the _____ and _____ of Yoga.

3. Integral psychology is an examination of _____ and _____ of consciousness as they are revealed to us by the _____ and _____ of Integral Yoga.

4. Integral psychology is the study of _____ and the _____ in the universe. Integral psychology is study of all planes and parts of _____ consciousness in context of all planes and parts of _____ consciousness, _____ consciousness and the _____ consciousness.

5. Integral psychology is the study of involution of the transcendental consciousness into _____ and _____ of that involved transcendental consciousness towards _____ consciousness.

6. Integral psychology is study of man as a _____ being in context of _____ and _____.

7. Evolution starts from _____ but _____ starts from _____. (inconscient, transcendental consciousness)

8. Systematic record of _____ experienced during performance of integral yoga is integral psychology.

9. Does integral psychology study only human consciousness? (Answer in a couple of sentences)

10. Integral psychology has nothing to do with God. (Answer in a couple of sentences).

Project

1. Make a list of all old as well as new yogic and rational scientific psychology.

II. THE SOURCE LITERATURE OF INTEGRAL PSYCHOLOGY

Short Answer Type Questions

1. Why should one say that the basic knowledge of integral psychology given by Sri Aurobindo and The Mother is vast?

2. Name a few branches of integral psychology that can be developed from the knowledge given by Sri Aurobindo and The Mother.

3. Why can Sri Aurobindo and The Mother be called the greatest modern psychologists?
4. Can it be said that Sri Aurobindo and The Mother are twin super-psychologists?
5. Is it true to say that The Mother's integral psychology and Sri Aurobindo's integral psychology are different?

III. SRI AUROMERE'S PSYCHOLOGY IS INTEGRAL IN NATURE

Short Answer Type Questions

1. Why it is said that field of study of integral psychology is integral? Give four reasons.
2. State definition of consciousness.
3. Who is the creator of the Creation – the universe or the cosmos according to Vedic Seers (*Rishis*)?
4. What is the relation between the world and the Divine?
5. When does consciousness become an unconscious energy?
6. When does consciousness become an atom?
7. Consciousness is a fundamental thing, the fundamental thing in existence." Explain giving examples.
8. Write a paragraph on *Adya Shakti.*
9. Is the Divine on all the planes of existence?
10. Is the Divine on all plane of existence in the same way and aspect?
11. Enumerate grades of consciousness.
12. Does consciousness depend on personality?
13. Who taught Gita's meaning to Sri Aurobindo?
14. Does God exist? Describe in short Dr. Eben's and Srinivas Ramanujan's experience of God.
15. What is the difference in aim of old yogic psychology and aim of integral psychology?
16. Give names of methods of integral psychology.
17. What is pre-vision? Describe The Mother's pre-vision of India's independence.

18. How and why Sri Aurobindo and the Mother helped the Allied powers in World War II?
19. Describe in short how infantryman Jon Kelly came to know about Sri Aurobindo?
20. How did The Mother misguide Hitler to attack Russia?
21. List five experiences of Dr. Eben that proves integral psychology to be true.
22. Does Ramanujan and Sri Ramakrishna's experience prove that method of direct knowledge is a valid method?

Essay Type Questions

1. The Consciousness (or, Adya Shakti) is the fundamental thing in all big and small things. Explain this statement giving example of the universe, unconscious unanimated matter, atom and man. Either use the word consciousness or use the word Adya Sakti everywhere in your essay.
2. Describe the field of the integral psychology.
3. What are the aims of integral psychology?
4. Describe the methods of integral psychology in short.
5. Why Sri Auromere's psychology is called integral psychology?
6. Bring out the nature of Integral Psychology.
7. With what attitude should one study and practice integral psychology?

IV. OTHER CHARACTERISTICS OF INTEGRAL PSYCHOLOGY

Short Answer Type Questions

1. Integral Psychology is compound of _____ and _____. (Fill in the gaps)
2. Why is integral psychology called evolutionary?
3. Why is integral psychology called yogic?
4. Why is integral psychology called experimental?
5. Why is integral psychology called global?

6. Practice of integral psychology would mean practice of _____.
   (Fill in the gaps)
7. Why the term psychology is applicable to integral psychology and not to scientific psychology?
8. Why can we say that integral psychology is fast developing?
9. Can one practice integral psychology for transforming oneself without depending on personal force of The Mother?

Essay Type Questions

1. Describe a few features of integral psychology.

V. INTEGRAL PSYCHOLOGY COMPARED TO SCIENTIFIC PSYCHOLOGY AND OTHER YOGIC PSYCHOLOGY

Short Answer Type Questions

1. Why have Western Psychologists, especially Professional Psychologists, started borrowing some aspects of Sri Auromere's integral psychology and other yogic psychologies?
2. Which two branches of Western psychology are more influenced by integral yogic psychology?
3. Explain the Heavenly Archetype of lotus.
4. Scientific psychology must be called mentology. Give the reason.
5. The word psychology is in fact applicable to integral psychology only. Is it true? Why?
6. What is the remark of The Mother on the study of psychology?

Essay Type Questions

1. State in your words Sri Aurobindo and The Mother's observations on the Freud's psychoanalysis.
2. Scientific psychology has started to be more complete? Explain.

Exercise

1. Create a table showing the similarity and differences between integral psychology and scientific psychology. A model of the table is given below:

Table

Integral Psychology and Scientific Psychology

Aspects to be Compared	Integral Psychology	Scientific Psychology
Aim		
Field: Subject of Study		
Method		
Approach & Method		

SELF TEST

Fill the gaps in the following sentences with the correct word/s

1. Integral psychology studies _____. (Individual, Universal, Transcendental, all three)
2. The literature of Auromere's psychology is _____. (meager, abundant)
3. The theme of The Mother's and Sri Aurobindo's writings is _____. (sociological, philosophical, religious, psychological)
4. Vedic and integral psychology's categories of consciousness are _____. (similar, same)
5. The Book *Essays on the Gita* contains the message of _____. (Sri Aurobindo, Sri Krishna)
6. In the west the Greek Philosopher _____ and his followers first time coined the word Psychology to name "the study of self of man" that was being carried out as a part of _____.

7. The subject matter of study of psychology in the West went on changing from study of _____, to_____, to _____, to _____ and it started returning back towards the ancient *vedic* knowledge of Inner-self (*Antaratma*) from the time of the psychoanalyst Freud of Germany and now it has been made to reach at the old starting place "self" by transpersonal and humanistic psychologists influenced by Sri Auromere's integral psychology.

8. Integral psychology can really be called _____, and the current scientific psychology should be called _____.

9. Sri Aurobindo and The Mother are really super psychologists, because_____.

10. Integral psychology is called Auromere's psychology, because _____.

11. _____ is the guiding force of practical integral psychology.

12. Sri Aurobindo has recognised the limitations of all world psychologies. Three of them as noted in this book are _____, _____, _____.

13. Aim of integral psychology is to divine the _____, _____ and ____.

14. Two Methods of integral psychology are _____ and _____.

15. _____ is evolving from the Inconscient.

16. Which God came to meet Sri Aurobindo in the Alipore jail?

17. Integral psychology is joint creation of _____ and _____.

18. _____ and _____ are two spiritual psychology of West.

19. Help of the force of _____ is a must for transformation of Personality.

20. According to Sri Aurobindo the field of old Psychoanalysis is _____, _____ and _____.

21. According to The Mother, old Psychoanalysis is _____. (useful, dangerous)

CHAPTER III

CREATION OF THE UNIVERSE AND
THE EARTH AND EVOLUTION OF
THE HUMAN BEING

I.   INADEQUATE KNOWLEDGE OF RATIONALISTIC
     SCIENCE ABOUT EVOLUTION

II. THE CREATION OF THE CONSCIENT GLORIOUS
     UNIVERSE

III. DEVOLUTION OF THE CONSCIENT UNIVERSE INTO THE
     INCONSCIENT UNIVERSE

IV. INVOLUTION OF *ADYA MATRI SHAKTI* IN THE
     INCONSCIENT FOR ITS REDEMPTION

V.   THE TERRESTRIAL EVOLUTION

   1. The involved Shakti Initiates Evolution Step by Step
   2. The Mother's Words on the Terrestrial Evolution
   3. Sri Aurobindo on Evolution
   4. The Mother's Story of the Creation of the Conscient Universe:
      The Process of Devolution, Involution and the Terrestrial
      Evolution

VI. EVOLUTION AND THE AVATAR

   1. Definition of the Avatar
   2. The Object of Avatarhood
   3. An Illustration of the Ten Avatars
   4. The Recent Latest Biune Avatar (Kalki): Sri Aurobindo and
      the Mother

Boxes:

(3.1) *The Mother, the Creator of the Universe*

(3.2) *The sacrifice of the Divine Shakti: Involution of Para-Prakriti for Effecting the Evolution on Earth*

(3.3) *The object of Avatarhood Given in the Bhagavad-Gita and as Stated by Sri Aurobindo*

(3.4) *Sri Aurobindo on "Ten Incarnations and the Evolution"*

(3.5) *Gita and Ten Incarnations*

(3.6) *Sri Aurobindo is the Latest Avatar: an Announcement by the Mother*

(3.7) *The Mother and Sri Aurobindo are Kalki Avatar*

(3.8) *Sri Aurobindo on the Mother*

Tables:

(3.1) *The Mother (परमेश्वरी) manifests four Beings to create a Glorious Universe*

(3.2) *The Devolution: Four Divine Powers turn into Four Hostile Powers (Four Asuras)*

(3.3) *Involution and Descending planes of Consciousness*

(3.4) *The Gradual Steps of Involution and Evolution in The Mother's Story*

Pictures:

(3.1) *Sri Aurobindo*

(3.2) *The Mother: Kali Puja, 10th November 1958*

(3.3) *Vaman Avatar*

(3.4) *Buddhavatar*

(3.5) *Krishnavatar*

(3.6) *Sri Aurobindo and The Mother: Darshan Photo*

Appendices:

(3.1) *Sri Aurobindo's Words on Involution and Evolution*

I. INADEQUATE KNOWLEDGE OF RATIONALISTIC SCIENCE ABOUT THE CREATION AND TERRESTRIAL EVOLUTION

In this chapter different planes or grades of the consciousness and beings will be explained, as they are created during the process of devolution and terrestrial evolution.

The rationalistic materialistic science (तार्किक भौतिक विज्ञान) believes that the matter is the only primary original existence and from it vegetation, animal and man have evolved on earth. But, in fact, the matter has evolved from the Inconscient (असत्), which itself has devolved from the superconscient Sachchidananda (सच्चिदानंद), from which all other existences, visible and invisible, have developed, and thus Sachchidananda is the only primary original existence or Being. Sachchidananda (सच्चिदानंद) has three triune aspects: (i) *Sat, (ii) Chit and (iii) Anand. Sat* may be called in English the Transcendent Existence or Being[81] (परम अस्तित्व, परम पुरुष, पुरुषोत्तम, परमात्मा), *Chit* may be called the Transcendent Consciousness (*Parameshvari, Adya Shakti,* परम चेतना, परा-प्रकृति) and *Anand* may be called the Transcendent Bliss or Delight (परम आनन्द). Sachchidananda is infinite triune oneness,

---

[81] [Unknown Author] *A Glossary of Sanskrit terms in The Synthesis of Yoga,* (Pondicherry-605 002, India: Sri Aurobindo Ashram 1969) , p. 61

एकमेवाद्वितीयम **and** cause of everything in this visible and other invisible worlds.

The phenomena of devolution of Inconscient (अचित) from the Superconscient Sachchidananda and gradual evolution of matter, vegetation, animal and man from the inconscient is an occult and enigmatic secret knowledge which is beyond the rational means of knowledge, such as rational mind, physical senses and material instruments of observation. This secret knowledge is revealed to the psychic, spiritual, and supramental senses and consciousness only. So, it has been missed by the rational science. **Darwin's scientific theory of evolution** has described the evolution of forms of living organisms on earth, but has not given the cause of evolution of the forms; it means *the theory* **has not been able to explain the phenomena of evolution.** It has not been able to cognize that it is actually the consciousness in the forms that has been evolving itself and its own forms and this evolving consciousness is the cause of the evolution of the forms. Thus it has missed the main aim of the science, the aim of explaining phenomena. Of course, recently Western psychologists have realised the inadequacy of rational psychology and they have begun to employ super-rational methods of knowledge and search out a greater and truer psychology. This inadequacy of rational method and knowledge has been already noted while discussing the method of integral psychology in the sub-section 3 of the section III of chapter II, and while discussing how the Western scientific psychology is now becoming more complete in the sub-section 2 of the section V of chapter II.

Ancient Vedic seers (ऋषि) of the Pre-Historic Era had this super-rational psychological knowledge (तर्कातीत, तर्कोपरि ज्ञान). It was preserved with oral tradition and documentation and passed on by one generation to the next generation by select groups of Brahmins in its original words and sound until it got documented on paper. The Vedic Texts are garbed in a mystical symbolic language and are synoptic expressions. **Now, Sri Aurobindo and The Mother**[82] **have updated the ancient Vedic psychological knowledge of evolution and rendered in a language that the modern mind can understand.** The Mother and Sri Aurobindo are thus modern super-psychologists, for they have given a greater and higher psychology than the materialistic rational psychologists have given. In this chapter, Sri Aurobindo and The Mother's Knowledge (दर्शन) about Devolution, Involution, and Evolution is briefly given.

II. THE CREATION OF THE CONSCIENT GLORIOUS UNIVERSE

As noted above, the Sachchidananda is the trinity of transcendent divine existence, transcendent divine consciousness and transcendent divine bliss manifesting the universe. The transcendent consciousness (*the Adya Shakti*, the Mother, the *para-prakriti*) manifests the universe that is sanctioned by the Supreme. When the Supreme Divine (*Parameshvar* or Sachchidananda) wanted to objectivise Himself to see Himself as a universe, He asked His Creatrix Divine Consciousness the *Adya Shakti*, the *Parameshvari*, to create the universe as He wished. *See Box 3.1.* So She emanates four Beings to start this universal development which was to be the progressive objectivisation of all that is potentially contained in the Supreme. These Beings were, in the principle of their existence: Consciousness and Light, Life, Bliss and Love, and Truth. *See Table 3.1.* They set to develop the universe which was in the beginning a Glorious Golden Divine Universe. This, so to say, was the beginning of a Conscient

---

[82] For elaborate reading refer: CWM, Vol. 4, pp. 241-42; CWM, Vol. 9, pp. 205-7 and CWM, Vol. 8, pp. 339-40. SABCL Vol. 19, Chs. 16 & 23-28

Glorious Universe (दिव्य जगत). But unfortunately they took a wrong turn and it devolved into a dark inconscient universe.

Box 3.1

The Mother, *आद्या शक्ति*, the Creator of the Universe

Sri Aurobindo writes in his book *The Mother*, "The one original transcendent Shakti, the Mother stands above all the worlds and bears in her eternal consciousness the Supreme Divine. Alone, she harbours the absolute Power and the ineffable Presence; containing or calling the Truths that have to be manifested, she brings them down from the Mystery in which they were hidden into the light of her infinite consciousness and gives them a form of force in her omnipotent power and her boundless life and a body in the universe. The Supreme is manifest in her forever as the everlasting Sachchidananda, manifested through her in the worlds as the one and dual consciousness of Ishwara-Shakti and the dual principle of Purusha-Prakriti, embodied by her in the Worlds and the Planes and the Gods and their Energies and figured because of her as all that is in the known worlds and in unknown others. All is her play with the Supreme; all is her manifestation of the mysteries of the Eternal, the miracles of the Infinite. **All is she, for all are parcel and portion of the divine Conscious-Force. Nothing can be here or elsewhere but what she decides and the Supreme sanctions**; nothing can take shape except what she moved by the Supreme perceives and forms after casting it into seed in her creating Ananda." [Bold letters are ours.]

From: Sri Aurobindo; The Mother with Letters on the Mother; CWSA Vol. 32 (Sri Aurobindo Ashram Publication Department, Sri Aurobindo Ashram, Pondicherry, 605 002, India, 2002); pp. 14-15

Table 3.1

The Mother (परमेश्वरी) manifests four Beings to create a Glorious Universe

---

1. The Being of Consciousness and Light (परम चेतना-प्रकाश)

2. The Being of Life (अमर जीवनम)

3. The Being of Bliss and Love (परम आनन्द एवं परम प्रेम)

4. The Being of Truth (परम सत्य)

III. DEVOLUTION OF THE CONSCIENT UNIVERSE INTO THE INCONSCIENT UNIVERSE

Now, these four powers were all-powerful and had full freedom, so they had their own conception of how it had to be done. Instead of acting as servant and instrument of the Supreme Creatrix Shakti (*Adya Shakti*), they chose to do it independently according to their own conceptions and whims. As soon as there was this separation between the Supreme and what had been emanated, all the four divine Beings (*called चत्वारो देवाः, Chatvaro Devah; or पूर्वे देवाः, Purve Devah in Veda*) devolved into four *Asuras:* Consciousness changed into inconscience (*Achit*), Light (*Param Prakash*) into Darkness (अंधकार), Life (अमर जीवनम) turned into Death (मृत्यु, मर्त्य जीवनम), Love (*Param Prem*) turned into Hatred (धिक्कार), Bliss (Param Anand) turned into Suffering (दुखः), and Truth (*Param Satya*) into Falsehood (असत्य). *See Table 3.2.* As a result the glorious divine conscious universe turned into a pitch-black undivine inconscient universe (तमोग्रस्त विश्व). There was now darkness covered with greater darkness: तमः आसित तमसा निगूढम (*Tamah Aasit Tamasah Nigudham)* as it is said in the Veda.

Table 3.2

The Devolution: Four Divine Powers turn into
Four Hostile Powers (Four Asuras)

1. Consciousness turned into Inconscience (*Achit*) and Light into Darkness (अंधकार)

2. Life (अमर-शाश्वत- जीवनम्) turned into Death (मृत्यु, मर्त्य- क्षणिक- जीवनम्)

3. Love (*Param Prem*) turned into Hatred (धिक्कार), Bliss (*Param Anand*) into Suffering (दुखः)

4. Truth (*Param Satya*) turned into Falsehood (असत्य)

On gazing this dark creation, the Creatrix Mother turned to the Supreme for a remedy, and the Supreme asked Her to precipitate herself, to involve herself, into the Inconscience to redeem it. So She initiates the process of involution or descent, as described below.

IV. INVOLUTION OF *ADYA MATRI SHAKTI* (आद्या मातृ शक्ति) IN THE INCONSCIENT FOR ITS REDEMPTION

"On receiving command from the Supreme the original superconscient Divine Shakti, the Mother Energy (मातृ शक्ति) or the Original Shakti (आदि शक्ति) descends downwards step by step and plunges into the Inconscience. In the first step of descent she creates the subtle universal plane of the Sachchidananda consciousness and in it forms Anandamaya Worlds and individual beings proper to those Anandamaya worlds. Then descends step by step through subtle planes of the supramental, the overmental (spiritual), the mental, the vital and the physical consciousness forming corresponding Supramental, Overmental, Mental, Vital and Physical subtle Worlds and in those worlds beings and powers proper to them and finally culminated in and involved herself completely in the Inconscient Universe. This is termed as involution."[83] *See Box 3.2 and Table 3.3*

Box 3.2

The sacrifice of the Divine Shakti: Involution of Para-Prakriti for Effecting the Evolution on Earth

Describing the involution of The Mother in the Inconscient Sri Aurobindo writes in his book *The Mother*, "The Mother not only governs all from above but she descends into this lesser triple universe. Impersonally, all things here, even the movements of the Ignorance, are herself in veiled power and her creations in diminished substance, her Nature body and Nature-force, and they exist because, moved by the mysterious fiat of the Supreme to work out something that was there in the possibilities of the Infinite, she has consented to the great sacrifice and has put on like a mask the soul and forms of the Ignorance. But personally too she has stooped to descend here into the Darkness that she may lead it to the Light, into the Falsehood and Error that she may convert it to the Truth, into this Death that she may turn it to godlike Life, into this world-pain and its obstinate sorrow and suffering that she may end it in the transforming ecstasy of her sublime Ananda. In her deep and great love for her children she has consented to put on herself the cloak of this obscurity, condescended to bear the attacks and torturing influences of the powers of the Darkness and the Falsehood,

---

[83] Patel C. P.; *Psychological Foundation of the "Free Progress System" as Evolved in Sri Aurobindo International Centre of Education* (Publisher: Sri Aurobindo Study Circle (Bokhira-Porbandar), Bokhira, Gujarat, 360579, India, 1986); p. 56 (the quoted text is updated version)

borne to pass through the portals of the birth that is a death, taken upon herself the pangs and sorrows and sufferings of the creation, since it seemed that thus alone could it be lifted to the Light and Joy and Truth and eternal Life. This is the great sacrifice called sometimes the sacrifice of the Purusha, but much more deeply the holocaust of Prakriti, the sacrifice of the Divine Mother."

From: Sri Aurobindo, *The Mother with Letters on The Mother: CWSA Vol.32* (Sri Aurobindo Ashram Publication Department, Sri Aurobindo Ashram, Pondicherry, 605002, India, 2011); p. 17

Table 3. 3

Involution and Descending Planes of Consciousness

The Transcendent Divine Trinity: Sachchidananda

Adya Chit Shakti of the Trinity Descends Step by Step Creating Descending Planes of the Universal Consciousness

1. The Universal Divine Plane of Sachchidananda Consciousness

2. The Universal Plane of Supramental Consciousness and in it Supramental Worlds & beings and forces proper to them

3. The Universal Plane of the Spiritual (Overmental) Consciousness and Overmental Worlds and beings and forces proper to them

4. The Universal Plane of Mental Consciousness and in it Mental Worlds & beings and forces proper to them

5. Universal Plane of Vital Consciousness and in it Vital Worlds & beings and forces proper to them

6. Universal Plane of Physical Consciousness and in it Physical Worlds & beings and forces proper to them

7. Universal Plane of the Subconscious Consciousness and in it Subconscious Worlds & beings and forces Proper to them

Then,

   She plunges into the Inconscient (*Achit*) and in it Inconscient Worlds & individual beings and forces proper to them

---

From the Inconscience, then the involved Shakti initiates the return journey towards the Superconscient Divine in a similar reverse gradual movement and that process is called the terrestrial evolution. Thus the Superconscient is prior to the Inconscient and both are prior to involution and evolution.

V. THE TERRESTRIAL EVOLUTION

1. THE INVOLVED SHAKTI INITIATES EVOLUTION STEP BY STEP

The plunged consciousness has made the inconscient to release progressively on earth

(i) the subconscious physical being and consciousness and world and material things in it, then

(ii) the vital being and consciousness, vital world and vegetation and animals in it, and next

(iii) the mental being and consciousness, mental world and human being in it, and then

(iv) the psychic being and consciousness, psychic world and human being secretly governed by their more or less developed personal psychic being and consciousness. The psychic starts becoming active at the nexus of the vital and mental planes of consciousness to lead the evolution mostly covertly from behind the veil of physical-vital-mental nature in it. The progressive evolution raises mental being into

(v) the overmental spiritual being and consciousness and spiritual world. The overmental being and consciousness will then lead the evolution to the next stage of

(vi) the supramental being and consciousness and the supramental world. This step will begin the cycle of the *satya yuga*, the

Golden Age and progressively lead to the full realisation of an age which ancients called the Golden Age, the *Satya yuga, (Suvarna yuga, krita yuga)*. When man and the world will attain the supramental consciousness they will have totally got rid of inconscient (*Achetana*) and ignorance (*Avidya*). The Vidya will rule the life of man and the world. The Creatrix would have accomplished its task of redeeming the Inconscient world. But evolution would not stop here; it will proceed to the next stage of

(vii) the plane of the superconscient Sachchidananda, the divine world and the divine-being. But again

(viii) **it will not be the end of evolution of consciousness, for the Divine Consciousness has infinite possibilities.** And so as envisioned by **Vedic Seers** new evolutionary cycle must start. Quoting Vedic poets, Sri Aurobindo states in his book *The Human Cycle* that

" … This ascent to the first spiritual levels would not be the end of the divine march, a culmination that left nothing more to be achieved on earth. For there would be still yet higher levels within the supramental realm, as the old Vedic poets knew when they spoke of the spiritual life as a constant ascent —

> *brahmā́ṇas tvā śatakrato*
> *úd vaṃśám iva yemire;*
> *yát sā́noḥ sā́num ā́ruhad,*
> *bhū́ry áspaṣṭa kártvam.*

> ब्रह्माणस त्वा शतक्रतो
> उद् वंशम् इव येमिरे।
> यत्सानोः सानुम् आरुहद्
> भूरि अस्पष्ट कर्त्वम॥   (ऋ १.१०.१ & १.१०.२)[84]

---

[84] શ્રી સુન્દરમના પુસ્તક *"ધ્યાત્મિક સમાજ"* (દક્ષિણા કાર્યાલય, શ્રી અરવિન્દ આશ્રમ, પૉન્ડિચેરી, ૬૦૫૦૦૨, ઇન્ડિયા) માંથી શ્લોકનો ઋગ્વેદમાંની સંદર્ભસંખ્યા મળી છે.

'The priests of the word climb thee like a ladder, O hundred-powered. As one ascends from peak to peak, there is made clear the much that has still to be done.'

"But once the foundation has been secured, the rest develops by a progressive self-unfolding and the soul is sure of its way. As again it is phrased by the ancient Vedic singers,—

abhy àvasthâḥ prá jāyante,
prá vavrér vavrís ciketa;
upásthe mātúr ví caṣṭe,

अभ्यवस्थाः प्र जायन्ते
प्र वव्रेर वव्रिश चिकेत।
उपस्थे मातुर वि चष्टे॥   (ऋ. ५.१९.१)[85]

'State is born upon state; covering after covering becomes conscious of knowledge; in the lap of the Mother the soul sees.'

"This at least is the highest hope, the possible destiny that opens out before the human view, and it is a possibility which the progress of the human mind seems on the way to redevelop. If the light that is being born increases, if the number of individuals who seek to realise the possibility in themselves and in the world grows large and they get nearer the right way, then the Spirit who is here in man, now a concealed divinity, a developing light and power, will descend more fully as the Avatar of a yet unseen and unguessed Godhead from above into the soul of mankind and into the great individualities in whom the light and power are the strongest. There will then be fulfilled the change that will prepare the transition of human life from its present limits into those larger and purer horizons; the

---

[85] એજન

90

earthly evolution will have taken its grand impetus upward and accomplished the revealing step in a divine progression of which the birth of thinking and aspiring man from the animal nature was only an obscure preparation and a far-off promise."[86]

2. THE MOTHER'S WORDS ON THE TERRESTRIAL EVOLUTION

Hereunder is quoted the lucid, succinct, convincing, optimistic and assuring and encouraging description of terrestrial evolution given by The Mother in Her book *Ideal Child*.

"There is an ascending evolution in nature which goes from the stone to the plant, from the plant to the animal, from the animal to man. Because man is, for the moment, the last rung at the summit of the ascending evolution, he considers himself as the final stage in this ascension and believes there can be nothing on earth superior to him. In that he is mistaken. In his physical nature he is yet wholly an animal, thinking and speaking animal, but still an animal in his material habits and instincts. Undoubtedly, nature cannot be satisfied with such an imperfect result; she endeavours to bring out a being who will be to man what man is to animal, a being who will remain a man in its external form, and yet whose consciousness will rise far above the mental and its slavery to ignorance.

"Sri Aurobindo came upon earth to teach this truth to man. He told them that man is only a transitional being living in a mental consciousness, but with the possibility of acquiring a new consciousness, the truth consciousness, and capable of living a life perfectly harmonious, good and beautiful, happy and fully conscious. During the whole of his life upon earth, Sri Aurobindo gave all his time to establish in himself this

---

[86] SABCL Vol.15; pp. 253-254

consciousness which he called the supramental, and to help those gathered around him to realise it."[87]

These words are addressed to the resident children (students) of Sri Aurobindo Ashram and all children (students) outside of Sri Aurobindo. Let us view them as addressed to us all, for She is mother of all, of the earth and of the universe, the whole earth is Her Ashram.

3. SRI AUROBINDO ON EVOLUTION

Picture 3.1 Sri Aurobindo

---

[87] The Mother; *Ideal Child* (Sri Aurobindo Ashram, Pondicherry, 605 002, India, 1978); pp.11-12

Describing the terrestrial evolution, Sri Aurobindo writes,

"In the descent into the material plane of which our natural life is a product, the lapse culminates in a total Inconscience out of which an involved Being and Consciousness have to emerge by a gradual evolution. This inevitable evolution first develops, as it is bound to develop, Matter and a material universe; in Matter, Life appears and living physical beings; in Life, Mind manifests and embodied thinking and living beings; in Mind, ever increasing its powers and activities in forms of Matter, the Supermind or Truth-Consciousness must appear, inevitably, by the very force of what is contained in the Inconscience and the necessity in Nature to bring it into manifestation. Supermind appearing manifests the Spirit's self-knowledge and whole knowledge in a supramental living being and must bring about by the same law, by an inherent necessity and inevitability, the dynamic manifestation here of the divine Existence, Consciousness and Delight of existence. It is this that is the significance of the plan and order of the terrestrial evolution; it is this necessity that must determine all its steps and degrees, its principle and its process. Mind, Life and Matter are the realised powers of the evolution and well-known to us; Supermind and the triune aspects of Sachchidananda are the secret principles which are not yet put in front and have still to be realised in the forms of the manifestation, and we know them only by hints and a partial and fragmentary action still not disengaged from the lower movement and therefore not easily recognisable. But their evolution too is part of the destiny of the soul in the Becoming, — there must be a realisation and dynamisation in earth-life and in Matter not only of Mind but of all that is above it, all that has descended indeed but is still concealed in earth-life and Matter".[88]

This being the plan of evolution, Sri Aurobindo says in his epic poem *Savitri*:

"We are sons of God and must be even as he:
His human portion, we must grow divine."[89]

The Mother has said the same thing in a story-telling style. Her story is quoted below.

Picture 3.2 The Mother Kali Puja, 10 November 1958[90]

---

[88] SABCL Vol. 19; pp. 663-4

[89] Sri Aurobindo; *Savitri: SABCL Vol. 28* (Sri Aurobindo Ashram Trust, Pondicherry, 605002, India; 1970); p.67

[90] CWM Vol. 9; p iii

4. THE MOTHER'S STORY OF THE CREATION OF THE CONSCIENT UNIVERSE: THE PROCESS OF DEVOLUTION, INVOLUTION AND THE TERRESTRIAL EVOLUTION

The Mother had answered questions received from students of her class on 16 October 1957; Her answer is quoted below:

"I have received four questions. Naturally they are not about what I have just read, and they are on three different subjects. And each one needs a very lengthy answer. But still, I am going to take the first two which go together. They are about the involution of the Spirit[91].

The first question:

"If all that is to manifest is already involved in Matter, are there, hidden in it, other principles besides the supermind which will be revealed when it has been fully manifested?"

Logically speaking, "yes", for essentially, there is an identity between Matter and the Supreme. [For Matter is a form of the Supreme and the Supreme is in Matter.] But – and this brings in the second question:

"Did the involution take place in Time and does it have a history as evolution has?"

"It could almost be said that the answer to this question depends on the mental attitude of the person who asks it.... Scholars will tell you that there are different schools which have spoken about these things in ways that are also very different. There are the metaphysicians who deny any history, minds that

---

[91] Sri Aurobindo tells us that evolution is the result of an involution. Thus, life is involved in Matter, mind is involved in life and supermind is involved in mind. Nothing can come out of nothing; it is because the Supreme is involved in Matter that the Supreme can emerge from Matter. — Editor

are essentially speculative, philosophical and, as I said, metaphysical, abstract, who consider that histories are only for children. There are the psychologists who translate everything into movements of consciousness, and finally there are those who love images and for whom universal history is a great development which might be described as "cinematographic", and this development in pictures is for them something much more living and tangible, for even if it is only symbolic, it makes them understand things in a more intimate and real way.

"It goes without saying that the three explanations are equally true, and that the important thing is to be able to synthesise and harmonise them in one's thought. But we shall put aside the rigidities of metaphysics, for it is better to read about them in the books of scholars who tell you things in a very precise, very exact and very dry fashion! The psychological point of view... it is better to live it than speak about it.

"So we are left with the story for children. It is good to be always a child. And although we must take care not to believe in it as a dogma in which nothing should be changed if one doesn't want to be sacrilegious, we can at least take these stories as a means to make living to our childlike consciousness something which would otherwise be too remote from us.

"There *we can choose from many stories that have been told, stories more or less true, more or less complete, more or less expressive. ...* if one can relive this story, at least partially and in its broad outlines, it helps one to understand and hence to master the how and why of things. Some people have done that, they are the ones usually considered as initiates, occultists and prophets at the same time – and very beautiful stories have been told.

"I am going to tell you one, very succinctly. Don't take it as a gospel! Take it rather as a story.

"When the Supreme decided to exteriorise Himself in order to be able to see Himself, the first thing in Himself which He exteriorised was the Knowledge of the world and the Power to create it. This Knowledge-Consciousness and Force began its work; and in the supreme Will there was a plan, and the first principle of this plan was the expression of both the essential Joy and the essential Freedom, which seemed to be the most interesting feature of this creation.

"So intermediaries were needed to express this Joy and Freedom in forms. And at first four Beings were emanated to start this universal development which was to be the progressive objectivisation of all that is potentially contained in the Supreme. These Beings were, in the principle of their existence: Consciousness and Light, Life, Bliss and Love, and Truth.

"You can easily imagine that they had a sense of great power, great strength, of something tremendous, for they were essentially the very principle of these things. Besides, they had full freedom of choice, for this creation was to be Freedom itself. ... As soon as they set to work – they had their own conception of how it had to be done – being totally free, they chose to do it independently. Instead of taking the attitude of servant and instrument ... they naturally took the attitude of the master. Mistake – as I may call it – was the first cause, the essential cause of all the disorder in the universe. As soon as there was separation – for that is the essential cause, separation – as soon as there was separation between the Supreme and what had been emanated, Consciousness changed into inconscience (*Achit*), Light (*Param Prakash*) into darkness, Love (*Param Prem*) into hatred, Bliss (*Param Anand*) into suffering, Life (*Amartyata*) into death and Truth (*Param Satya*) into falsehood. And they proceeded with their creations independently, in separation and disorder."

97

"The result is the world as we see it. It was made progressively, stage by stage, and it would truly take a little too long to tell you all that, but finally, the consummation is Matter – obscure, inconscient, miserable.... The creative Force which had emanated these four Beings, essentially for the creation of the world, witnessed what was happening, and turning to the Supreme she prayed for the remedy and the cure of the evil that had been done.

"Then she was given the command to precipitate her Consciousness into this inconscience, her Love into this suffering, and her Truth into this falsehood. And a greater consciousness, a more total love, a more perfect truth than what had been emanated at first, plunged, so to say, into the horror of Inconsciousness in order to awaken in it consciousness, love and truth, and to begin the movement of Redemption which was to bring the material universe back to its supreme origin.

"So, there have been what might be called "successive involutions" in Matter, and a history of these involutions. The present result of these involutions is the appearance of the Supermind emerging from the inconscience; **but there is nothing to indicate that after this appearance there will be no others... for the Supreme is inexhaustible and will always create new worlds.**

"That is my story"[92]

Steps of successive involution and evolution narrated in this story are itemised in the *Table 3.4.*

---

[92] CWM Vol. 9, pp. 204-207

Table 3.4

The Gradual Steps of Involution and Evolution in The Mother's Story

---

Phase 1
CREATION OF THE CONSCIENT UNIVERSE
(सत अस्तित्व, दिव्य विश्व)

(1) The Supreme exteriorised Himself to see Himself: He exteriorised consciousness (शक्ति):

> (i) The Knowledge of the world, The Knowledge Consciousness and
> (ii) The Power to create it, The Power Consciousness.

Plan in the Supreme Will and the first principle of the plan is to express both the

> (i) essential Joy and
> (ii) essential Freedom

(2) For this work four intermediary Beings (पूर्वे देवाः Purve Devah) were emanated: in the principle of their existence they were

> (i) Consciousness,
> (ii) Life,
> (iii) Bliss and Love and
> (iv) Truth.

Their function was to express

> (i) essential Joy and
> (ii) essential Freedom

in forms and start the creation of the conscient universe (**सत अस्तित्व, दिव्य विश्व**) by progressively objectivising what is potentially contained in the Supreme.

Phase 2
DEVOLUTION: THE DIVINE CONSCIENT EXISTENCE BECOMES INCONSCIENT EXISTENCE (**असत अस्तित्व, अदिव्य विश्व**)

These **four Beings** were tremendously powerful and had full freedom of choice, for the creation was form of "Essential Freedom" itself. They chose to create the universe independently: They ceased to be servant of The Supreme and assumed the role of Masters. This separation turned them into *four Asuras* (असुराः)

  (i)   Consciousness turned into **inconscience**
  (ii) Life turned into **darkness**
  (iii) Bliss and Love turned into suffering and **hatred**, and
  (iv) Truth turned into **falsehood**

This deformation progressively proceeded to ultimately result in the creation of subconscious material universe, obscure, dark and miserable.

Phase 3
INVOLUTION: THE CREATIVE FORCE INVOLVES ITSELF IN THE INCONSCIENT EXISTENCE TO TURN IT INTO THE DIVINE EXISTENCE (**दिव्य अस्तित्व**)

Seeing the evil creation, the Creatrix Force which had emanated these four Beings, turns to The Supreme and prayed for the remedy: The Supreme commanded Her to precipitate

(i) Her greater Consciousness in the inconscience,

(ii) Her Life in the darkness

(iii) Her more total Bliss and Love in the suffering and hatred *(Refer Appendix: 3.3:* "Love is the Cause of the Evolution according to The Mother," *at the end of this chapter)*, and

(iv) Her more perfect Truth in the falsehood

So, the Creatrix plunged into the horror of Matter in order to awaken in it consciousness, love, life and truth and to begin the movement of Redemption which was to bring the material universe back to its supreme origin. Sri Aurobindo[93] defines this sacrifice of the Divine Shakti as holocaust of Prakriti (The Transcendental Nature, पराशक्ति, पराप्रकृति). *Please refer Box 3.2:* "The sacrifice of the Divine Shakti: Involution of Para-Prakriti for Effecting the Evolution on Earth" in this chapter.

Phase 4
EVOLUTION

From the inconsciousness gradually emerges matter, vital, mind, overmind and supermind one by one and after that the evolution must continue, for as The Mother tells in Her story, "but there is nothing to indicate that after this appearance there will be no others... for the Supreme is inexhaustible and will always create new worlds." (*Refer above Section V: The Terrestrial Evolution, sub-section 1 – (viii), and below Section VI: Evolution and the Avatar, sub-section 4 – Kalki – (iv)*).

Please refer to Appendix 3.1: "Sri Aurobindo's Words on Involution and Evolution" *at the end of this chapter for more*

---

[93] Sri Aurobindo, *The Mother, deluxe edition 1953* (Sri Aurobindo Ashram, Pondicherry, 605002, India; 1953); pp. 50-52

details of the description of involution and evolution and the Appendix 3.2: "Sri Aurobindo's Description of the Material Universe that First Evolved from the Inconscient: Evolution of the Matter from the Inconscience" at the end of this chapter for description of the manifested Material Universe from the Inconscient.

VI. EVOLUTION AND THE AVATAR

1. DEFINITION OF THE AVATAR

Defining an Avatar in a letter to a Sadhak, Sri Aurobindo writes, "An Avatar, roughly speaking, is one who is conscious of the divine born in him or descended into him and governing from within his will, life, and action; he feels identified inwardly with this divine power and presence."[94] Sri Ram, Sri Krishna, The Mother & Sri Aurobindo are examples of such Avatars.

2. THE OBJECT OF AVATARHOOD

An Avatar of the Supreme descends, generally, at the time of a crisis of evolution to carry forward the evolution, for establishing the next stage of evolution, the next *Yuga:* there are five objectives of the descent of the Avatar on earth says Sri Aurobindo: (*Refer Box 3.3*)[95]:

(i) To exemplify to man that the Divine can manifest in a human body, so that man, after knowing the personality of the divine

---

[94] Sri Aurobindo; Letters on Yoga: SABCL Vol. 22 (Sri Aurobindo Ashram, Pondicherry, 605002, India, 1970); p. 406

[95] Sri Aurobindo; Essays on the Gita: SABCL Vol. 13 (Sri Aurobindo Ashram, Pondicherry, 605002, India, 1970); pp. 150-151

Avatar, may be encouraged to grow personality in himself like that of the divine Avatar.

(ii) It is also to leave the influence of that manifestation vibrating in the earth-nature and the soul of that manifestation presiding over its upward endeavour.

(iii) It is to present a spiritual model of divine manhood, so that man can remodel his ordinary manhood into a figure of that spiritual divine life.

(iv) It is to give a dharma, a religion, – not a mere creed, but a method of inner and outer living, – a way, a rule and law of self-moulding by which he can grow towards divinity.

(v) It is too to hold the society together in its great crises, to support the collective social progress, to break the Asuric forces of the downward gravitation when they grow too insistent, to uphold or restore the great dharma of the Godward law in man's nature, to initiate the work of establishing the kingdom of God (सत्ययुग, कृतयुग, सुवर्णयुग), to ensure victory of the seekers of light and perfection, *sādhūnām* (साधुनाम), and the overthrow of those who fight for the continuance of the evil and the darkness.

Box 3.3:

The object of Avatarhood Given in the Bhagavad-Gita and as Stated by Sri Aurobindo

"But it is to assist that ascent or evolution the descent is made or accepted; that the Gita makes very clear. It is, we might say, (i) to exemplify the possibility of the Divine manifest in the human being, so that man may see what that is and take courage to grow into it. (ii) It is also to leave the influence of that manifestation vibrating in the earth-nature and the soul of that manifestation presiding over its upward endeavour. (iii) It is to give a spiritual mould of divine manhood into which the seeking soul of the human being can cast itself. (iv) It is to give a dharma, a religion, – not a mere creed, but a method of inner and outer living, – a way, a rule and law of self-moulding by which he can grow towards divinity. (v) It is too, since this growth, this ascent is no mere isolated and individual phenomenon, but like all in the divine world-activities a collective business, a work and the work for the race, to assist the human march, to hold it together in its great crises, to break the forces of the downward gravitation when they grow too insistent, to uphold or restore the great dharma of the Godward law in man's nature, to prepare even, however far off, the kingdom of God, the victory of the seekers of light and perfection, *sādhūnām* (साधुनाम्), and the overthrow of those who fight for the continuance of the evil and the darkness. All these are recognised objects of the descent of the Avatar, and it is usually by his work that the mass of men seek to distinguish him and for that that they are ready to worship him. It is only the spiritual who see that this external Avatarhood is a sign, in the symbol of a human life, of the eternal inner Godhead making himself manifest in the field of their own human mentality and corporeality so that they can grow into unity with that and be possessed by it. The divine manifestation of a Christ, Krishna, Buddha in external humanity has for its inner truth the same manifestation of the eternal Avatar within in our own inner humanity. That which has been done in the outer human life of earth, may be repeated in the inner life of all human beings. This is the object of the incarnation, ..."

From: Sri Aurobindo; Essays on the Gita: SABCL Vol. 13 (Sri Aurobindo Ashram, Pondicherry, 605002, India, 1970); pp. 150-151

This Gita's view is well-known to Indians. Now even the theory of Avatarhood is known to people of the world, especially to persons who have interest in Indian spiritual knowledge. Below in Section 3 are depicted Sri Aurobindo's own views on the objectives of ten Hindu Avatars of Vishnu (विष्णु) – (*Refer Box 3.4 and 3.5*).

3. AN ILLUSTRATION OF THE TEN AVATARS

Ten Avatars are listed below in chronological order. We can identify five main stages in the Incarnations of Avatarhood and in evolution on earth: (1) Animal Stage, (2) Animal-Man Stage, (3) Man Stage, (4) Spiritual Man Stage (5) Supramental Man Stage. One need not rule out the next stages of Incarnations, Avatars (*See Box 3.6*).

(1) ANIMAL STAGE

There are <u>three</u> Avatars in animal Stage:

(i) The Fish Avatar *(Matsy-Avatar)*, the animal living in water, then

(ii) The Tortoise Avatar *(Kachchhap-Kurmma-Avatar)*, the amphibious animal living in water and on land, then

(iii) The Boar Avatar *(Varah-Avatar)*, the land animal, then

(2) ANIMAL-MAN STAGE

In the stage bridging animal and man, there is <u>one</u> Avatar:

(iv) The Man-Lion Avatar *(Nrisinh -Avatar)*, bridging man and animal, then

(3) MAN STAGE

In the stage of Man, there are <u>three</u> Avatars:

(v) The Man as dwarf *(Vaman-Avatar)*, small and undeveloped and **physical** but containing in himself the godhead and taking possession of existence, then

Picture 3.3 Vaman Avatar

(vi) The man as **vital-mental** man (*Rajasic Parshuram-Avatar*, then

(vii) The **mental** man, *(Sattwic Ram-Avatar)*, then

(4) SPIRITUAL MAN STAGE

In the stage of spiritual man, there are <u>two</u> Avatars:

(viii) Buddha-Avatar: the **awakened spiritual man**

Picture 3.4 Buddhavatar

(ix) Krishna-Avatar: The overmental Man, The superman,
The complete spiritual man *(Adhimanas-Avatar)*

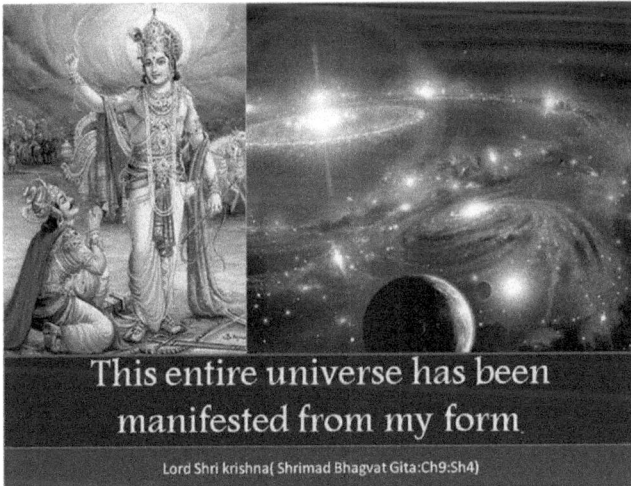

This entire universe has been
manifested from my form

Lord Shri krishna(Shrimad Bhagvat Gita:Ch9:Sh4)

Picture 3.5 Krishnavatar

Krishna establishes and dynamises the spiritual consciousness on earth. A disciple had once asked Sri Aurobindo, if Krishna is the supramental Godhead or the overmind Godhead. Sri Aurobindo had answered:

"Krishna is not the supramental light. The descent of Krishna would mean the descent of the overmind Godhead preparing, though not itself actually, the descent of Supermind and Anand. Krishna is the Anandamaya; he supports the evolution through the overmind leading it towards the Anand."[96]

(5) SUPRAMENTAL MAN STAGE.

In the stage of Supramental Man, there is one Avatar:

(x) Sri Aurobindo and the Mother, the biune Supramental Avatar, the supermind divine-man: The Kalki Avatar: Sri Krishna, the overmind Godhead, descends in Sri Aurobindo's physical on November 24, 1926[97], and then Sri Aurobindo retires completely for concentrated sadhana for the descent of the Supramental Godhead, and that happens on December 5, 1950; he becomes the Supramental-Man, the supramental Avatar. In 1956, The Mother and Sri Aurobindo make The Supramental Shakti descend on earth in its subtle physical consciousness and put the evolution in its charge.

[96] Sri Aurobindo; Letters on Yoga: SABCL Vol. 22 (Sri Aurobindo Ashram, Pondicherry, 605002, India, 1970); p. 405
[97] SABCL Vol. 30: Index and Glossary (Sri Aurobindo Ashram, Pondicherry, 605002, India, 1970); p. 13

Picture 3.6 Sri Aurobindo and The Mother
(Darshan Photo)

Box 3. 4

Sri Aurobindo on "Ten Incarnations and the Evolution"

Avatar is necessary when a special work is to be done and in crises of evolution. The Avatar is a special manifestation while for the rest of the time it is the Divine working within the ordinary human limits as a Vibhuti.

***

Avatarhood would have little meaning if it were not connected with the evolution. *The Hindu procession of the ten Avatars is itself, as it were, a parable of evolution.* First the Fish Avatar, then the amphibious animal between land and water, then the land animal, then the Man-Lion Avatar, bridging man and animal, then man as dwarf, small and undeveloped and physical but containing in himself the godhead and taking possession of existence, then the rajasic, sattwic, nirguna Avatars, leading the human development from the vital rajasic to the sattwic mental man and again the overmental superman. Krishna, Buddha and Kalki depict the last three stages, the stages of the spiritual development – Krishna opens the possibility of overmind, Buddha tries to shoot beyond to the supreme liberation but that liberation is still negative, not returning upon earth to complete positively the evolution; Kalki is to correct this by bringing the Kingdom of the Divine upon earth, destroying the opposing Asura forces. The progression is striking and unmistakable.

As for the lives in between the Avatar lives, it must be remembered that Krishna speaks of many lives in the past, not only a few supreme ones, and secondly that while he speaks of himself as the Divine, in one passage he describes himself as a Vibhuti, *vrishrinam vasudevah*, वृष्णीनाम् वासुदेवः. We may therefore fairly assume that in many lives he manifested as the Vibhuti veiling the fuller Divine Consciousness. If we admit that the object of Avatarhood is to lead the evolution, this is quite reasonable, the Divine appearing as Avatar in the great transitional stages and as Vibhutis to aid the lesser transitions.

From: Sri Aurobindo; *Letters on Yoga*: SABCL Vol. 22 (Sri Aurobindo Ashram, Pondicherry, 605002, India, 1970); p. 401-2

Box 3.5

Gita and Ten Incarnations

In Gita, Sri Krishna says: धर्मसंस्थापनार्थाय सम्भवामि युगे युगे (अध्याय ४, श्लोक ८). In Hindu Vaishnavite Traditional Theory, it means Lord Vishnu reincarnates himself as different animal and human forms according the need and pace of the stage of animal and human evolution. Gita has applied the doctrine of reincarnation, boldly enough, to the Avatar himself. In this regard, Sri Aurobindo wrote a reply-letter to one of his disciples in which he says, "some would interpret **the ten incarnations of Vishnu, first in animal forms, then in the animal man, then in the dwarf man-soul, Vaman, the violent Asuric man, Rama of the axe, the divinely-natured man, a greater Rama, the awakened spiritual man, Buddha, and, preceding him in time, but final in place, the complete divine manhood, Krishna, – for the last Avatar, Kalki, only accomplishes the work Krishna began, – he fulfils in power the great struggle which the previous Avatars prepared in all its potentialities. It is a difficult assumption to our modern mentality, but the language of the Gita seems to demand it.**"

Quoted Sentences From: Sri Aurobindo; *Essays on the Gita:* CWSA Vol. 19: (Sri Aurobindo Ashram, Pondicherry, 605002, India, 1997); pp. 165-167

4. THE KALKI AVATAR: SRI AUROBINDO AND THE MOTHER

Ancient Indian and modern Indian spiritual mystic knowledge have always asserted certain characteristics of Kalki Avatar, which all are applicable to Sri Aurobindo and The Mother.

(i) *Kalki Avatar* will be a female Avatar, and achieve two special works mentioned below in para (ii) and (iii). *(Refer Box 3.4, 3.5, 3.7 & 3.8)*

(ii) Kalki's special work is to gain decisive victory over the dark Asuric forces that oppose the progression of spiritual evolution and ultimately destroy them. *(Refer Box 3.4, 3.5, 3.7 & 3.8). See Box 3.7* to know that Sri Aurobindo and The Mother has accomplished this work.

(iii) Kalki will initiate the Golden Age; Kalki will work for supramental divinisation of individual and the collective humanity *(Refer Box 3.4, 3.5, 3.7 & 3.8). See Box 3.7* to know that Sri Aurobindo and The Mother has accomplished this work.

(iv) Kalki is the last, rather the latest, 10th Avatar, the latest because further new Avatars cannot be ruled out. For The Mother says, "In the eternity of becoming each avatar is only the announcer, the forerunner of a more perfect future realisation." *See Box 3.6.*

Box 3.6

Sri Aurobindo is the Latest Avatar: an Announcement by the Mother

"In the eternity of becoming each avatar is only the announcer, the forerunner of a more perfect future realisation.

And yet men have always the tendency to deify the Avatar of the past in opposition to the Avatar of the future.

Now again Sri Aurobindo has come announcing to the world the realisation of tomorrow; and again his message meets with the same opposition as of all those who preceded him.

But tomorrow will prove the truth of what he revealed and his work will be done".

The Mother

Reference: Shree; *"Bunch of Thoughts in the Light of Sri Aurobindo and other Articles:* (Publisher: Sabnis Anil; 523, 4th main 8th cross, J. P. Nagar 3rd Phase, Bangalore, Karnataka, 560 078); 4th cover Page

---

Box 3.7

The Mother and Sri Aurobindo are Kalki Avatar

The Mother and Sri Aurobindo began partnership in supramental yoga on April 24, 1920 for establishing "victory over the adverse forces", – a work expected from Kalki Avatar by ancient Indian scriptures – is clearly stated by Amal Kiran (K. D. Sethna) in these words:

"It was on April 24 in 1920 that the Mother came finally to settle in Pondicherry by the side of Sri Aurobindo and work with him to establish on earth what he called the Supramental or Truth-Consciousness. It was on April 24, 1937, that she described her "return to Pondicherry" as "the tangible sign of the sure Victory over the adverse forces". And it was on April 24, 1956 that she at last announced the event which had taken place nearly two months earlier: the manifestation of the Supermind in the earth-atmosphere – that is, in the subtle physical layer of terrestrial existence – as a new Power permanently settled to evolve the Divine Superman. In her message she called it "a living fact and a reality" and said that a day would come when even the blindest would recognise the presence of this Power."

Reference: Amal Kiran (K. D. Sethna); Article: *"A Living Fact, A Reality" – Reflections apropos the message of 24 April, 1956* in MOTHER INDIA Vol. LVII, No. 4, 24 April 2015; pp. 291-293

Box 3.8

Sri Aurobindo on the Mother

"What is known as Sri Aurobindo's Yoga is the joint creation of [me], Sri Aurobindo, and the Mother. There is no difference between the Mother's path and mine, we have and have always had the same path, the path that leads to the supramental change and the divine realisation; not only at the end, but from the beginning they have been the same. When I came to Pondicherry a programme was dictated to me from within for my Sadhana. I followed it and progressed for myself but could not do much by the way of helping others. Then came the Mother and with her help I found the necessary method. The Mother's consciousness and mine are the same, the one Divine Consciousness in two, because that is necessary for the play."

From: Vrekhem, Georges Van; *The Mother; The Divine Shakti* (Rupa & Co, 7/16, Ansari Road, Daryaganj, New Delhi, 110002, India); pp. 4-5

VII. EVOLUTION AND VIBHUTI

Distinguishing an avatar from a Vibhuti Sri Aurobindo wrote,

"The Avatar is necessary when a special work is to be done and in crises of the evolution. The Avatar is a special manifestation, while for the rest of the time it is the Divine working within the ordinary human limits as a Vibhuti.

***

"An Avatar, roughly speaking, is one who is conscious of the presence and power of the Divine born in him or descended into him and governing from within his will and life and action; he feels identified inwardly with this divine power and presence. **A Vibhuti is supposed to embody some power of the Divine and is enabled by it to act with great force in the world but that is all that is necessary to make him a Vibhuti: the power may be very great but the consciousness is not that of an inborn or indwelling Divinity.** This is the distinction we can gather from the Gita which is the main authority on this subject. If we follow this distinction, we can confidently say from what is related of them that Rama and Krishna can be accepted as Avatars; Buddha figures as such although with a more impersonal consciousness of the Power within him; Ramakrishna voiced the same consciousness when he spoke of him who was Rama and who was Krishna being within him … **Shankara** and **Vivekananda** were certainly Vibhutis; they cannot be reckoned as more, though as Vibhutis they were very great."[98] As to "**Mahomed and Christ:** Mahomed would himself have rejected the idea of being an Avatara, so we have to regard him only as the prophet, the instrument, the Vibhuti. Christ

---

[98] CWSA Vol. 28: Letters on Yoga I; p. 485-6

realised himself as the Son who is one with the Father—he must therefore be an *aṁśa avatāra*, a partial incarnation."[99]

It means the man who is an Avatar is conscious of the divinity within, while the Vibhuti, a man with a very great power, is not conscious of the divinity within; he is like ordinary person, but has extraordinary power. About Arjun Sri Aurobindo writes, "Arjun himself is a Vibhuti, he is a man high in spiritual evolution, a figure marked out in the crowd of his contemporaries, a chosen instrument of the divine Narayana, the Godhead in humanity."[100] He was the main instrument of the Avatar Sri Krishna and helped him to carry forward the evolution, the spiritual stage – while Sri Krishna knew himself as the embodied divinity. "Ramakrishna was certainly quite as much an Avatar as Christ or Chaitanya." Swami Vivekananda was a Vibhuti, had highly dynamic spiritual intelligence and power and extended Sri Ramakrishna's work all over the earth and suddenly awakened earth-people to spiritual knowledge. These are two examples of Avatar and Vibhuti working hand in hand.

But the Divine appears as Vibhuti in absence of an Avatar also to help evolution to progress in between the Avatar lives also says Sri Aurobindo,

> "As for the lives in between the Avatar lives, it must be remembered that Krishna speaks of many lives in the past, not only a few supreme ones, and secondly that while he speaks of himself as the Divine, in one passage he describes himself as a Vibhuti, *vṛṣṇīnāṁ vāsudevaḥ*, वृष्णीनाम वासुदेव:. We may therefore fairly assume that in many lives he manifested as the Vibhuti veiling the fuller Divine Consciousness. If we admit that the object of Avatarhood is to lead the evolution, this is quite reasonable, the Divine appearing as Avatar in the great

---

[99] Ibid.; p. 501
[100] SABCL Vol. 13; p. 361

transitional stages and as Vibhutis to aid the lesser transitions."[101]

All great persons who advance civilisation are such Vibhutis, for "All greatness is the Vibhuti of the Divine, says the Gita."[102] Valmiki, Vyas, Tagore and Shakespeare are literary Vibhutis[103]. Napoleon, Augustus Caesar and Leonardo da Vinci, Raman, Ramanujan, Einstein, Tulsi, Mirabai of Chittodgadha, all saints, Mahatma Gandhi, Chhatrapati Shivaji, Abraham Lincoln and so many other great personalities are Vibhutis. Mahatma Gandhi is a spiritual-political Vibhuti: He introduced non-violence, voice of inner soul, love, civil dis-obedience, peace as instruments for political activity in the world political culture. About Augustus Caesar and Leonardo da Vinci Sri Aurobindo says,

> "Augustus Caesar organised the life of the Roman Empire and it was this that made the framework of the first transmission of the Graeco-Roman civilisation to Europe – he came for that work and the writings of Virgil and Horace and others helped greatly towards the success of his mission. After the interlude of the Middle Ages, this civilisation was reborn in a new mould in what is called the Renaissance, not in its life-aspects but in its intellectual aspects. It was therefore a supreme intellectual, Leonardo da Vinci, who took up again the work and summarised in himself the seeds of modern Europe.

***

Never heard before of my declaring or anybody declaring such a thing [*that a divine descent was attempted*

---

[101] CWSA Vol. 28: Letters on Yoga I; p. 487

[102] CWSA Vol. 28: Letters on Yoga I; p. 504

[103] Ibid.; p. 505-506; and Sri Aurobindo; SABCL vol. 9: The Future Poetry pp. 333-335

during the Renaissance with Leonardo da Vinci as its centre]. What Leonardo da Vinci held in himself was all the new age of Europe on its many sides. But there was no question of Avatarhood or consciousness of a descent or pressure of spiritual planes. Mysticism was no part of what he had to manifest."[104]

As there are Vibhutis of the Divine Purushottam, there are Vibhutis of the Divine Mother also, who all lead the terrestrial evolution.

VIII. NOW IS THE TIME WHEN HUMANITY NEEDS TO ATTEMPT TO REALISE THE SUPRAMENTAL

Pointing to the evolutionary accomplishment of Sri Aurobindo, The Mother tells to people that,

"Sri Aurobindo incarnated in a human body the supramental consciousness and has not only revealed to us the nature of the path to follow and the method of following it so as to arrive at the goal, but has also by his own personal realisation given us the example; he has provided us with the proof that the thing can be done and the time is now to do it."[105]

She has also described the method of how to begin the sadhana for reaching the goal of supramental realisation:

---

[104] CWSA Vol. 28: Letters on Yoga I; p. 502
[105] CWM Vol. 13: Words of The Mother - I; p.21

"Concentrate in the heart. Enter into it; go within and deep and far, as far as you can. Gather all the strings of your consciousness that are spread abroad, roll them up and take a plunge and sink down.

"A fire is burning there, in the deep quietude of the heart. It is the divinity in you – your true being. Hear its voice, follow its dictates."[106]

This effort will initiate three processes which are basic for the achievement of the goal of the practice of integral psychology and integral yoga. Efforts for the realisation has to be based on three things, says Sri Aurobindo:

> "You know the three things on which the realisation has to be based: (1) on a rising to a station above the mind and on the opening out of the cosmic consciousness; (2) on the psychic opening; and (3) on the descent of the higher consciousness with its peace, light, force, knowledge, Ananda etc. into all the planes of the being down to the most physical. All this has to be done by the working of the Mother's force aided by your aspiration, devotion and surrender. **That is the Path**. The rest is a matter of the working out of these things for which you have to have faith in the Mother's working."[107]

So, for performing *tapasya* for the supramental consciousness one must aspire to do three actions, *kriyas*: (i) to open the psychic, (ii) to take station above the mind and to widen in the cosmic consciousness and (iii) to receive the descent of the higher consciousness into all the planes of our being down to body; this has be done with the working of the Mother's force (*Shakti of Para-Prakriti*) with the aid of one's aspiration, devotion and surrender to the Mother; three things are worked out by the Mother's force only, one's personal aspiration,

---

[106] CWM Vol. 3: Questions and Answers 1929-1931; p. 1
[107] CWSA Vol 30: Letters on Yoga III; p. 319

devotion and surrender are only aids to the Mother's workings, they on their own are not capable to achieve the goal of supramental transformation of one's human nature (*apara* or lower *prakriti*); so, one needs to maintain constant faith in the Mother's working and to have infinite patience for reaching the destiny, for journey may be too long.

In other words, as The Mother says, one has to go within ones deepest heart, meet the path-leader Light (*Purohit Agni*) and follow this torch-bearer to the end.

Numerous individuals and various spiritual social groups have developed and are developing under Sri Aurobindo and The Mother's spiritual influence, such as, Sri Aurobindo ashram, Pondicherry; Sri Aurobindo Ashram (Delhi Branch), New Delhi; Sri Aurobindo Society, Pondicherry; Sri Aurobindo Action, Pondicherry; International Town Auroville, Tamil Nadu; Sri Aurobindo International Centre of Education, Pondicherry; *Auro University, Surat*; Sri Aurobindo Sadhana Peetham, Lodi, U.S.A. and thousands of Integral Yoga Centers all over the world. Humanity seems to have responded to The Mother's call.

Integral psychology is getting applied in almost all fields of life now: There are families who are trying to practice collectively integral psychology; There are universities that teach courses based on Sri Aurobindo and The Mother's teachings; Educational organisations have sprung up that apply integral psychology in their educational activities; Sri Aurobindo International Centre of Education, Pondicherry, India (The SAICE) is developing the "Free Progress System of Education" based on integral psychology; Former students of The SAICE Vijay and Gita, now working for Sri Aurobindo Society, Pondicherry India have established an online forum of Integral Management; Anand Reddy, a former student of The SAICE, has established an International University at Pondicherry to teach various courses prepared in the light of integral knowledge given by Sri Aurobindo and The Mother. Auroville Citizens have taken up projects of social reconstruction. These are the few examples among many more efforts pursued by devotees in many countries. The pace of expansion is significantly fast; it creates a confidence in our heart that Sri Aurobindo and The Mother's work for evolution will be carried on by people and one day humanity will realise supramental consciousness and there will dawn on earth the Golden Age.

If one is inspired to practice integral psychology sincerely, one should always remember The Mother's advice quoted above; one must always remember that **the personal psychic divine** seated in the heart always enables a person to walk securely on the razor edge path and helps the person to unite ultimately with the supramental divine.

SUMMARY

I. Inadequate knowledge of Rationalistic reductionist science: It wrongly believes that Matter is the original existence, for Sachchidananda (सच्चिदानन्द) is the only primary existence and the origin from which everything material or subtle is evolved. Darwin's theory describes evolution of forms and does not explain it by giving its cause. The cause of evolution is the original mother consciousness (आद्या शक्ति आदि चित). Ancient Vedic knowledge knew this; Sri Aurobindo and The Mother have explained this thing now.

II-III-IV. Creation of Conscient Glorious Universe, its devolution into Inconscient Universe and Involution of *Adya Matri Shakti* in it for its Redemption: The original eternal transcendent Adya Shakti created a conscient glorious universe but it devolved into an inconscient universe. So, she descends in the inconscient universe creating on the way one by one subtle Universal planes of sachchidandmaya, supramental, overmental, mental, vital, physical, subconscious matter.

V. The Terrestrial Evolution: The original divine consciousness dispersed and hidden in the inconscient makes the inconscient to release first the plane of subconscious physical consciousness, world and beings in it. Next the plane of vital consciousness, world and beings in it are evolved and then the plane of mental consciousness, world and beings in it (– the plane of psychic consciousness, world and beings manifest at the nexus of the mental and vital plane, it is portion of the Divine behind the external physical-vital-mental triple consciousness and not part of the hierarchy of the triple nature –) and the plane of overmental consciousness, world and beings in it are evolved one by one. Thus far evolution has been accomplished on earth. Now, overmental consciousness has begun to evolve into the supramental consciousness and world and beings as a result of integral yoga performed by the latest Avatars Sri Aurobindo and the Mother.

VI. Evolution and the Avatar: Avatarhood is connected with evolution. *"The Hindu procession of the ten Avatars is itself, as it were, a parable of evolution.* First the Fish Avatar, then the amphibious animal between land and water, then the land animal, then the Man-Lion Avatar, bridging man and animal, then man as dwarf, small and undeveloped and physical but containing in himself the godhead and taking possession of existence, then the rajasic, sattwic, nirguna Avatars, leading the human development from the vital rajasic to the sattwic mental man and again the overmental superman. Krishna, Buddha and Kalki depict the last three stages, the stages of the spiritual development – Krishna opens the possibility of overmind, Buddha tries to shoot beyond to the supreme liberation but that liberation is still negative, not returning upon earth to complete positively the evolution; Kalki is to correct this by bringing the Kingdom of the Divine upon earth, destroying the opposing Asura forces. The progression is striking and unmistakable." (*See box 3.4*). Sri Aurobindo and The Mother are Kalki Avatar, they realised supramental consciousness and manifested it in earth's subtle physical and opened the way for the Kingdom of the Divine.

VII. Evolution and Vibhuti: A Vibhuti embodies certain divine quality in an extra-ordinary measure, but he is not conscious of the divinity within and leads the terrestrial evolution in lesser transitions. For example, Arjun is Vibhuti and Krishna is Avatar.

VIII. Now is the time when humanity needs to attempt to realise the Supramental: Humanity must now embark on the path revealed to it by Sri Aurobindo for realising the supramental transformation, for by incarnating supramental consciousness in his body, he has also provided a proof that the transformation can be achieved by a human being. The path's beginning terminal is in the heart's Light, which will lead to the goal, if one maintains faith in The Mother's workings.

Suggestions for Further Reading

1. SABCL Vol. 13: Essays on the Gita: In chapters XI – XVII Sri Aurobindo has discussed the possibility, the purpose and the process of Avatarhood. In chapters VIII - IX of the second Series he has discussed the emanation of the Divine as *Vibhutis.*

2. Sri Aurobindo; CWSA Vol. 28: Letters on Yoga I: In the section two of part five of this book, Sri Aurobindo has explained the meaning and purpose of Avatarhood and the Vibhuti and written on specific Avatars and Vibhutis.

3. SABCL Vol. 19, Chs. 16, 23, 24 & 21, 25, 26, 27 & 28

4. CWM Vol. 9, pp. 204-242

5. CWM Vol. 9, pp. 190-244 (The Mother's talks on intermediate being, The "Mind of Light", Passage to higher hemisphere, Story of successive involution, Terrestrial evolution, Individual and cosmic evolution, and Supramental power)

6. CWM Vol. 4; pp. 217-256 (The Mother's talks on The Universe, Mental worlds and the Psychic being)

7. CWM Vol. pp. 173-174 (The Mother's talk on Supermind and overmind)

8. SABCL Vol. 28; pp. 95-304 (Sri Aurobindo's last writing: Savitri. Sri Aurobindo in these pages unveils all planes of the World in poetry.)

9. Sri Aurobindo & The Mother; *Avtarvad Translated in Gujarati by Ambubhai Purani, Sundaram, Amidhar Bhatt* (Sri Aurobindo Society (Branch), Sri Hasmukh Shah, "Centre" Bungalow, Kochrab Pahelo Dhal, Ahmadabad, 6, India)

10. Georges Van Vrekhem (Editor); *The Mother's Vision* (Publisher: Sri Aurobindo Ashram, Pondicherry, 605002, India; 2005); Ch.1: The Divine and His Creation: Pp. 1-54

11. SABCL Vol. 26: Sri Aurobindo on Himself; Part Two: Section One of it describes Sri Aurobindo and The Mother as Leaders of Evolution and Section Two describes Identity of their Consciousness & its New edition CWSA Vol. 35: Sri Aurobindo on Himself and The Ashram: Part three of it introduces Sri Aurobindo as Guru, Guide and Avatar.

12. SABCL Vol. 25: The Mother & its new edition CWSA Vol. 32: The Mother with letters on the Mother; Sri Aurobindo has described Adi Shakti as the creatrix and as Avatar and Vibhutis leading the evolution.

13. The Mother; The Mother's Vision: Selection from Questions and Answers Compiled by Georges Van Vrekhem (Sri Aurobindo Ashram, Pondicherry, 605002, India, 2005): Chapter 1 is on The Divine and His Creation, Ch. 2 on The Universe.

14. The Mother; Creation and Creator (Sri Aurobindo Society, Pondicherry, 605002, India, August 2002); p. 112

15. The Mother on Herself; The Mother (Sri Aurobindo Ashram, Pondicherry, 605002, India, 1977); p. 46

WORKBOOK: QUESTIONS FOR PREVIEW AND REVIEW

I. INADEQUATE KNOWLEDGE OF RATIONAL SCIENCE ABOUT THE CREATION AND THE TERRESTRIAL EVOLUTION

Short Answer Type Questions and Objective Questions

1. What is the primary existence according to the rationalistic science?
2. What is the primary existence according to the Vedic spiritual psychology and integral psychology?
3. Sachchidananda is the infinite triune oneness. (True or False)
4. Does Darwin's theory of evolution explain the terrestrial evolution?
5. What is the origin of the inconsciousness?
6. Give English words for Sat, Chit and Anand.
7. Why rationalistic science cannot explain the phenomena of the devolution and the terrestrial evolution.
8. Why can Sri Aurobindo and The Mother be called the super-psychologists? Give two reasons.
9. Name the four stages of terrestrial evolution from inconsciousness to man.
10. The individual is set in the _____.
11. Who has created this earth and life on it?
12. Vedic texts can be understood by average intelligence. (True or False)

Essay Type Questions

1. The knowledge of the rationalistic science is inadequate. Discuss.

II-III. THE CREATION OF THE CONSCIENT GLORIOUS UNIVERSE AND ITS DEVOLUTION

Essay Type Questions

1. How was the inconscient universe created?

Short Answer Type Questions and Objective Questions

1. Whom did the Supreme Divine direct to create a universe? by the Supreme Divine?
2. How many Powers were emanated to create the universe?
3. The first principle of the plan of the creation was expression of Essential _____ and essential _____.
4. The First four Beings created by The Supreme's Consciousness, The Creatrix, were 1. _____, 2. _____ 3. _____ 4. _____ .
5. Why the first created Divine Beings separated themselves from the Supreme Divine?
6. When Divine Beings separated themselves from the Supreme Divine Shakti, The Divine Being of Light turned into _____, Love turned into _____, Truth turned into _____.
7. Super Consciousness devolved into Inconscience due to the process of involution. (True or False)
8. Inconscient is dark and inert. So, it does not contain inside it light, love knowledge and force. (True or False)
9. To express _____ and _____ was the first principle of plan of the first creation by the Divine Shakti.

IV-V. INVOLUTION OF *ADYA MATRI SHAKTI* AND TERRESTRIAL EVOLUTION

Short Answer Type Questions

1. Where did the evolution start in the universe?
2. Which of the two is prior to involution and evolution, Inconscient or Super-conscient?
3. The Involutionary stages or planes appeared in _____ order and the evolutionary stages appeared in _____ order. (descending, ascending)

4. Name the Involutionary stages of the consciousness in order of their gradual appearance.
5. Name the evolutionary stages in order of their appearance on the earth.
6. Are there beings in the involutionary planes of consciousness?
7. Name the last rung of ascending evolutionary ladder. _____. Will there be no more further evolution?
8. What did the Vedic poets knew?
9. How is the spiritual evolution of humanity to proceed?
10. Why does The Mother say that man is still in his nature wholly an animal?
11. According to The Mother, what was the purpose of Sri Aurobindo's coming upon earth?
12. According to Sri Aurobindo, after manifestation of supramental beings on earth, evolution will proceed to manifest the dynamic _____.

Essay Type Questions

1. Describe the process of involution
2. Describe the process of terrestrial evolution.
3. Describe The Mother's story of devolution involution and terrestrial evolution in your own words.

Exercises

1. Make a table showing the stages of involution and evolution in the serial order of their successive creation.
2. Make a figure of involution using the figure of the human body.
3. Make a figure of evolution using the figure of the human body.
4. Make a figure of the sun family showing evolution on earth only.
5. Present the process of creation in the form of a drama.

VI. EVOLUTION AND THE AVATAR

Short Answer Type Questions

1. Write definition of Avatar given by Sri Aurobindo.
2. Enumerate the five objects of Avatarhood?
3. Give the meaning of *dharma* and *adharma* (धर्म च अधर्म च). - (hint: See Box 3.3)
4. Give the meaning of *Sadhunam and Duskritam* (साधुनाम च दुष्कृताम च).- (hint: See Box 3.3)
5. Which is the great dharma that an Avatar comes to establish on earth? - (hint: See Box 3.3)
6. (1) _____, (2) _____, (3) _____, (4) _____ and (5) _____ are the five stages of Avatars.
7. (1)_____, (2)_____, (3) _____ are three Avatars of animal stage.
8. _____ is an Avatar bridging animal and _____.
9. (1)_____, (2)_____, (3)_____, are three Avatars of mental stage.
10. In the stage of spiritual stage there are two Avatars: 1. _____ and 2. _____.
11. Sri Aurobindo and The Mother as Avatar belongs to the _____ stage and can be named as _____ Avatar.
12. The awakened spiritual man is _____ Avatar, the complete spiritual man is _____ and the supramental persons are _____ and _____. (Fill gaps with one of these words Buddha, Sri Aurobindo & The Mother)
13. Sri Krishna prepared the descent of _____ and _____.
14. Sri Krishna descends in Sri Aurobindo's physical on _____ (fill in the date). Sri Aurobindo retires completely for concentrated _____ for the descent of _____ and the supramental consciousness descends in his body on _____ (fill in the date). In the year _____ the supramental consciousness descends in the subtle physical consciousness of earth and takes over the charge of further evolution.

15. What is the function of the Kalki Avatar?
16. Are the yoga of Sri Aurobindo and the yoga of The Mother two different yogas? Explain. (Hint: See Box 3.8)
17. What has been pronounced by The Mother about Sri Aurobindo as an Avatar?
18. What does K. D. Sethna have to say about The Mother and Sri Aurobindo?

Essay Type Questions

1.   Explain the role of Avatar in Evolution.
2.   Write a story of terrestrial evolution describing the ten Avatars
3.   Write an essay on Kalki Avatar.

VII. EVOLUTION AND VIBHUTI

Short Answer Type Questions

1.   What is the difference between an Avatar and a Vibhuti?
2.   Vibhutis come with Avatars only to lead the terrestrial evolution. (True or False)
3.   Name pairs of Vibhuti and Avatar that came on earth together.

Essay Type Questions:

1.   Name a few old and modern Vibhutis and describe their contributions in the evolution of society.

Project:

1.   Write names of Avatars and Vibhutis of each of the countries in a sketch of the world map.
2.   Make a table showing Vibhutis of different societal areas.

VIII. NOW IS THE TIME WHEN HUMANITY NEEDS TO ATTEMPT TO REALISE THE SUPRAMENTAL

Short Answer Type Questions

1. The Mother says that humanity should now choose to perform sadhana to realise the supramental. Why does she say so?
2. In which part of oneself one should concentrate and do *karma* under the guidance of its Light, if one wants to progress towards the supramental consciousness?
3. Describe all aspects of the path that leads to the supramental.
4. Can austerity for the supramental be performed by one's own strength?
5. How to take psychic attitude in living the day to day life, so that one may advance towards the supramental transformation?
6. Why one has to depend on the Mother's force solely to achieve the transformation of the human *prakriti*? Why one needs to cultivate infinite patience on the path to the supramental?

SELF TEST

1. Who is creator of the universe?
2. Arrange the phenomena noted *below* in chronological order: Beginning of terrestrial evolution, Creation of Conscient Glorious Universe, Beginning of Involution, The Divine Shakti
3. Name four Devas who started the creation of the Glorious World?
4. Name four Asuras who created the Inconscient universe?
5. Has scientific psychology got the truth of life?
6. Which aspect of Sachchidananda is creator of the Universe?
7. Name the subtle worlds of the universe.
8. Name the planes of consciousness that have ascended from the inconsciousness.
9. Is the terrestrial evolution still continuing?

10. Name the next stage of the terrestrial evolution.
11. Why there cannot be the end of the movement of the terrestrial evolution?
12. Did Vedic seers have knowledge of the terrestrial evolution?
13. Put in chronological order these three things: evolution, involution and devolution.
14. List ten Avatars in the ascending order of consciousness planes.
15. In between Avatar lives who leads the evolution?
16. Name the latest Avatar. What knowledge has he given to humanity?
17. Why does Mother say that now is the time for mental humanity to try for becoming supramental humanity?
18. Can one realise the supramental perfection of one's nature without solely relying on the Mother?

Appendix 3.1

Sri Aurobindo's Words on Involution and Evolution

"This Divine Being, Sachchidananda, is at once impersonal personal: it is an Existence and the origin and foundation of all truths, forces, powers, existences, but it is also the one transcendent Conscious Being and the All-Person of whom all conscious beings are the selves and personalities; for He is their highest Self and the universal indwelling Presence. It is a necessity for the soul in the universe—and therefore the inner trend of the evolutionary Energy and its ultimate intention—to know and to grow into this truth of itself, to become one with the Divine Being, to raise its nature to the Divine Nature, its existence into the Divine Existence, its consciousness into the Divine Consciousness, its delight of being into the divine Delight of Being, and to receive all this into its becoming, to make the becoming an expression of that highest Truth, to be possessed inwardly of the Divine Self and Master of its existence and to be at the same time wholly possessed by Him and moved by His Divine Energy and live and act in a complete self-giving and surrender. On this side the dualistic and theistic views of existence which affirm the eternal real existence of God and the Soul and the eternal real existence and cosmic action of the Divine Energy, express also a truth of the integral existence; but their formulation falls short of the whole truth if it denies the essential unity of God and Soul or their capacity for utter oneness or ignores what underlies the supreme experience of the merger of the soul in the Divine Unity through love, through union of consciousness, through fusion of existence in existence.

"The manifestation of the Being in our universe takes the shape of an involution which is the starting-point of an evolution,—Matter the nethermost stage, Spirit the summit. In the descent into involution there can be distinguished seven principles of manifested being, seven gradations of the manifesting Consciousness of which we can get a perception or a concrete realisation of their presence and immanence here or a reflected experience. The first three are the original and fundamental principles and they form universal states of consciousness to which we can rise; when we do so, we can become aware of supreme planes or levels of fundamental manifestation or self-formulation of the spiritual reality in which is put in front the unity of the Divine Existence, the power of the Divine Consciousness, the bliss of the Divine Delight of existence,— not concealed or disguised as here, for we can possess them in their full independent reality. A fourth principle of supramental truth-consciousness is associated with them; manifesting unity in infinite multiplicity, it is the characteristic power of self-determination of the Infinite. This quadruple power of the supreme existence, consciousness and delight constitutes an upper hemisphere of manifestation based on the Spirit's eternal self-knowledge. If we enter into these principles or into any plane of being in which there is the pure presence of the Reality, we find in them a complete freedom and knowledge. The other three powers and planes of being, of which we are even at present aware, form a lower hemisphere of the manifestation, a hemisphere of Mind, Life and Matter. These are in themselves powers of the superior principles; but wherever they manifest in a separation from their spiritual sources, they undergo as a result a phenomenal lapse into a divided in place of the true undivided existence: this lapse, this separation creates a state of limited knowledge exclusively concentrated on its own limited world order and oblivious of all that is behind it and of the underlying unity, a state therefore of cosmic and individual Ignorance.

"In the descent into the material plane of which our natural life is a product, the lapse culminates in a total Inconscience out of which an involved Being and Consciousness have to emerge by a gradual evolution. This inevitable evolution first develops, as it is bound to develop, Matter and a material universe; in Matter, Life appears and living physical beings; in Life, Mind manifests and embodied thinking and living beings; in Mind, ever increasing its powers and activities in forms of Matter, the Supermind or Truth-Consciousness must appear, inevitably, by the very force of what is contained in the Inconscience and the necessity in Nature to bring it into manifestation. Supermind appearing manifests the Spirit's self-knowledge and whole knowledge in a supramental living being and must bring about by the same law, by an inherent necessity and inevitability, the dynamic manifestation here of the divine Existence, Consciousness and Delight of existence. It is this that is the significance of the plan and order of the terrestrial evolution; it is this necessity that must determine all its steps and degrees, its principle and its process. Mind, Life and Matter are the realised powers of the evolution and well-known to us; Supermind and the triune aspects of Sachchidananda are the secret principles which are not yet put in front and have still to be realised in the forms of the manifestation, and we know them only by hints and a partial and fragmentary action still not disengaged from the lower movement and therefore not easily recognisable. But their evolution too is part of the destiny of the soul in the Becoming, —there must be a realisation and dynamisation in earth-life and in Matter not only of Mind but of all that is above it, all that has descended indeed but is still concealed in earth-life and Matter."[108]

---

[108] CWSA Vol. 22; pp. 688-690

Appendix 3.2

Sri Aurobindo's Description of the Material Universe that First Evolved from the Inconscient: Evolution of the Matter from the Inconscience

"In the earliest stages of evolutionary Nature we are met by the dumb secrecy of her inconscience; there is no revelation of any significance or purpose in her works, no hint of any other principles of being than that first formulation which is her immediate preoccupation and seems to be forever her only business: for in her primal works Matter alone appears, the sole dumb and stark cosmic reality. A Witness of creation, if there had been one conscious but uninstructed, would only have seen appearing out of a vast abyss of an apparent non-existence an Energy busy with the creation of Matter, a material world and material objects, organising the infinity of the Inconscient into the scheme of a boundless universe or a system of countless universes that stretched around him into Space without any certain end or limit, a tireless creation of nebulae and star-clusters and suns and planets, existing only for itself, without a sense in it, empty of cause or purpose. It might have seemed to him a stupendous machinery without a use, a mighty meaningless movement, an aeonic spectacle without a witness, a cosmic edifice without an inhabitant; for he would have seen no sign of an indwelling Spirit, no being for whose delight it was made. A creation of his kind could only be the outcome of an inconscient Energy or an illusion-cinema, a shadow play or puppet play of forms reflected on a superconscient indifferent Absolute. He would have seen no evidence of a soul and no hint of mind or life in this immeasurable and interminable display of Matter. It would not have seemed to him possible or imaginable that there could at all be in this desert universe forever inanimate and insensible an outbreak of teeming life, a first vibration of something occult and incalculable, alive and conscious, a secret spiritual entity feeling its way towards the surface.

"But after some aeons, looking out once more on that vain panorama, he might have detected in one small corner at least of the universe this phenomenon, **a corner**[109] **where Matter had been prepared, its operations sufficiently fixed, organised, made stable, adapted as a scene of a new development,—the phenomenon of a living matter,** a life in things that had emerged and become visible: but still the Witness would have understood nothing, for evolutionary Nature still veils her secret. He would have seen a Nature concerned only with establishing this outburst of life, this new creation, but life living for itself with no significance in it,—a wanton and abundant creatrix busy scattering the seed of her new power and establishing a multitude of its forms in a beautiful and luxurious profusion or, later, multiplying endlessly genus and species for the pure pleasure of creation: a small touch of lively colour and movement would have been flung into the immense cosmic desert and nothing more. The Witness could not have imagined that a thinking mind would appear in this minute island of life, that a consciousness could awake in the conscient, a new and greater subtler vibration come to the surface and betray more clearly the existence of the submerged Spirit. It would have seemed to him at first that Life had somehow become aware of itself and that was all; for this scanty new-born mind seemed to be only a servant of life, a contrivance to help life to live, a machinery for its maintenance, for attack and defense, for certain needs and vital satisfactions, for the liberation of life-instinct and life-impulse. It could not have seemed possible to him that in this little life, so inconspicuous amid the immensities, in one sole species out of this petty multitude, a mental being would emerge, a mind serving life still but also making life and matter its servants, using them for the fulfilment of its own ideas, will, wishes,—a mental being who would create all manner of utensils, tools, instruments out of Matter for all kinds of utilities, erect out of it cities, houses, temples, theatres, laboratories, factories, chisel from it statues and carve cave-cathedrals, invent architecture, sculpture, painting, poetry and a hundred crafts and arts, discover the mathematics and

---

[109] Sri Aurobindo is referring to The Earth formed in the universe. Refer CWM Vol. 5 and Vol. 7 to know that The Earth is the only material stage in the material universe made for the evolution.

physics of the universe and the hidden secret of its structure, live for the sake of mind and its interests, for thought and knowledge, develop into the thinker, the philosopher and scientist and, as a supreme defiance to the reign of Matter, awake in himself to the hidden Godhead, become the hunter after the invisible, the mystic and the spiritual seeker."[110]

[110] CWSA Vol. 22; pp.881-883

Appendix 3.3

Love is the Cause of the Evolution According to The Mother[111]

"Consciousness is indeed the creatrix of the universe, but love is its saviour. Conscious experience alone can give a glimpse of what love is, of its purpose and process. Any verbal transcription is necessarily a mental travesty of something which eludes all expression in every way. Philosophers, mystics, occultists, have all tried to define love, but in vain. I have no pretension of succeeding where they have failed. But I wish to state in the simplest possible terms what in their writings takes such an abstract and complicated form. My words will have no other aim than to lead towards the living experience, and I wish to be able to lead even a child to it.

"Love is, in its essence, the joy of identity; it finds its ultimate expression in the bliss of union. Between the two lie all the phases of its universal manifestation.

"At the beginning of this manifestation, in the purity of its origin, love is composed of two movements, two complementary poles of the urge towards complete oneness. On one hand there is the supreme power of attraction and on the other the irresistible need for absolute self-giving. No other movement could have better bridged the abyss that was created when in the individual being consciousness was separated from its origin and became unconsciousness.

"What had been projected into space had to be brought back to itself without, however, annihilating the universe which had thus been created. That is why love burst forth, the irresistible power of union.

"It brooded over the darkness and the inconscience; it was scattered and fragmented in the bosom of unfathomable night. And then began the awakening and the ascent, the slow formation of Matter and its endless progression. It is indeed love, in a corrupted and darkened

---

[111] The Mother; *On Education: CWM Vol. 12, Travel Size* (Publisher: All India Book, Pondicherry, 605002, India,1984); pp. 62-69

form that is associated with all the impulses of physical and vital Nature, as the urge behind all movement and all grouping, which becomes quite perceptible in the plant kingdom. In trees and plants, it is the need to grow in order to obtain more light, more air, more space; in flowers, it is the offering of their beauty and fragrance in a loving efflorescence. Then, in animals, it is love that lies behind hunger and thirst, the need for appropriation, expansion, procreation, in short, behind every desire, whether conscious or not. And among the higher species, it is in the self-sacrificing devotion of the female to her young. This brings us quite naturally to the human race in which, with the triumphant advent of mental activity, this association reaches its climax, for it has become conscious and deliberate. Indeed, as soon as terrestrial development made it possible, Nature took up this sublime force of love and put it at the service of her creative work by linking and mixing it with her movement of procreation. This association has even become so close, so intimate that very few human beings are illumined enough in their consciousness to be able to dissociate these movements from each other and experience them separately. In this way, love has suffered every degradation; it has been   based to the level of the beast.

"From then on, too, there clearly appears in Nature's works the will to rebuild, by steps and stages and through ever more numerous and complex groupings, the primordial oneness. Having made use of the power of love to bring two human beings together to form the biune group, the origin of the family, after having broken the narrow limits of personal egoism, changing it into a dual egoism, Nature, with the appearance of children, brought forth a more complex unit, the family. And in course of time, with multifarious associations between families, individual interchanges and   mingling of blood, larger groupings were formed: clans, tribes, castes, classes, leading to the   creation of nations. This work of group formation proceeded simultaneously in the various parts of the world, crystallising in the different races. And little by little, Nature will fuse these races too in her endeavour to build a real and material foundation for human unity.

"In the consciousness of most men, all this is the outcome of chance; they are not aware of the existence of a global plan and take circumstances as they come, for better or for worse according to their temperament: some are satisfied, others discontented.

"Among the contented, there is a certain category of people who are perfectly adapted to Nature's ways: these are the optimists. For them the days are brighter because of the nights, colours are vivid because of the shadows, joy is more intense because of suffering, pain gives a greater charm to pleasure, illness gives health all its value; I have even heard some of them say that they are glad to have enemies because it made them appreciate their friends all the more. In any case, for all these people, sexual activity is one of the most enjoyable of occupations, satisfaction of the palate is a delight of life that they cannot go without; and it is quite normal to die since one is born: death puts an end to a journey which would become tedious if it were to last too long.

"In short, they find life quite all right as it is and do not care to know whether it has a purpose or a goal; they do not worry about the miseries of others and do not see any need for progress.

"Never try to "convert" these people; it would be a serious mistake. If they were unfortunate enough to listen to you, they would lose the balance they have without being able to find a new one. They are not ready to have an inner life, but they are Nature's favourites; they have a very close alliance with her, and this realisation should not be needlessly disturbed.

"To a lesser degree, and above all, in a less durable way, there are other contented people in the world whose contentment is due to the magic effect of love. Each time an individual breaks the narrow limitations in which he is imprisoned by his ego and emerges into the open air, through self-giving, whether for the sake of another human being or his family, his country or his faith, he finds in this self-forgetfulness a foretaste of the marvellous delight of love, and this gives him the impression that he has come into contact with the Divine. But most often it is only a fleeting contact, for in the human being love is immediately mixed with lower egoistic movements which debase it and rob it of its power of purity. But even if it remained pure, this contact with the divine existence could not last forever, for love is only one aspect of the Divine, an aspect which here on earth has suffered the same distortions as the others.

"Besides, all these experiences are very good and useful for the ordinary man who follows the normal way of Nature in her stumbling march towards the future unity. But they cannot satisfy those who want to hasten the movement, or rather, who aspire to belong to another line of more direct and rapid movement, to an exceptional movement that will liberate them from ordinary mankind and its interminable march, so that they may take part in the spiritual advance which will lead them along the swiftest paths towards the creation of the new race, the race that will express the supramental truth upon earth. These rare souls must reject all forms of love between human beings, for however beautiful and pure they may be, they cause a kind of short-circuit and cut off the direct connection with the Divine.

"For one who has known love for the Divine, all other forms of love are obscure and too mixed with pettiness and egoism and darkness; they are like a perpetual haggling or a struggle for supremacy and domination, and even among the best they are full of misunderstanding and irritability, of friction and incomprehension.

"Moreover, it is a well-known fact that one grows into the likeness of what one loves. Therefore if you want to be like the Divine, love Him alone. Only one who has known the ecstasy of the exchange of love with the Divine can know how insipid and dull and feeble any other exchange is in comparison. And even if the most austere discipline is required to arrive at this exchange, nothing is too hard, too long or too severe in order to achieve it, for it surpasses all expression.

"This is the marvellous state we want to realise on earth; it is this which will have the power to transform the world and make it a habitation worthy of the Divine Presence. Then will pure and true love be able to incarnate in a body that will no longer be a disguise and a veil for it. Many a time, in order to make the discipline easier and to create a closer and more easily perceptible intimacy, the Divine has sought, in his highest form of love, to assume a physical body similar in appearance to the human body; but each time, imprisoned within the gross forms of Matter, he was able to express only a caricature of himself. And in order to manifest in the fullness of his perfection he waits only for human beings to have made some indispensable progress in their consciousness and in their bodies; for the vulgarity of man's vanity and the stupidity of his conceit mistake the sublime divine love, when it expresses itself in a human form, for a sign of weakness and dependence and need.

"And yet man already knows, at first obscurely, but more and more clearly as he draws nearer to perfection, that love alone can put an end to the suffering of the world; only the ineffable joy of love in its essence can sweep away from the universe the burning pain of separation. For only in the ecstasy of the supreme union will creation discover its purpose and its fulfilment.

"That is why no effort is too arduous, no austerity too rigorous if it can illumine, purify, perfect and transform the physical substance so that it may no longer conceal the Divine when he takes on an outer form in Matter. For then this marvellous tenderness will be able to express itself freely in the world, the divine love which has the power of changing life into a paradise of sweet joy.

"This, you will say, is the culmination, the crown of the effort, the final victory; but what must be done in order to achieve it? What is the path to be followed and what are the first steps on the way?

"Since we have decided to reserve love in all its splendour for our personal relationship with the Divine, we shall replace it in our relations with others by a total, unvarying, constant and egoless kindness and goodwill that will not expect any reward or gratitude or even any recognition. However others may treat you, you will never allow yourself to be carried away by any resentment; and in your unmixed love for the Divine, you will leave him sole judge as to how he is to protect you and defend you against the misunderstanding and bad will of others.

"You will await your joys and pleasures from the Divine alone. In him alone will you seek and find help and support. He will comfort you in all your sorrows, guide you on the path, lift you up if you stumble, and if there are moments of failure and exhaustion, he will take you up in his strong arms of love and enfold you in his soothing sweetness.

"To avoid any misunderstanding, I must point out here that because of the exigencies of the language in which I am expressing myself, I am obliged to use the masculine gender whenever I mention the Divine. But in fact the reality of love I speak of is above and beyond all gender, masculine or feminine; and when it incarnates in a human body, it does so indifferently in the body of a man or a woman according to the needs of the work to be done.

"In summary, austerity in feelings consists then of giving up all emotional attachment, of whatever nature, whether for a person, for the family, for the country or anything else, in order to concentrate on an exclusive attachment for the Divine Reality. This concentration will culminate in an integral identification and will be instrumental to the supramental realisation upon Earth."

Appendix 3.4

Chapter VI of the Life Divine[112]

Man in the Universe

*The Soul of man, a traveller, wanders in this cycle of Brahman,
huge, a totality of lives, a totality of states, thinking itself different
from the Impeller of the journey. Accepted by Him, it attains its
goal of Immortality.*

(Swetaswatara Upanishad. [1.6])

THE PROGRESSIVE revelation of a great, a transcendent, a
luminous Reality with the multitudinous relativities of this world that
we see and those other worlds that we do not see as means and material,
condition and field, this would seem then to be the meaning of the
universe,—since meaning and aim it has and is neither a purposeless
illusion nor a fortuitous accident. For the same reasoning which leads
us to conclude that world-existence is not a deceptive trick of Mind,
justifies equally the certainty that it is no blindly and helplessly self-
existent mass of separate phenomenal existences clinging together and
struggling together as best they can in their orbit through eternity, no
tremendous self-creation and self-impulsion of an ignorant Force
without any secret Intelligence within aware of its starting-point and its
goal and guiding its process and its motion. An existence, wholly self-
aware and therefore entirely master of itself, possesses the phenomenal
being in which it is involved, realises itself in form, unfolds itself in the
individual.

That luminous Emergence is the dawn which the Aryan
forefathers worshipped. Its fulfilled perfection is that highest step of the
world-pervading Vishnu which they beheld as if an eye of vision
extended in the purest heavens of the Mind. For it exists already as an

---

[112] SABCL Vol. 18; pp.42-50

all-revealing and all-guiding Truth of things which watches over the world and attracts mortal man, first without the knowledge of his conscious mind, by the general march of Nature, but at last consciously by a progressive awakening and self-enlargement, to his divine ascension. **The ascent to the divine Life is the human journey, the Work of works, the acceptable Sacrifice. This alone is man's real business in the world and the justification of his existence, without which he would be only an insect crawling among other ephemeral insects on a speck of surface mud and water which has managed to form itself amid appalling immensities of the physical universe.**

This Truth of things that has to emerge out of the phenomenal world's contradictions is declared to be an infinite Bliss and self - conscious Existence, the same everywhere, in all things, in all times and beyond Time, and aware of itself behind all these phenomena by whose intensest vibrations of activity or whose largest totality it can never be entirely expressed or in any way limited; for it is self-existent and does not depend for its being upon its manifestations. They represent it, but not exhaust it; point to it, but do not reveal it. It is revealed only to itself within their forms. The conscious existence involved in the form comes, as it evolves, to know itself by intuition, by self-vision, by self-experience. It becomes itself in the world by knowing itself; it knows itself by becoming itself. Thus possessed of itself inwardly, it imparts also to its forms and modes the conscious delight of Sachchidananda. This becoming of the finite Bliss-Existence-Consciousness in mind and life and body,—for independent of them it exists eternally,—is the transfiguration intended and the utility of individual existence. Through the individual it manifests in relation even as of itself it exists in identity.

The Unknowable knowing itself as Sachchidananda is the one supreme affirmation of Vedanta; it contains all the others or on it they depend. This is the one veritable experience that remains when all appearances have been accounted for negatively by the elimination of their shapes and coverings or positively by the reduction of their names and forms to the constant truth that they contain. For fulfilment of life or for transcendence of life, and whether purity, calm and freedom in the spirit be our aim or puissance, joy and perfection, Sachchidananda is the unknown, omnipresent, indispensable term for which the human consciousness, whether in knowledge and sentiment or in sensation and action, is eternally seeking.

The universe and the individual are the two essential appearances into which the Unknowable descends and through which it has to be approached; for other intermediate collectivities are born only of their interaction. This descent of the supreme Reality is in its nature a self-concealing; and in the descent there are successive levels, in the concealing successive veils. Necessarily, the revelation takes the form of an ascent; and necessarily also the ascent and the revelation are both progressive. For each successive level in the descent of the Divine is to man a stage in an ascension; each veil that hides the unknown God become for the God-lover and God-seeker an instrument of His unveiling. Out of the rhythmic slumber of material Nature unconscious of the Soul and the Idea that maintain the ordered activities of her energy even in her dumb and mighty material trance, the world struggles into the more quick, varied and disordered rhythm of Life labouring on the verges of self-consciousness. Out of Life it struggles upward into Mind in which the unit becomes awake to itself and its world, and in that awakening the universe gains the leverage it required for its supreme work, it gains self-conscious individuality. But Mind takes up the work to continue, not to complete it. It is a labourer of acute but limited intelligence who takes the confused materials offered by Life and, having improved, adapted, varied, classified according to its power, hands them over to the supreme Artist of our divine manhood. That Artist dwells in supermind; for supermind is superman. Therefore our world has yet to climb beyond Mind to a higher principle, a higher status, a higher dynamism in which universe and individual become aware of and possess that which they both are and therefore stand explained to each other, in harmony with each other, unified.

The disorders of life and mind cease by discerning the secret of a more perfect order than the physical. Matter below life and mind contains in itself the balance between a perfect poise of tranquillity and the action of an immeasurable energy, but does not possess that which it contains. Its peace wears the dull mask of an obscure inertia, a sleep of consciousness or rather of a drugged and imprisoned consciousness. Driven by a force which is its real self but whose sense it cannot yet seize nor share, it has not the awakened joy of its own harmonious energies.

Life and mind awaken to the sense of this want in the form of a striving and seeking ignorance and a troubled and baffled desire which are the first steps towards self-knowledge and self-fulfillment. But where then is the kingdom of their self-fulfilling? It comes to them by the exceeding of themselves. Beyond life and mind we recover consciously in its divine truth that which the balance of material Nature grossly represented,—tranquillity which is neither inertia nor a sealed trance of consciousness but the concentration of an absolute force and an absolute self-awareness, and an action of immeasurable energy which is at the same time an out-thrilling of effable bliss because its every act is the expression, not of a want and an ignorant straining, but of an absolute peace and self-mastery. In that attainment our ignorance realises the light of which it was a darkened or a partial reflection; our desires cease in the plenitude and fulfilment towards which even in their most brute material forms they were an obscure and fallen aspiration.

The universe and the individual are necessary to each other in their ascent. Always indeed they exist for each other and profit by each other. Universe is a diffusion of the divine All in infinite Space and Time, the individual its concentration within limits of Space and Time. Universe seeks in infinite extension the divine totality it feels itself to be but cannot entirely realise; for in extension existence drives at a pluralistic sum of itself which can neither be the primal nor the final unit, but only a recurring decimal without end or beginning. Therefore, it creates in itself a self-conscious concentration of the All through which it can aspire. **In the conscious individual Prakriti turns back**

147

to perceive Purusha, World seeks after Self; God having entirely become Nature, Nature seeks to become progressively God.

On the other hand it is by means of the universe that the individual is impelled to realise himself. Not only is it his foundation, his means, his field, the stuff of the divine Work; but also, since the concentration of the universal Life which he is takes place within limits and is not like the intensive unity of Brahman free from all conception of bound and term, he must necessarily universalise and impersonalise himself in order to manifest the divine All which is his reality. Yet is he called upon to preserve, even when he most extends himself in universality of consciousness, a mysterious transcendent something of which his sense of personality gives him an obscure and egoistic representation. Otherwise he has missed his goal, the problem set to him has not been solved, the divine work for which he accepted birth has not been done.

The universe comes to the individual as Life,—a dynamism the entire secret of which he has to master and a mass of colliding results, a whirl of potential energies out of which he has to disengage some supreme order and some yet unrealised harmony. This is after all the real sense of man's progress. It is not merely a restatement in slightly different terms of what physical Nature has already accomplished. Nor can the ideal of human life be simply the animal repeated on a higher scale of mentality. Otherwise, any system or order which assured a tolerable well-being and a moderate mental satisfaction would have stayed our advance. The animal is satisfied with a modicum of necessity; the gods are content with their splendours. But man cannot rest permanently until he reaches some highest good. He is the greatest of living beings because he is the most discontented, because he feels most the pressure of limitations. He alone, perhaps, is capable of being seized by the divine frenzy for a remote ideal.

To the Life-Spirit, therefore, the individual in whom its potentialities centre is pre-eminently Man, the Purusha. It is the Son of Man who is supremely capable of incarnating God. This Man is the

Manu, the thinker, the Manomaya Purusha, mental person or soul in mind of the ancient sages. No mere superior mammal   he, but a conceptive soul basing itself on the animal body in Matter. He is conscious me or Numen accepting and utilising form as a medium through which Person can deal with substance. The animal life emerging out of Matter is only the inferior term of his existence. The life of thought, feeling, will, conscious impulsion, that which we name in its totality Mind, that which strives to seize upon Matter and its vital energies and subject   them to the law of its own progressive transformation, is the middle term in which he takes his effectual station. But there is equally a supreme term which Mind in man searches after so that having found he may affirm it in his mental and bodily existence. This practical affirmation of something essentially superior to his present self is the basis of the divine life in the human being.

Awakened to a profounder self-knowledge than his first Mental idea of him, Man begins to conceive some formula and to perceive some appearance of the thing that he has to affirm. But it appears to him as if poised between two negations of itself. If, beyond his present attainment, he perceives or is touched by the power, light, bliss of a self-conscious infinite existence and translates his thought or his experience of it into terms convenient for his mentality,—Infinity, Omniscience, Omnipotence, Immortality, Freedom, Love, Beatitude, God,—yet does this sun of his seeing appear to shine between a double Night,—darkness below, a mightier darkness beyond. For when he strives to know it utterly, it seems to pass into something which neither any one of these terms nor the sum of them can at all represent. His mind at last negates God for a Beyond, or at least it seems to find God transcending Himself, denying Himself to the conception. Here also, in the world, in himself, and around himself, he is met always by the opposites of his affirmation. Death is ever with him, limitation invests his being and his experience, error, inconscience, weakness, inertia, grief, pain, evil are constant oppressors of his effort. Here also he is driven to deny God, or at least the Divine seems to negate or to hide itself in some appearance or outcome which is other than its true and eternal reality.

And the terms of this denial are not, like that other and remoter negation, inconceivable and therefore naturally mysterious, unknowable to his mind, but appear to be knowable, known, definite,— and still mysterious. He knows not what they are, why they exist, how they came into being. He sees their processes as they affect and appear to him; he cannot fathom their essential reality.

Perhaps they are unfathomable, perhaps they also are really unknowable in their essence? Or, it may be, they have no essential reality, are an illusion, Asat, non-being. The prior Negation appears to us sometimes as a Nihil, a Non-Existence; this inferior negation may also be, in its essence, a Nihil, a nonexistence. But as we have already put away from us this evasion of the difficulty with regard to that higher, so also we discard it for this inferior Asat. To deny entirely its reality or to seek an escape from it as a mere disastrous illusion is to put away from us the problem and to shun our work. For Life, these things seem to deny God, to be the opposites of Sachchidananda, are real, even if they turn out to be temporary. They and their opposites, good, knowledge, joy, pleasure, life, survival, strength, power, increase, are the very material of her workings.

It is probable indeed that they are the result or rather the inseparable accompaniments, not of an illusion, but of a wrong relation, wrong because it is founded on a false view of what the individual is in the universe and therefore a false attitude both towards God and Nature, towards self and environment. Because that which he has become is out of harmony both with what the world of his habitation is and what he himself should be and is to be, therefore man is subject to these contradictions of the secret Truth of things. In that case they are not the punishment of a fall, but the conditions of a progress. They are the first elements of the work he has to fulfill, the price he has to pay for the crown which he hopes to win, the narrow way by which Nature escapes out of Matter into consciousness; they are at once her ransom and her stock.

For out of these false relations and by their aid the true have to be found. **By the Ignorance have to cross over death. So too the Veda speaks cryptically of energies that are like women evil in impulse, wandering from the path, doing hurt to their Lord, which yet, though themselves false and unhappy, build up in the end "this vast Truth"**, the Truth that is the Bliss. It would be, then, not when he has excised the evil in Nature out of himself by an act of moral surgery or parted with life by an abhorrent recoil, but when he has turned Death into a more perfect life, lifted the small things of the human limitation into the great things of the divine vastness, transformed suffering into beatitude, converted evil into its proper good, translated error and falsehood into their secret truth that the sacrifice will be accomplished, the journey done and Heaven and Earth equalised join hands in the bliss of the Supreme.

Yet how can such contraries pass into each other? By what alchemy shall this lead of mortality be turned into that gold of divine Being? But if they are not in their essence contraries? If they are manifestations of one Reality, identical in substance? Then indeed a divine transmutation becomes conceivable.

We have seen that the Non-Being beyond may well be an inconceivable existence and perhaps ineffable Bliss. At least the Nirvana of Buddhism which formulated one most luminous effort of man to reach and to rest in this highest Non-Existence, represents itself in the psychology of the liberated yet upon earth as an unspeakable peace and gladness; its practical effect is the extinction of all suffering through the disappearance of all egoistic idea or sensation and the nearest we can get to a positive conception of it is that it is some inexpressible Beatitude (if the name or any name can be applied to a peace so void of contents) into which even the notion of self-existence seems to be swallowed up and disappear. It is a Sachchidananda to which we dare no longer apply even the supreme terms of Sat, of Chit and of Ananda. For all terms are annulled and all cognitive experience is overpassed.

On the other hand, we have hazarded the suggestion that since all is one Reality, this inferior negation also, this other contradiction or non-existence of Sachchidananda is none other than Sachchidananda itself. It is capable of being conceived by the intellect, perceived in the vision, even received through the sensations as verily that which it seems to deny, and such would it always be to our conscious experience if things were not falsified by some great fundamental error, some possessing and compelling Ignorance, Maya or Avidya. In this sense a solution might be sought, not perhaps a satisfying metaphysical solution for the logical mind,—for we are standing on the border-line of the unknowable, the ineffable and straining our eyes beyond,—but a sufficient basis in experience for the practice of the divine life.

To do this we must dare to go below the clear surfaces of things on which the mind loves to dwell, to tempt the vast and obscure, to penetrate the unfathomable depths of consciousness and identify ourselves with states of being that are not our own. Human language is a poor help in such a search, but at least we may find in it some symbols and figures, return with some just expressible hints which will help the light of the soul and throw upon the mind some reflection of the ineffable design.

CHAPTER IV

HEREDITY AND ENVIRONMENT:
TWO BASIC FACTORS INFLUENCING
INDIVIDUAL'S DEVELOPMENT

I.   THE ENVIRONMENTAL UNIVERSE AND THE HUMAN INDIVIDUAL AND THE DIVINE

II.   THE TRANSCENDENTAL ENVIRONMENT: THE ONE ORIGINAL TRANSCENDENTAL SHAKTI: (एकमेव परात्पर आद्याशक्ति, The Mother)

III. ELEVEN (or 12) TYPES OF UNIVERSAL ENVIRONMENTS

IV. FOUR TYPES OF HEREDITY: THE INHERENT DEVELOPMENTAL FORCES INFLUENCING THE EVOLUTION OF AN INDIVIDUAL

     1. Physical (Genetic) Heredity
     2. Atavistic Heredity
     3. Pre-birth Heredity
     4. Heritage from Subhuman Origins of Man's Life

        Table:

        (4.1) Planes and Parts of Consciousness of the Individual and his Environing universe: (A Schematic Presentation)

I. THE ENVIRONMENTAL UNIVERSE AND THE HUMAN INDIVIDUAL AND THE DIVINE

The aim of the creation and evolution is to progressively divinise man's and the universal Nature. Aim of Integral Psychology is same: It has been already noted in the *"Section III-1-(iv)*: *It is Integral for it studies man in the universe"* of the previous Chapter II* that the central aim of integral psychology is to help nature of man and the society to grow progressively into divinity, so that the environmental universal nature, of whose they are the parts, also achieves its divine fulfilment progressively for it cannot achieve it by itself. Man is a special concentration created in itself by the universal Nature so that through him and with him it can progressively ascend the ladder of evolution step by step and reach the summit of the supramental Nature. Explaining the relation among the man, the universe and the Divine and interdependence of the man and the universe on each other and the ultimate evolutionary goal of the human being and consciousness and the universal being and consciousness, Sri Aurobindo writes in the sixth chapter of his book: *The Life Divine,*

> **"The universe and the individual are necessary to each other in their ascent. Always indeed they exist for each other and profit by each other.** Universe is a diffusion of the divine All in infinite Space and Time, the individual its concentration within limits of Space and Time. Universe seeks in infinite extension the divine totality it feels itself to be but cannot entirely realise; for in extension existence drives at a pluralistic sum of itself which can neither be the primal nor the final unit, but only a recurring decimal without end or beginning. Therefore, it creates in itself a self-conscious concentration of the All through which it can aspire. **In the conscious individual Prakriti turns back to perceive Purusha, World seeks after Self; God having entirely become Nature, Nature seeks to become progressively God.**

"On the other hand it is by means of the universe that the individual is impelled to realise himself. Not only is it his foundation, his means, his field, the stuff of the divine Work; but also, since the concentration of the universal Life which he is takes place within limits and is not like the intensive unity of Brahman free from all conception of bound and term, **he must necessarily universalise and impersonalise himself in order to manifest the divine All** which is his reality. Yet is he called upon to preserve, even when he most extends himself in universality of consciousness, a mysterious transcendent something of which his sense of personality gives him an obscure and egoistic representation. Otherwise he has missed his goal, the problem set to him has not been solved, the divine work for which he accepted birth has not been done."[113] [*Bold letters are of the author of this book.*]

Here, Sri Aurobindo tells us that the universe is an infinitely extended form of the Divine All (समग्र भगवान, परब्रह्म, ब्रह्मन, Brahman) in infinite space and time; and the universe has created in itself the man, through whom it can aspire for the Divine and evolve into the Divine and feel identity with man and the Divine; further he says the man is self-conscious concentration of the All and by means of the universe, the individual man can develop and ultimately evolve into the Divine and feel identity with the universe and the Divine.

The individual human being is a self-limitation of the universe within itself. So, in principle, the planes and parts of the man's nature and those of the universal nature are the same and coextensive, interpenetrative, interconnected and interdependent and separated only by ultra-thin ultra-transparent ultra-subtle consciousness-membrane. All planes and parts of the universal nature are invisibly manifest but in

---

[113] SABCL Vol. 18; pp. 45-46; For reading complete chapter refer to Appendix 3.4 in the chapter III of this book.

the man a few are manifest and the others are waiting to manifest. *Table 4.1 shows some of these facts of the man and the universe.* As if man is a bubble (जल-बुदबुद) of sea-water in the universal blue great ocean (महासागर); as if an individual person is a miniature form of the universal infinite personality (लघुरूप of विराट व्यक्तित्व) harboured in and moving in the oceanic infinite expanse; or say, man is within the universal nature and a finite personality of the infinite universal personality. Positive as well as hostile negative forces of the universal nature constantly enter in and go out from the individual's mental-vital-physical nature, and either help or obstruct his upward evolution. The individual does the same thing *vice versa;* he also reciprocates the movements of the universal nature; he also sends out positive and negative hostile forces from his/her personal consciousness into the universe and either helps or retards the upward evolution of the universe. *Refer Appendix 3.4 in the chapter III of this book for reading Sri Aurobindo's narration.*

Table 4.1

Planes and Parts of Consciousness of the Individual and his Environing Universe
(A Schematic Presentation)

(The Divine, ब्रह्म or परमात्मा, stands above all things, but holds & guides them also. Thus as the Divine influences an individual person, He is the transcendental environment for a person. See section II that follows.)

TYPES OF PLANES	THE PLANES AND PARTS OF THE UNIVERSE: THE ENVIRONMENT AROUND THE MAN	THE PLANES AND PARTS OF THE INDIVIDUAL
The Bliss Plane	1. The Sachchidananda Plane आनन्दलोक	1.The Sachchidananda Plane (unmanifest in Man, but realisable by man)
The Supramental Plane	2. The Supramental Plane अतिमनसलोक	2. The Supramental Plane (unmanifest in Man, but realisable by man)
The Spiritual Plane	3. The Overmental Plane अधिमनसलोक (Four Parts of It in Descending Order: The Overmind, The Intuitive Mind the Illumined Mind, and the Higher Mind)	3. The Spiritual Plane (Four Parts of It in Descending Order: The Overmind, The Intuitive Mind the Illumined Mind, and the Higher Mind) (unmanifest in man, but realisable by man)

The Inmost Conscient Plane		4. The Psychic Plane (unmanifest in man, but realisable by man)
The Conscient Plane	5. The Mental Plane: मनोमयलोक	5. The Mental Plane (manifest in man)
The Conscient Plane	6. The Vital Plane: प्राणमयलोक	6.The Vital Plane (manifest in man)
The Conscient Plane	7. The Subtle Physical Plane: सूक्ष्म पार्थिवलोक 8. The Material Physical Plane: जड पार्थिवलोक 9. The Social Plane: समाजलोक (It consists of the people on earth & subtle beings in the universe on all of its planes; e.g. gods, goddesses, Asuras on the overmental level)	7. The Subtle Physical Plane 8. The Physical Plane 9.The Social Plane: It consists of the people on earth & subtle beings in the universe on all of its planes; e.g. gods & goddesses in the overmental plane (all planes are accessible to man)
Under The Conscient Plane	10. The Subconscient Plane अवचेतनलोक 11. The Inconscient Plane	10. The Subconscient, nether part not accessible to mind 11. The Inconscient Plane. Not accessible to mind So, there are 12 environments for a person.

Let us consider a real incidence that exemplifies the interaction between an individual consciousness and universal consciousness around him.

A father is helping his child to complete his homework and the child, due to some disturbance in the mind that has entered from the surrounding universal consciousness, is not able to concentrate and work speedily and without mistakes. The child often makes mistakes, which his father gets him to correct. The work progresses at slow speed. The father feels that his departure to office will be delayed and he will not be able to reach his office in time. His mind feels worry and frustration and his vital being becomes prey to impatience and anger that arise from within and anger that enters from without from the surrounding universal nature. He can no longer restrain his mind and vital and starts shouting, "What is wrong with you today? Hurry up. Go fast, I have to go to the office soon. I do not want to be late". Remembering past experiences, the child expects more attacks of angry words coupled with physical punishment from his father and so his mind and emotion get more worried and more disturbed. As a result, he makes mistakes even more. The completion of homework is slowed down even more. The force of anger, frustration and exasperation and helplessness increases and takes possession of the father's mind and vital, as his departure is getting increasingly delayed, he loses control over his mind and abruptly yells to his wife, "I am going, you take care of your child, help him to complete the work."

The father leaves for his office in anger. For the feeling of frustration aroused and activated the dormant force of anger lodged in his personality, which had created cracks and holes in his being and consciousness, rather in his personal environmental consciousness; the universal force of irritation and anger had rushed through those openings in him and united with and augmented the already active inner anger in his vital being and these increased force of anger in his vital being had overpowered the force of peace in his mind and so he had abused his child and had angrily given charge of the child to his wife. He had allowed the play of his habit of anger and thus strengthened it.

The father has increased and strengthened the negative forces of anger, helplessness and violence in the child, in himself and around in the universe, for the vibrations of such consciousness forces naturally go out and travel around into the universal consciousness. He has increased and strengthened in himself, in the child and in the universe the forces of the vital level – the vital forces of anger, fear, frustration and helplessness – which is below the mental level in the evolutionary scale. Thus, he has allowed himself to be a retarding force acting against the evolutionary upward movement of himself, child and the universal consciousness around. Moreover, he has taught the child a dangerous principle: The practice of the use of violent force as a tool to control other's behaviours.

If his mind would have noticed the arising vibrations of inner dormant anger and immediately applied the mental peace-force, soul's psychic peace force and over-soul's spiritual peace force to control and hold and offer them to the inner soul and upper Spirit and also to the transcendental Divine Mother above (आद्या शक्ति), he would have extradited his habit of anger or at least degraded and weakened his habit of anger, strengthened and upgraded his habit of peace and thus purified and strengthened his vital emotional being and upgraded and evolved his nature of peace. If his mind would have noticed the universal force of anger trying to enter in him from the outer universal consciousness, he should have barred its entry and pushed it back into the universe around him and saved himself from being more polluted by anger; but if while pushing it back he had pushed it up and offered it to the transcendental Divine Mother, the universal force of anger would have weakened and universal force of peace would have been augmented and thus he would have helped the Universal Nature to evolve.

The child's mother speaks to him from the kitchen in a tone full of filial love, "Be quiet, try to concentrate and quietly continue your work. I will be with you in a minute and help you". She reaches the child in a minute, puts and moves her hand softly on the back of the child and encourages and guides the child in the work. Thus she removes the distraction created by the father's anger in the mind of the child. The mother, by treating the child with positive feelings, words and actions, creates positive forces in her child; the child now works with peaceful concentration. She leaves for the kitchen. The child's heart has been soothed, his mind has become a settled concentrated force and he finishes the work in no time. When his mother comes back, she only has to help the child correct a few errors. Now, they are both happy and the child leaves for school filled with happiness and enthusiasm. Thus the mother has helped the child to cultivate and feel forces of love, self-confidence, forgiveness, silence, concentration, happiness and enthusiasm. The child also has sent out of himself these forces into the universe. The mother has worked to promote the upward progress of the individual and the universe; while, the father had done something contrary.

As we have seen above (*Refer Table 4.1*), The One Divine Power (आद्याशक्ति, The Mother) and the eleven universal environments surround the man and develop him. In other words, the man, The One Divine Power (आद्याशक्ति, The Mother) and the eleven universal environmental powers form human personality. There is one more factor, the factor of heredity that also determines human personality. We shall consider this phenomenal fact much briefly next.

II. THE TRANSCENDENTAL ENVIRONMENT: THE ONE ORIGINAL TRANSCENDENTAL SHAKTI (एकमेव परात्पर आद्याशक्ति, The Mother)

1. The Supreme Divine (परमात्मा) is the creator of the universe and everything in the universe and is the creator of the earth and everything on it. He is not an absentee landlord of the universe and earth and man: He through his Shakti, the Mother, holds and dominates the universe, earth and the man and guides them in their evolution towards the next evolutionary stage of the supramental consciousness. *Refer to the Chapter III Section V: The Terrestrial Evolution for detailed explanation.*

2. The Divine and the Mother come on earth as Avatars; they take birth in human body as the divine man and divine woman at the time of crisis on earth and work resolutely and relentlessly to lift the existing life to new upper stage of evolution, to establish a new age on earth. Sri Ram, Sri Krishna, Buddha, and Sri Aurobindo and The Mother of Pondicherry are such Avatars. *Refer to "Chapter III Section VI: Evolution and The Avatar" for detailed explanation.*

3. The Divine and the Mother have emanated many Vibhutis that are incarnations of their particular qualities to effect some required limited change in the life throughout human history. Arjun of the ancient Mahabharata time, Swami Vivekananda of modern time are two such examples. *Refer to chapter III for detailed explanation.*

4. The Supreme Divine through the Mother emanates a part of himself and his agent called the cosmic Soul (विश्वात्मा, जीवात्मा, आत्मा) in the universal nature; this cosmic Soul also as an assistance of the Divine holds, dominates and guides the universe towards the goal of its evolution.

5. The Supreme Divine through the Mother partially (अंशरूपेण) descends in man's subtle-heart centre (हृदृपद्म) as his soul and the psychic (अन्तरात्मा), that holds, dominates and guides him to his evolutionary destiny, the supramental realisation.

162

III. ELEVEN (or 12) TYPES OF UNIVERSAL ENVIRONMENTS

We have mentioned eleven (rather twelve) types of universal environments of man in Table 4.1 in the first section of this chapter, namely (1) the Supreme Divine, (2) bliss, (3) supramental, (4) overmental, (5) psychic, (6) mental, (7) vital, (8) subtle physical, (9) material physical, (10) social, (11) subconscient and (12) inconscient. Only the material physical and the social environments are included in the field of study of the materialistic science and psychology. Other ten subtle environments are excluded from the field of study. Man and his universe must be studied also in reference to these ten environments, that is man and his universe must be studied with reference to all twelve environments. All twelve environments really exist in the universe around the man and the society and all impact the life of the individual and the society. So only such kind of holistic study can provide integral knowledge, perfect knowledge, wholistic knowledge, पूर्णज्ञान, the true knowledge, सत्यज्ञान about the individual, the society and the universe.

Such a knowledge is preserved in ancient Vedic, Upanishadic literature and recent large number of spiritual cum pragmatic studies in India and it would be profitable for the scientists and psychologists to study them and on the basis of them enlarge their method and field of study.

This study on integral psychology is based on integral knowledge about the man, the society and the universe given by Sri Aurobindo and The Mother and attempts to arrive at a statement of psychology, that presents a wholistic description of man and the universe and a wholistic description of the progressing evolution of the individual man, the society and the universe from the material stage to the mental stage and to the destined next supramental stage.

IV. FOUR TYPES OF HEREDITY: THE INHERENT DEVELOPMENTAL FORCES INFLUENCING THE EVOLUTION OF AN INDIVIDUAL

Physical heredity, atavistic heredity, heredity from sub-human origins and pre-birth heredity are four types of heredity. First three are received by a person at the time of his conception and the last one is received at the time of his birth, when his soul enters his body and takes possession of it.

1. THE PHYSICAL (GENETIC) HEREDITY

At the moment of conception two germ cells, one a sperm cell from the father and the other an egg cell (ovum) from the mother unite to form a new individual organism, which is called a zygote. The mother's germ cell carries her personality-characteristics and the father's germ cell carries his personality-characteristics. It means the zygote, the new person born, inherits personality-characteristics from both the parents: In other words, the zygote, the new person born, inherits the genetic heredity from both the parents. But the mechanism of which parental characteristics would appear and which would not appear in the life of the offspring is not known to the science of Genetics and the science of psychology. It is an enigma for them. So they assume that appearance of inherited characteristics in a person is determined by the CHANCE. But the spiritual psychology will say it is determined by the will of the cosmic Mother Nature or by the Time Spirit or the Divine or the Power of Grace of the Supreme Mother, the *Adya Shakti*.

Physical heredity received is the cumulative heredity of the past seven generations in the lines of the father and the mother. Of course, the child receives different amount of genetic heredity from each of the past seven generations through the parents. That is why there may be some resemblances between the child and his previous grandparents. And that is why persons in the same line of seven generations have a kind of similarity in their heredity. It has been found that parents having similar genetic heredity do not produce children of good quality. So, a person should not marry within one's own seven generations, within blood-relation of seven generations, so as to avoid creation of a line of less quality children. More dissimilarity in heredity ensures higher quality in children. Vedic Hindu Dharma knew this truth and so there is a bar on marriage within seven generations. The material science have only recently found this truth.

All types of heredity in environments jointly determine the development of personality traits. Materialistic rational psychology accepts the role of the genetic heredity and the role of the physical and social environments only. Hence, the validity of its knowledge is much less and is less useful for practical life.

The phenomena of mutation or mitosis proves that there is no fixed hereditary mechanism and determinism. The rational science of genetics and psychology have not been able to explain the genetic mutation. But integral psychology has explained it. Integral psychology knows that the forces of the subtle worlds enter in the organism and effect genetic mutation.

Particular forces at their own will can enter in the organism to change a particular heredity, particular genetic code and particular characteristic of personality. Or, if a person aspires for a particular change in particular heredity and genetic code, particular characteristic of personality and particular behaviours and life and by means of *sadhana, yoga,* prayer, meditation, *Japa,* etc. call the particular divine forces from the subtle worlds to help him, they may help him to realise the aspired changes. In fact, it is the force of the divine Grace acting from behind the environmental forces and man's own inner powers – mental will, quality of perseverance, courage, etc. – that effect required change in man's traits and behaviours.

In short, one can call one's own inner physical, vital, mental, psychic and spiritual forces and also outer physical, vital, mental, psychic and spiritual, overmental and supramental forces in order to make desired changes in oneself and in one's environment. Man and the universe are not fixed system. They are existences in transition.

2. THE ATAVISTIC HEREDITY

Psychological personality characteristics of previous generations received by the organism at the time of its conception is called Atavistic heredity. It is received at the time when a male parent and female parent sexually unite. The particular consciousness characteristic a zygote receives depends on what type of consciousness vibrations the male and the female would emit from their own being and consciousness consciously, unconsciously impulsively and self-willingly. The process of transferring this heredity is almost an occult phenomena and almost all parents are ignorant about it at the moments of mating. They do not mate with any conscious mental will but to satisfy greedily the vital sexual sensational joy and to feel sudden thrill of impulsive sex. This seems to be the view of The Mother and Sri Aurobindo with regard to Atavism or atavistic heredity. The Mother was asked the following question by a student, which she answered extempore: The question and answer is given below:

Question:

"Is the vital distorted from the very birth?"

Answer:

"If your birth was not an accident, you could very well think there was no distortion, but what you are at your birth is most of the time almost absolutely what your mother and father have made you, and also, through them, what your grandparents have made you. There are certain <u>vital traditions in families and, besides, there is the state of consciousness in which you were formed, conceived — the moment at which you were conceived — and that, not once in a million times does that state conform to true aspiration</u>; and it is only a true aspiration which could make your vital pure of all mixture, make the vital element attracted for the formation of the being a pure element, free from all contagion; I mean that if a psychic being enters there, it can gather elements favourable to its growth. In the world as it is, things are so mixed up, have been so mixed up in every way, that it is almost impossible to have elements of the vital sufficiently pure not to suffer the contagion of all other contaminated beings.

"I think I have already spoken about that, I have said what kind of aspiration ought to be there in the parents before the birth; but as I said, this does not happen even once in a hundred thousand instances. The willed conception of a child is extremely rare; mostly it is an accident. Among innumerable parents it is quite a small minority that even simply bothers about what a child could be; they do not even know that what the child will be depends on what they are. It is a very small elite which knows this. Most of the time things go as they can; anything at all happens and people don't even realise what is happening. So, in these conditions how do you expect to be born with a vital being sufficiently pure to be of help to you? One is born with a slough to clean before one begins to live. And once you have made a good start on the way to the inner transformation and you go down to the subconscient root of the being — that exactly which comes from parents, from **ATAVISM** — well, you do see what it is! And all, almost all difficulties are there, there are very few things added to existence after the first years of life. This happens at any odd moment; if you keep bad company or read bad books, the poison may enter you; but there are all the imprints deep-rooted in the subconscient, the dirty habits you have and against which you struggle. For instance, there are people who can't open their mouth without telling a lie, and they don't always do this deliberately (that is the worst of it), or people who can't come in touch with others without quarrelling, all sorts of stupidities — they are there in the subconscient, deeply rooted. Now, when you have a goodwill, externally you do your best to avoid all that, to correct it if possible; you work, you fight; then become aware that this thing always keeps coming up, it comes up from some part which escapes your control. But if you enter this subconscient, if you let your consciousness infiltrate it, and look carefully, gradually you will discover all the sources, all the origins of all your difficulties; then you will begin to understand what your fathers and mothers, grandfathers and grandmothers were, and if at a certain moment you are unable to control yourself, you will understand, "I am like that because they were like that."

"If you have within you a psychic being sufficiently awake to watch over you, to prepare your path, it can draw towards you things which help you, draw people, books, circumstances, all sorts of little coincidences which come to you as though brought by some benevolent will and give you an indication, a help, a support to take decisions and turn you in the right direction. But once you have taken this decision, once you have decided to find the truth of your being, once you start sincerely on the road, then everything seems to conspire to help you to advance, and if you observe carefully you see gradually the source of your difficulties: Ah! Wait a minute, this defect was in my father; oh! this habit was my mother's; oh! my grandmother was like this, my grandfather was like that." Or it could well be the nurse who took care of you when you were small, or brothers and sisters who played with you, the little friends you met, and you will find that all this was there, in this person or that or the other. But if you continue to be sincere, you find you can cross all this quite calmly, and after a time you cut all the moorings with which you were born, break the chains and go freely on the path.

"If you really want to transform your character, it is that you must do. It has always been said that it is impossible to change one's nature; in all books of philosophy, even of yoga, you are told the same story: "You cannot change your character, you are born like that, you are like that." This is absolutely false, I guarantee it is false; but there is something very difficult to do to change your character, because it is not your character which must be changed, it is the character of your antecedents. In them you will not change it (because they have no such intention), but it is in you that it must be changed. It is what they have given you, all the little gifts made to you at your birth — nice gifts — it is this which must be changed. But if you succeed in getting hold of the thread of these things, the true thread, since you have worked upon this with perseverance and sincerity, one fine morning you will be free; all this will fall off from you and you will be able to get a start in life without any burden. Then you will be a new man, living a new life, almost with a new nature. And if you look back you will say, "It is not possible, I was never like that!"[114]

The above explanation makes it clear that the zygote gets the essence of personality characteristics from the parents, grandparents, great grandparents and so on, perhaps of seven previous generations like the way it is asserted in the case of physical heredity by genetic science.

As an illustration of this principle of atavism, Chandrakant[115] observes, "If one can enter into one's sub-consciousness, one would know that his certain personality characteristics are similar to certain forefathers." This second kind of heredity explains similarity in consciousness and mental and emotional behaviours of genetically related individuals, which the rational psychology has not been able to explain well.

The author of this book has observed closely and studied some common qualities and behaviours of a few persons over a long period of time; his study suggests that instinctive or spontaneous and unconscious habit of asserting lies which is a routine response of ego's defense mechanism (of Freudian Analytical Psychology), and other pre-

---

[114] CWM Vol.4 – Travel size Edition; pp. 260-262

[115] Patel Chandrakant P.; *Samanya Manovignan* (Publisher: University Book Production Board, Gujarat Govt., Ahmedabad, Gujarat, 380 006, India, 1991); p. 12

neurotic mental behaviours of defense mechanism, such as, regression, rationalization, etc. have roots in the atavistic heredity, for the persons observed had some common ancestry and they had lived right from their birth in different environments away from each other and yet both had in their nature the same above-mentioned personality traits.

The author of this book has also come across a striking example of atavistic heredity: Two ladies, who had lived quite far away from each other in very different social environments but had common genealogical ancestry, happen to come together to live under the same roof later on during their adulthood; they had never met before; it is surprising that both should have certain common characteristics; such as, argumentativeness, closed mind, lack of plasticity, lack of emotional control, hyper-sensitivity, sulking, tendency of withdrawal, anger and depression and attitude of domination, possessiveness, finding faults of others but overlooking one's own faults, harshness, disregard of other's feelings, shrewdness, attitude of projection and rationalization, proneness to underrate expertise of others, paranoid tendencies and paradoxical co-existence of opposite traits in the personality. The similarity in their character is so striking that we have to deduce that the similarity of their traits is due to common atavistic heredity. For, as they had grown in insulation of each other in different places, they had not leant those qualities from each other, neither they were sibling nor of same age.

3. THE PRE-BIRTH HEREDITY

The psychic being of the human organism, when takes birth, carries with it the essence of the developments of psychic, mental, vital and physical consciousness that has been accrued during the previous births for further developments in the new life. This constitutes pre-birth heredity, according to Auromere's psychology, says Patel Chandrakant.[116] Sri Aurobindo says,

---

[116] Ibid.

"It is true that we bring most of ourselves, – or rather most of our predispositions, tendencies of reaction to the universal Nature, from past lives. Heredity only affects strongly the external being; besides, all the effects of heredity are not accepted even there, only those that are in consonance with what we are to be or not preventive of it at least."[117]

Prof. Mukherjee had studied rebirth using research method of Case-History a long time ago. His studies of cases were serially reported in the newspapers of India and were read, liked and discussed with a lot of interest by psychologists. Birth of genius children of ordinary, unintelligent and economically backward parents can be explained with the principle of pre-birth heredity only.

Professor Indra Sen[118] is the first person to investigate a case of incarnation, which was known as "Shanti Devi" case. The study report stands even today as a significant scientific document.

Anyway, one thing is clear here that this problem of rebirth and heredity and environment is a rich, large and interesting field for study.

4. THE HERITAGE FROM THE SUBHUMAN ORIGINS OF MAN'S LIFE

Matter, vegetation and animal are evolutionary sub-human origins of man. So, naturally human nature has received some natural qualities of his sub-human origins. Commenting on semi-barbaric and semi-civilised nature of man Sri Aurobindo observes,

"The course of evolution proceeding from the vegetable to the animal, from the animal to the man, starts in the latter from the subhuman; he has to take up into him the

---

[117] SABCL Vol. 22; pp. 359-360

[118] Sen Indra; *Integral Psychology: The Psychological System of Sri Aurobindo* (Publisher: Sri Aurobindo International Centre of Education, Pondicherry, INDIA, 1986); p. vi of Preface.

animal and even the mineral and vegetable: they constitute his physical nature, they dominate his vitality, they have their hold upon his mentality. His proneness to many kinds of inertia, his readiness to vegetate, his attachment to the soil and clinging to his roots, to safe anchorages of all kinds, and on the other hand his nomadic and predatory impulses, his blind servility to custom and the rule of the pack, his mob-movements and openness to subconscious suggestions from the group-soul, his subjection to the yoke of rage and fear, his need of punishment and reliance on punishment, his inability to think and act for himself, his incapacity for true freedom, his distrust of novelty, his slowness to seize intelligently and assimilate, his downward propensity and earthward gaze, his vital and physical subjection to his heredity, all these and more are his heritage from the subhuman origins of his life and body and physical mind. It is because of this heritage that he finds self-exceeding the most difficult of lessons and the most painful of endeavours. Yet it is by exceeding of the lower self that Nature accomplishes the great strides of her evolutionary process. To learn by what he has been, but also to know and increase to what he can be, is the task that is set for the mental being."[119]

"To take the body and the physical life as the one thing important, to judge manhood by the physical strength, development and prowess, to be at the mercy of the instincts which rise out of the physical inconscient, to despise knowledge as a weakness and inferiority or look on it as a peculiarity and no necessary part of the conception of manhood, this is the mentality of the barbarian. It tends to reappear in the human being in the *atavistic* period of boyhood, — when, be it noted, the development of the body is of the greatest importance, — but to the adult man in civilised humanity it is ceasing to be possible. For, in the first place, by the stress of modern life even

---

[119] CWSA Vol. 25; p. 74; SABCL Vol.15; p. 67

the vital attitude of the race is changing. Man is ceasing to be so much of a physical and becoming much more of a vital and economic animal. Not that he excludes or is intended to exclude the body and its development or the right maintenance of and respect for the animal being and its excellences from his idea of life; the excellence of the body, its health, its soundness, its vigour and harmonious development are necessary to a perfect manhood and are occupying attention in a better and more intelligent way than before. But the first rank in importance can no longer be given to the body, much less that entire predominance assigned to it in the mentality of the barbarian."[120]

Review of books[121] of the rational materialistic scientific psychology shows that it has identified only one type of heredity – the physical heredity – and only two types of environments – the physical & social environments – of man, and explains human nature in this partial and inadequate context, while integral psychology[122] of Sri Aurobindo and The Mother has identified all the four kinds of Heredity

---

[120] CWSA Vol. 25; pp. 67-68

[121] Patel Chandrakant P.; *Samanya Manovignan – General Psychology – (*Publisher: University Granthnirman Board, Gujarat Rajya, Ahmedabad, India, 1991); Chapter 3: pp.158-210; Garret Henry E.; *General Psychology* (Publisher: Eurasia Publishing House (Pvt.) Ltd., Ram Nagar, New Delhi-110055, India,1975); Chapter 2: pp. 33-66; Krech David and Crutchfield Richard S.; *Elements of Psychology;* (New York: Alfred A. Knopf, U.S.A.,1958); Chapter XXI, pp. 563-585; Morgan Clifford T.; *Introduction to Psychology* (Publisher: McGraw-Hill Book Company, Inc., New York, U.S.A., 1961); Chapter 2: pp. 29-64; Morgan Clifford T. and King R. A.; *Introduction to Psychology* (Publisher: Tata McGraw-Hill Publishing Company Ltd., Bombay, India, 1971); Chapter 2: pp. 33-62; Carmichael (Ed.); *Introduction to Psychology* (Oxford & IBH Publishing Co. Pvt. Ltd., New Delhi, India, 1967); pp. 80-103

[122] SABCL Vol. 3, pp. 67-70; SABCL Vol. 16, pp.72, 83-84, 96, 97, 100-102, 108-109, 158, 226, 230, 260; SABCL Vol. 18, pp. 299; SABCL Vol. 19, pp.743, 825-826, 828; SABCL Vol. 22, pp. 360, 476-477; (i) SABCL Vol. 22 (1970), pp. 359-360 & 476-77; SABCL Vol. 16 (1971), pp. 83-84, 96-101; SABCL Vol. 18 (1970), pp. 299; SABCL Vol. 19 (1970), pp. 743, 825-26, 828 SABCL Vol. 20, (1970), pp. 427-437; SABCL Vol. 22 (1970), pp. 233-380; (ii) CWM Vol. 4; pp. 191-194 & 260-262; CWM Vol. 5- Travel Size Edition; pp. 359-361; (iii) Patel Chandrakant P; p. 53

and 11 or 12 kinds of environments of man and explains human nature in complete context of hereditary and environment. So, integral psychology is able to explain better the human nature and to provide truly effective process of development and evolution of human nature. The statement of integral psychology given in this book is derived from Sri Aurobindo and The Mother's psychological writings spread over approximately *17562* pages. *(Refer to "Section II: Source literature of Integral Psychology" in the chapter II: The Definition and Nature of Integral Psychology).* In this book of integral psychology, the author has described a basic theory and practice of Yoga of Self-Perfection. If one studies and practices the integral psychology given in this book in the spirit of a seeker seeking truth of life, he is likely to make an adventurous attempt to self-perfect, spiritualise and to realise the final goal of life, the supramental life. Considering this importance of integral psychology Chandrakant Patel[123] advises to scientific psychology that

> "If men's growth is to be studied properly and helped effectively so as to further his evolution, the psychology needs to accept holistic concept of heredity and environment and expand its subject-matter and method: It must admit in its field and scope of study the intuitional and metaphysical knowledge and yogic method of research — yogic introspection and observation and direct cognition — in addition to empirical ones."

---

[123] Patel C. P.; *Studies in Integral Psychology, Integral Education and Integration of the Nation and the World* (Publisher: Sri Aurobindo Society Centre, B-305, Galaxy Apartments, Wadi Plot, Porbandar, Gujarat, 360575, India, 1999); pp. 13-14

SUMMARY

1. Twelve Types of Environment of Man

Universe is the environment of man. There are eleven parts and planes of universal consciousness: (i) the inconscient, (ii) the subconscious, (iii) the subtle physical, (iv) the vital, (v) the mental, (vi) the psychic, (vii) the spiritual (the worlds of the higher mind, the illumined mind, the intuitive mind and the overmind), (viii) the supramental and (ix) the Sachchidananda. These nine levels of the universe are subtle. There are two gross ones also; they are (x) the physical and (xi) the social. The individual and the universe are interdependent on each other for their evolutionary development. Both are inseparably and integrally connected and to ascend to divinity step by step is the purpose of their life.

2. Four types of Heredity of Man

(i) Physical heredity is received by an individual at the time of his conception from parents through their germ cells. (ii) Atavistic heredity is genealogical inheritance of mental nature received at the time of conception from parents; it depends on the quality of consciousness that parents have during the sexual union. (iii) Pre-birth heredity is the essence of the psychological development of previous births that the psychic being carries with it and establishes in the individual when it enters the individual's body, and (iv) The Heritage from The Subhuman Origins of Man's life.

Suggestions for Further Reading

1. CWM Vol. 4; pp. 217-256 (The Mother's talks on The universe, Mental worlds and the psychic being.)

2. CWM Vol. 9; pp. 190-244 (The Mother's talks on intermediate being, The "Mind of Light", Passage to higher hemisphere, Story of successive involution, Terrestrial evolution, Individual and cosmic evolution, and Supramental power.)

3. CWM Vol. 3; pp. 173-174 (The Mother's talk on Supermind and Overmind)

4. SABCL Vol. 28; pp. 95-304 (Sri Aurobindo's last writing: Savitri. Sri Aurobindo in these pages unveils all planes of the World in poetry.)

5. Van Vrekhem (Editor); *The Mother's Vision* (Publisher: Sri Aurobindo Ashram, Pondicherry, 605002, India; 2005); Ch. 2: The Universe: pp. 55-80

WORKBOOK: QUESTIONS FOR PREVIEW AND REVIEW

Essay Type Questions

1. The individual and the universe are integrally connected and are interdependent for higher development. Explain with an illustration.
2. Describe briefly four types of heredity. How can one change them?
3. Describe briefly twelve types of environments.

Short Answer Type and Objective questions

1. The individual and the universe are _____ and _____.
2. _____Consciousness forces help upward evolution, while _____ forces retard evolution.
3. Anger is a _____ force, while peace is a_____. (positive, negative)
4. Enumerate planes and parts of universal consciousness.
5. Enumerate planes and parts of individual consciousness. Which of them are manifested and which are waiting for manifestation?
6. Name three types of heredity.

7. Physical heredity received by child at the time of birth. Discuss.
8. Define Atavistic heredity.
9. Which two kinds of heredity are received from parent?
10. Pre-birth heredity is received by the child at the time of conception.
11. Physical and atavistic heredity consist of characteristics of _____ generation.

Exercises

1. Sri Aurobindo says, "The universe and the individual are necessary to each other in their ascent. Always indeed they exist for each other and profit by each other." Try to write in your words his explanation of the idea in this sentence.
2. Draw a ladder of planes and parts of consciousness.

SELF TEST

1. _____ psychology says man is in the society, but _____ psychology says man is in the universe.
2. _____ psychology says there are two types of environments, but _____ psychology says there are twelve.
3. _____ psychology says there is one type of heredity, but _____ psychology says there are four types of heredity.
4. Child receives _____ heredity at the time of conception, but receives _____ heredity at the time of birth.

CHAPTER V

THE PLANES AND PARTS OF A HUMAN BEING: THE STRUCTURE OF PERSONALITY AND THE METHOD OF ITS TRANSFORMATION

I. HUMAN BEING IS THE THIRD STEP OF THE EVOLVING DIVINE CONSCIOUSNESS ON THE EARTH

II. THE PLANES AND PARTS OF CONSCIOUSNESS OF HUMAN BEING

      1. The Inconscient and The Subconscient
      2. The Super-Conscient and The Conscient

III. SRI AUROBINDO AND THE MOTHER'S CONTRIBUTION TO PSYCHOLOGY

           Figure:
           (5.1) The Schematic Diagram of the Planes of
                Consciousness of Human Being

           Boxes:
           (5.1) A Scientist's Case for the Afterlife
           (5.2) Life after Death

I. HUMAN BEING IS THE THIRD STEP OF THE EVOLVING DIVINE CONSCIOUSNESS ON THE EARTH

As seen in *Sections IV-V of Chapter III*, the Divine Consciousness (or say the divine Love and the divine Anand) entered into the inconscient's expanse and started its redemption employing the process of upward evolution. The Upward push of the hidden super-consciousness impelled Inconsciousness to struggle for becoming conscious.

As a result, **from the Inconscient the sub-conscious** material physical world appeared and in it subconscious material things were created.

From the **material consciousness** came up **the Life (Vital) consciousness** (*Matsya → Kurma → Varah → Nrisinh*) and in it the botanical vegetable kingdom and zoological animal kingdom. *Refer "Section VI: Evolution and the Ten Avatars "in Chapter III for complete ascension of the consciousness.*

From the vital consciousness then emerged half-vital & half-mental plane of consciousness and in it half animal & half man, (*Nrisinh*).

Then from the half-vital & half-mental plane of consciousness evolved the **mental consciousness** and in it mental man (*Vaman → Parshuram → Rama*) and the mental world peopled with mental beings. Please refer *Appendix 3.2* placed at the end of the third chapter for the description of the evolutionary movement up to the mind given by Sri Aurobindo.

The next evolute is **the plane of spiritual consciousness** and in it spiritual man (*Sri Krishna*) and the spiritual world peopled with spiritual human beings.

The next evolute is **the plane of the supramental consciousness and in it supramental being** (*Sri Auromere*) and the

180

supramental world inhabited by supramental human beings. The Supramental World was made to descend in the earth subtle physical on 29th February 1956 by The Mother during the evening group meditation and the Mother Nature is awaiting the coming of the supramental living being in supramental body. Sri Aurobindo could invite supramental consciousness in his body on December 5th 1950, but the cells of the body could not safely hold it for more than five days and his physical body's cells dispersed and the body had to be laid into the Samadhi in the courtyard of the Ashram Main Building. Sri Aurobindo, like Sri Krishna, is still there in the earth's consciousness-atmosphere in his subtle physical consciousness supporting and leading the individual and universal mental consciousness to realise the supramental transformation in the body. The Mother had continued to supramentalise her body after Sri Aurobindo left body. She had talked to Satprem about her experiences received from her yoga of the body and Satprem had tape-recorded them, which were published in English by him under the title "Agenda'. Also, Sri Aurobindo Ashram's Management documented them in the volume eleven of *"The Collected Works of The Mother"* with the publisher's note,

> "We begin under this title to publish some fragments of conversations with The Mother. These reflections or experiences, these observations, which are very recent, are like landmarks on the way of Transformation: they were chosen not only because they illumine the work under way — a yoga of the body of which all the processes have to be established — but because they can be a sort of indication of the endeavour that has to be made."[124]

She left the scene of the material earth as her body could not stabilize permanently the supramental force in itself. Like previous Avatars, as is noted above, She still exists in her subtle body and is

---

[124] CWM Vol. 11; The Publisher's Note

supporting the upward evolution towards the supramental. Her helping presence has been experienced by many seekers and are documented in books and oral popular talk (लोकवाणी). The section of humanity trying to evolve further must continue the effort seeking help and guidance from them till the supramental is realised in the human physical consciousness for good.

There are worlds other than this physical world and in them there are angelic beings and man's forefathers, who help man; there are also devilish beings, who trouble mankind. This is known in India since pre-historic Vedic times. In recent times, in the West, materialistic scientists, physical doctors, have studied them using scientific research methods and found them to exist.

Box 5.1

A Scientist's Case for the Afterlife

Thousands of people have had near-death experiences, but scientists have argued that they are impossible. Dr. Eben Alexander was one of those scientists. A highly trained neurosurgeon, Alexander knew that NDEs feel real, but are simply fantasies produced by brains under extreme stress.

Then, Dr. Alexander's own brain was attacked by a rare illness. The part of the brain that controls thought and emotion — and in essence makes us human — shut down completely. For seven days he lay in a coma. Then, as his doctors considered stopping treatment, Alexander's eyes popped open. He had come back.

Alexander's recovery is a medical miracle. But the real miracle of his story lies elsewhere. While his body lay in coma, Alexander journeyed beyond this world and encountered an angelic being who guided him into the deepest realms of super-physical existence. There he met, and spoke with, the Divine source of the universe itself.

Alexander's story is not a fantasy. Before he underwent his journey, he could not reconcile his knowledge of neuroscience with any belief in heaven, God, or the soul. Today Alexander is a doctor who believes that true health can be achieved only when we realize that God and the soul are real and that death is not the end of personal existence but only a transition.

This story would be remarkable no matter who it happened to. That it happened to Dr. Alexander makes it revolutionary. No scientist or person of faith will be able to ignore it. Reading it will change your life.

From: Eben Alexander M. D.; Proof of Heaven (Publisher: Simon & Schuster Paperbacks, A Division of Simon and Schuster, Inc., 1230 Avenue of the Americas, New York, NY, 10020, U. S. A., 2012); 3rd Cover Page.

America's Neuro-Surgeon Dr. Eben Alexander, M. D. during his body's state of coma, happened to travel to one of the other subtle worlds, the heaven (स्वर्ग), where he met his forefathers (पितृन) and angelic being (देवता) who led him to "the Divine source of the universe itself", (आदि-शक्ति जगद्जननी अम्बा); the agnostic neurosurgeon then knew, "that true health can be achieved only when we realize that God and the soul are real and that death is not the end of personal existence but only a transition."[125] *Please refer Box 5.1 to read the full text in* which this sentence occurs. *आयुर्वेद, the Ayurveda, India's most ancient system of medicine knew this fact from the pre-historic vedic times; Allopathic science of medicine, after a millennium, now finds the Divine as a source of health; आयुर्वेद, the Ayurveda, has been proved to be the main medical system; of course it needs to assimilate by synthesising allopathic knowledge and practice within itself and also it needs to assimilate the knowledge of integral psychology (yoga) within itself and*

---

[125] Eben Alexander M. D.; Proof of Heaven (Publisher: Simon & Schuster Paperbacks, A Division of Simon and Schuster, Inc., 1230 Avenue of the Americas, New York, NY, 10020, U.S.A., 2012); 3rd Cover Page

renovate and enlarge itself. Allopathy should be now classified as an alternative medicine.

Dr. Raymond Moody has also studied his patients' experiences of other world in his book *"Life after Life"*. *Please Refer Box 5.2* for the introduction of his book. In the West, such experiences are called *"Near Death Experiences"*. Research literature of Transpersonal Psychology and Humanistic Psychology also contain studies of this kind. Super-physical phenomena has been studied recently by Indian psychologists also. In India, Sri Mukherjee, a psychologist, had studied the cases of persons who had "Memories of Previous Birth." They were reported in

---

Box 5.2

Life after Death

In *Life After Life*, Raymond Moody investigates more than one hundred case studies of people who experienced "clinical death" and were subsequently revived. First published in 1975, this classic exploration of life after death started a revolution in popular attitudes about the afterlife and established Dr. Moody as the world's leading authority in the field of near-death experiences. *Life after Life* forever changed the way we understand both death – *and life* – selling millions of copies to a world hungry for a greater understanding of this mysterious phenomenon.

The extraordinary stories presented here provide evidence that there is life after physical death, as Moody recounts the testimonies of those who have been to the "other side" and back – all bearing striking similarities of an overwhelming positive nature. These moving and inspiring accounts give us a glimpse of the peace and unconditional love that await us all.

Author: Raymond A. Moody: Publisher: Mockingbird Books (June 1981)

Gujarati newspaper also. Scientific psychology calls it Para-Psychology and does not accept it as one of the currents of its main stream. The field of integral psychology includes the field of parapsychology as an integral part of itself; that is why integral psychology is integral in nature. *(Please refer Section III-1 of Chapter II)*.

*In fact, **the aim of this book on Integral Psychology is to** convey some information on Sri Auromere's Practical Psychology to individuals and society, especially to management students of the Auro University, India which aims at transformative studies, education and life. They may include the transformative aspect of growth in their ongoing daily life. If it is done, the journey towards the Supramentalisation of the earth life and the universal consciousness will get decisively accelerated.*

II. THE PLANES OF CONSCIOUSNESS OF HUMAN BEING: THE STRUCTURE OF HUMAN PERSONALITY

1. THE INCONSCIENT AND THE SUBCONSCIENT

All upon earth is based on the inconscient, for the universe and earth have evolved from the inconscient. The inconscient had developed from the super-conscient due to the process of the devolution *(See section III chapter III)*. When the inconscient struggled into a half consciousness due to the process of evolution, the sub-conscient was formed first. (Please *refer figure 5.1)*. The inconscient is only universal and not individual.

But the sub-conscient[126] is universal as well as individual. Universal forces enter in an individual through his subconscient. The

---

[126] SABCL Vol. 22, pp. 353-64, 377; SABCL Vol. 23, p. 1088; SABCL Vol.24; pp. 1593-1612; SABCL Vol. 18, pp. 422-23

subconscient being of man is automatic, obscure, incoherent and a half conscious realm. It receives and stores up everything that is rejected by the waking consciousness and suppressed into it. It also receives and stores as obscure impressions everything that is consciously experienced. It is the main support of death and disease. Sri Aurobindo writes,

> "In the subconscient there is an obscure mind full of obstinate Sanskaras, impressions, associations, fixed notions, habitual reactions formed by our past, an obscure vital full of the seeds of habitual desires, sensations and nervous reactions, a most obscure material which governs much that has to do with the condition of the body. It is largely responsible for our illness; chronic or repeated illness are indeed mainly due to the subconscient and its obstinate memory and habit of repetition of whatever has impressed itself upon the body-consciousness."[127]

> Elsewhere, Sri Aurobindo has written, "Our ethical impulses and activities begin like all the rest in the infrarational and take their rise from the subconscient."[128]

Scientific Mentology studies it especially for counseling and therapy. This partial psychology knows that the subconscient sends out anything out of its stuff into the conscient in a disguised manner. But, it does not know that it has four parts: the subconscient physical, the subconscient vital and the subconscient mental and submental supramental.

It can be changed if it is opened to higher forces and the supramental light.

---

[127] SABCL Vol. 22; p. 353
[128] SABCL Vol. 15; p. 142

2. THE SUPER-CONSCIENT AND THE CONSCIENT

Above the individual subconscious being, there are the subliminal, the psychic, the conscient and the environmental consciousness of the individual. Outer triple personality, the physical-vital-mental complex of man, is in the front of his being and is the conscient. Behind it is the inner triple being, the inner physical-vital-mental personality. It is also called the subliminal. Behind it is the psychic being. Around the inner and outer beings is the environmental consciousness, and above them is the superconscient, which is universal and transcendental eternal original consciousness. This structure of human consciousness is pictured in *Figure 5.1.*

The conscient is the instrument of expression of the inner consciousness and the psychic. It receives influences from and is moulded by the inconscient and the subconscient from below, the subliminal from behind and the superconscient from above. Its each plane — "... mental, vital, physical — has its own consciousness separate though interconnected and interacting"[129] ... and interpenetrating; so each is subject to others in its working and each has formulation of others in itself. So there are physical mind, vital mind, mind proper, vital physical, etc. and yet each of them can act independently of others also. For the sake of brevity all the subparts will not be described in this chapter. Moreover, because the individual mostly lives in his outer triple consciousness, the general nature of the physical, the vital and the mental will be described in a little detail and the inner, the psychic, the spiritual and the supramental parts will be just sketched in a few words only. The survey of Auromere's psychology presented in this chapter and previous chapters makes us to identify Sri Aurobindo and The Mother's new findings in the following words.

---

[129] SABCL Vol. 22; pp. 347 & 177

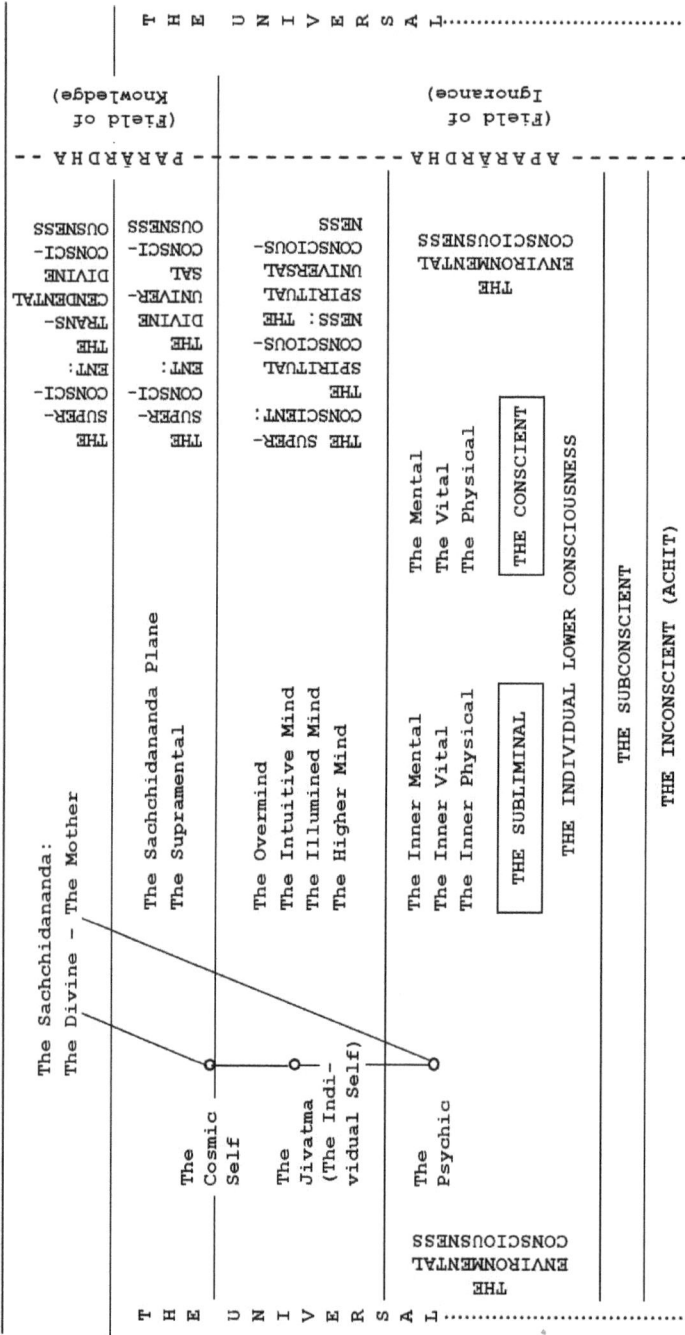

THE UNIVERSAL

(Field of Knowledge)   (Field of Ignorance)

— — PARARDHA — — — — — — — — — APARARDHA — — — — — —

THE SUPER-CONSCI-ENT: THE TRANS-CENDENTAL DIVINE UNIVER-SAL CONSCI-OUSNESS

THE SUPER-CONSCI-ENT: THE DIVINE UNIVER-SAL CONSCI-OUSNESS

THE SUPER-CONSCIENT: THE SPIRITUAL CONSCIOUS-NESS: THE SPIRITUAL UNIVERSAL CONSCIOUS-NESS

THE ENVIRONMENTAL CONSCIOUSNESS

The Sachchidananda:
The Divine – The Mother

The Sachchidananda Plane
The Supramental

The Overmind
The Intuitive Mind
The Illumined Mind
The Higher Mind

The Mental
The Vital
The Physical   THE CONSCIENT

The Inner Mental
The Inner Vital
The Inner Physical   THE SUBLIMINAL

THE INDIVIDUAL LOWER CONSCIOUSNESS

THE SUBCONSCIENT

THE INCONSCIENT (ACHIT)

The Cosmic Self

The Jivatma (The Indi-vidual Self)

The Psychic

THE ENVIRONMENTAL CONSCIOUSNESS

THE UNIVERSAL

Figure 5.1

The Simplified Schematic Diagram of the
Planes of Consciousness of Human Being

188

III. SRI AUROBINDO AND THE MOTHER'S CONTRIBUTION TO PSYCHOLOGY

They have provided far better, far wider, far deeper, far higher and far truer knowledge than any and all current and past disciplines of psychology and spirituality. Their knowledge is unprecedented knowledge. They have given exhaustive knowledge of the inconscient, the subconscient, the conscient (mental-vital-physical consciousness), the subliminal, the psychic, environmental consciousness of the individual that is around his personal conscient being, universal consciousness of the universe that is around and, the superconscient (spiritual, supramental and transcendental Sachchidananda consciousness). They are the first psychologists, who have explained the real cause of evolution and the destiny of man. Not only have they explained, but have also found out the method, the practical integral psychology which they called Integral Yoga that ensures the realisation of that destiny. That destiny is the liberation of soul and nature both from the rule of ignorance by changing and transforming the ignorant human nature into supramental nature and thus to make the earth atmosphere ready for the descent of the next species, the supramental being. These are their main contributions to the rational psychology and yogic metaphysical psychology.[130]

The following chapters will describe the nature of each of the parts of human individual in brief in ascending order from physical onward to supramental.

---

[130] SABCL Vol. 22; p. 364

SUMMARY

Inconscient was created from the super-conscient due to the process of devolution. Subconscious material things were created from the Inconscient due to the process of evolution. The inconscient is universal only, but the subconsciousness is universal as well as individual. Our habitual and repetitive movements and illness are due to the subconscient. From the **material consciousness** came up **the Life (Vital) consciousness** and vegetable and animal evolved. Next evolute is **the mental consciousness** and mental human being. Then the next evolute is **the spiritual consciousness** the spiritual human being. After that the next evolute is **the supramental consciousness**. Man is the third ascending step on evolutionary ladder.

Above the individual subconscious being, there are the subliminal, the psychic, the conscient and the environmental consciousness of the individual. Outer triple personality, the physical-vital-mental complex of man, is in the front of his being and is the conscient. Behind it is the inner triple being, the inner physical-vital-mental personality. It is also called the subliminal. Behind it is the psychic being. Around the inner and outer beings is the environmental consciousness, and above them is the superconscient. This structure of human consciousness is pictured in Figure 5.1 in this chapter.

Suggestions for Further Reading

1. Van Vrekhem (Editor); *The Mother's Vision* (Publisher: Sri Aurobindo Ashram, Pondicherry, 605002, India; 2005); Chapter 5: The Gradations of Existence and Their Expression in the Human Being; pp. 117-135 and Chapter 6: The Psychic Being or Soul; pp. 165-190

WORKBOOK: QUESTIONS FOR PREVIEW AND REVIEW

Essay Type Questions

1. Man is the third step of the evolution. Describe.

Short Answer Type Questions

1. What made the Inconsciousness to struggle for becoming conscious?
2. Name evolutionary steps of consciousness in the ascending order.
3. Has the plane of the supramental consciousness manifested on earth? Who made it to manifest?
4. Where does the Avatar reside permanently after leaving his body?
5. Whose Near Death Experience proves that there are other worlds than this visible earth?
6. Who has studied the phenomena of the life after the death?
7. List in ascending order the levels of consciousness of a human being.
8. What is the contribution of Sri Aurobindo and the mother to the science of psychology?
9. Behind the Conscient is the _____. And behind it is _____.
10. The super-conscient is _____ and _____; the inconscient is _____; but the subconscient is _____ and _____. (transcendental, universal and individual)
11. Our illness is mainly due to the support of the _____. (inconscient or conscient)

Exercise

1. Make a two column table of evolution in which the first column shows the steps of evolution and the second shows the Avatar/s causing the evolution of the particular stage. For example,

Column 1	*Column 2*
Stage of Evolution	The Avatar/s that cause the evolution

SELF TEST

1. Man appeared at the third stage of evolution. Illustrate and Explain.
2. _____ is between matter and the inconscient.
3. Death does not exist. Prove.
4. There is no life after death. (True or False)
5. In the sub-conscient there is no mind. (True or false)
6. _____ is only universal, but the _____ is universal as well as individual.
7. There is super-consciousness in man already. (True or False)
8. _____ is the highest plane of consciousness.
9. State Sri Aurobindo and The Mother's contribution to psychology.

CHAPTER VI

THE PHYSICAL CONSCIOUSNESS
OF AN INDIVIDUAL

I.   THE PHYSICAL CONSCIOUSNESS AND ITS RELATION
     WITH THE UNIVERSAL PHYSICAL CONSCIOUSNESS
     AND PSYCHIC BEING

II. THE PLANES AND PARTS OF THE PHYSICAL
     CONSCIOUSNESS

III. NEGATIVE AND POSITIVE QUALITIES OF THE
     PHYSICAL CONSCIOUSNESS

IV. A FEW OTHER CHARACTERISTICS

V.   PERFECTION OF THE PHYSICAL

> *Table:*
> *(6.1) The Five Parts of The Physical Consciousness Plane*
>
> *Picture:*
> *(6.1) The Mother teaching a class*

I. THE PHYSICAL CONSCIOUSNESS AND ITS RELATION WITH THE UNIVERSAL PHYSICAL CONSCIOUSNESS AND THE PSYCHIC BEING

There is the universal consciousness of Nature and our own individual physical consciousness is part of it, moved by it and used by our central being for the support of its expression in the physical world and for a direct dealing with all these external objects, movements and forces, says Sri Aurobindo.[131] It means our personal physical consciousness is intimately connected with the universal consciousness; it is used by our central being, the psychic being, for its dealings with other persons (such as child, wife, sister, enemy, etc.) and objects (such as flowers, trees, earthquake, etc.), external movements (such as wind, flying bird, singing bird, etc.) and forces (such as severe heat wave or cold wave, movements of a horse we are riding, movement of a dance-partner etc.). **Our physical is thus an instrument of our psychic being.**

As physical consciousness is **the basic important aspect of the individual's consciousness.** Other higher and subtler parts of consciousness, such as vital, mental, psychic and spiritual, would be inoperative in the physical world, if it is not there to support them. In absence of body, would one be able to talk to, play with or dine with other persons, make love with other person, express his mental thought? Without body, a man becomes absent in this world for others.

But it is not generally known that physical consciousness consists not only of physical body, but as we will see in this chapter it consists of many other physical parts also. The physical consciousness, like every other planes and parts of the individual, **has several sub-planes and parts and has dual qualities; positive and negative.**

---

[131] SABCL Vol. 22; p. 347

II. PLANES AND PARTS OF THE PHYSICAL CONSCIOUSNESS

The physical consciousness plane receives from the other planes their powers and influences and makes formations of them in its own province. Therefore there are (i) the mental physical, (ii) the vital physical, (iii) the psychic physical, (iv) the spiritual physical and (v) the supramental physical parts in it. The psychic physical, the spiritual physical and the supramental physical are developed still only minutely in the persons doing yoga of physical transformation; these parts are absent in ordinary people.

Body (or the subconscient material or the material physical or the subconscient physical or the mechanical physical) is its nethermost part; it is below its proper consciousness level and is the most tamasic part. Above the body are in the ascending order the physical vital, the mental physical and the psychic physical in its own province. The mental physical and the vital physical and the psychic physical are less tamasic and more conscious, more enlightened and more dynamic than the body, the tamasic part. The spiritual physical and the supramental physical are parts above the physical consciousness plane proper and are not still developed, but some sadhaks of yoga have them developed to an extent in their physical consciousness. *See Table 6.1.*

Table 6.1

The Six Parts of The Physical Consciousness Plane

(i)   The Supramental Physical
(ii) The Spiritual Physical
(iii) The Psychic Physical
(iv) The Mental Physical
(v)   The Vital Physical
(vi) The Subconscient Body

1. THE BODY OR THE GROSS PHYSICAL OR THE MATERIAL PHYSICAL[132]

(i) It is the most material and visible part of the physical being and has its own consciousness:

(a) Its own consciousness is obscure: If not attended by the mind consciously, it may not perceive properly and so it may not be able to maintain balance on a rugged road or on a staircase or escalator and fall down; even if then it is injured it may not feel the injury at that moment.

(b) Its limbs, cells, tissues, glands and organs have their own consciousness and personality proper to them: So each of its parts can act, feel and perceive almost independently in a sort of separation from the whole body and personality. For example, right shoulder of the author one day got stiff and would not move when he was doing his daily exercise; he tried to swing around the right hand, but would feel a lot of pain; so he concentrated and applied his mental will on the shoulder, told it to respond to the mind's order, receive the Mother's spiritual peace from above and make an effort to move; it worked: the consciousness of the right shoulder responded on its own and moved feeling less pain and distress. After a few repetitions, it started moving as it used to move normally before. Author has acted upon all of his body parts and achieved positive results: For example, his enlarged prostrate was told to reduce itself and it did so.

(c) As we have seen already, it is the flower of the material inconscient and the subconscient and so all in it is still half conscious. So, it is more influenced by the subconscient than by the mind or the vital, and it is routine-bound, rigid, inert, sluggish, and slow in progress and **subject to illness and the principle of decay and death**.

---

[132] SABCL Vol. 16, pp. 7 and 9-15; SABCL Vol. 22, pp. 328, 348 and 352; CWM Vol. 4, p. 367; CWM Vol. 5, pp. 295-96; CWM Vol. 10, pp. 30-31 and Tulsidas Chatterjee, *Sri Aurobindo's Yoga* (Pondicherry: Sri Aurobindo Books Distribution Agency, Sri Aurobindo Ashram, 1970), p. 74

(ii) It cannot progress as speedily as the vital and the mind and the soul progress. When one crosses adulthood, the body's metabolism decreases and so instead of progressing more, it stops progressing and starts regressing, which is called the aging process in the medical science. Now, when the soul sees that it is not useful, it leaves it. It was the soul that was the binding force agglomerating its elements and as soon as the soul departs, the elements of the body naturally start disintegrating and ultimately they change and merge into basic five elements: *jal (water), tej (light), vayu (air), akash (space) and prithvi (Matter)*. This temporary **disintegration of the body** is called death. But soul assumes another re-integrated body in the next birth. If it can develop psychic plasticity, it may progress at the rhythm of the soul and then soul will not leave it; there will be no death.[133] Thus the form of the body is permanent though it changes with time. There is no death of the form called body. So, logically death does not exist. This principle of the integral psychology makes mind understand the illusion of death and liberates it from pain-creating death-phobia.

(iii) It has got a very sure instinct, called physical instinct, and if one does not allow the mind, the vital and other universal forces to interfere in its natural instinctual action, it will act rightly. For example, never will it eat when it doesn't need to or eat something which will be harmful to it, says The Mother.[134] Perhaps here is the explanation of the phenomena found in the well-known cafeteria experiment.

(iv) It is inherently automatic in its functioning: Digestive, respiratory, glandular and other many functions of the body require no "mind-monitor". They all act even during sleep.

---

[133] SABCL Vol. 24; p. 1219
[134] CWM Vol. 5; pp. 295-296

(v) Its capacities of learning are almost amazing:

> (a) If it is blind, it can be taught how to move in public with the help of stick or trained dog.
>
> (b) It can learn to make different dance movements, assume different postures, etc., which are not natural to it if given proper training.

(vi) This gross physical body is actually encased in the subtle physical body (अन्नमय कोश - *annamaya kosha*): There is also a subtle physical body which contains the gross physical one. It surrounds the gross body and extends to some distance depending on the capacity of a person. Sometimes, we feel another person's presence behind us, when the other person comes near to us secretively, because this subtle physical body has touched it. The Mother could feel Sri Aurobindo's subtle physical from a distance of ten nautical miles[135], when she was coming from France to Pondicherry first time. *It is described in the section of the inner consciousness of which it is one of the parts.*

(vii) The physical consciousness and nature are shut up in their habits, they don't want to change them: Referring to this characteristic of the physical, The Mother told in 1951,

> "They accept only one regular routine. There is nothing more routine-bound than the body. If you change its habits in the least, it is quite bewildered, ... it doesn't know any longer what to do. Those whose vital being is very active and dominating may succeed in awakening the body, ... The physical obeys, it obeys the impulse, the inner order; then it consents to the change, the novelty, but it is an effort for it. But for the physical being and physical consciousness to be ready to receive the divine impulsion, they must be **extremely plastic**, because the vital uses coercion, it imposes its will, and the poor

---

[135] CWM Vol. 13; p. 73

body has but to obey, while the Divine just shows the light, gives the consciousness, and so one must obey consciously and willingly — it is a question of collaboration, it is no longer a question of coercion. The physical being and physical consciousness must be very plastic to be able to lend themselves to all the necessary changes, so as to be of one kind one day and another the next, and so on."[136]

Picture 6.1 The Mother teaching a Class

---

[136] CWM Vol. 4; pp. 367-368

For that plasticity one must open one's body to the psychic influence, so that it can partake some of the plasticity of the psychic and be more plastic, more refined, more luminous, more smooth and less gross. *(See below sub-section 4: The Psychic Physical)*

(viii) As we have noted above in (i) (b), it has many parts and they are generally at war with each other. This is called the internecine war in the physical: for example,

(a) The neurological part (the vital physical) and a material physical organ may be at war with each other. The penis may not get erect, even if the nervous system tells it to do so. And that causes problem of temporary impotency, sterilizes an erection, which may result in "war" between husband and wife and divorce.

(b) Sensational vital physical (the sexual organs) desire to have sex and sensational pleasure and would not like and may not submit to the restraint of the mental physical (brain) and would quarrel with it and disobey it and force on a person to perform sex. Sometimes, a man's penis will get aroused and be erect and eject the seminal fluid, even if his mind is against the act.

(c) So, it is very difficult to achieve a harmonious individualized physical being and consciousness. Even the most healthy and strong persons have some parts weaker than others and his parts may be pulling at each other. Of course one can control them and put them in harmony, but that would require a prolonged sincere effort to make them learn to surrender to the psychic and spiritual consciousness.

2. THE VITAL PHYSICAL BODY

The Neurological System, lower brain and Glandular System is called the vital physical part of the gross body: This part only makes the body alive and is responsible for body's impulsive actions.

3. THE MENTAL PHYSICAL OR BODY-MIND

The Cortex, the brain proper, is called the mental physical and governs the conscious movements of the material body: For example, when one's brain is affected as it happened to Dr. Eben the body is paralysed. *(See Chapter II – Section III – 1 – (i) Field of Integral Psychology is Consciousness and all Grades of Consciousness).* Our conscious perception of objects and routine thinking and actions are governed by this body-mind.

According to Sri Aurobindo[137], it is fixed on physical objects and happenings only, sees and understands these only and deals with them according to their own nature. Physical mind would see mob riot as a group's irrational violence and would try to curb it with suppressive strong police or military action. It will not see and understand that riot is caused by group mind influenced by forces of strife in the Universal Nature. It can with difficulty respond to higher forces; it will find it very difficult to receive higher spiritual force of peace and love and hold it. It is skeptical of supraphysical things. It would always doubt that world war is caused by the descent of the universal vital forces on earth.

It has two parts: (i) the true physical mind and (ii) the mechanical physical mind. Making clear the different functions of these two minds, Sri Aurobindo writes,

> "There is a mechanical mental physical or body-mind, which when left to itself simply goes on repeating the past customary thoughts and movements or at most adds to them such further mechanical reactions to things and reflexes as are in the round of life. **The true physical mind** is the receiving and externalising intelligence which has two functions – first, to work upon external things and give them a mental order with a way of practically dealing with them and, secondly, to be the channel of materializing and putting into effect whatever the

---

[137] SABCL Vol. 22; pp.347-348

thinking and dynamic mind sends down to it for the purpose. The mechanical mind is a sort of engine – whatever comes to it it puts into the machine and goes on turning it round and round no matter what it is."[138]

For example, many a times certain particular thought about a person or an animal or an object or a phenomena keeps on recurring round and round without stopping. This is the work of the mechanical physical mind when it is left to itself and is not under conscious control of the mind proper. The true physical mind receives ideas from the higher mind and expresses them as speech or written text. When an author, a researcher, a scientists or a poet writes something, it is the work of his true physical mind.

4. THE PSYCHIC PHYSICAL

Sri Aurobindo says,

> "There is a part of ... the body which is or can be influenced by the psychic, ... can be called the psychic-physical. According to the personality or the degree of evolution of each person, this can be small or large, weak or strong, covered up and inactive or prominent and in action. When it acts the movements of the physical accept the psychic motives or aims, partake of the nature of the psychic or follow its aims but with a modification in the manner which belongs to the physical."[139]

5-6. THE SPIRITUAL PHYSICAL AND THE SUPRAMENTAL PHYSICAL *are described later on in this chapter.*

---

[138] SABCL Vol. 22; pp. 328-329
[139] SABCL Vol. 24; pp. 1111-1112

III. POSITIVE AND NEGATIVE QUALITIES AND FORCES OF THE PHYSICAL

1. Negative Qualities:

According to Sri Aurobindo and the Mother[140] there are many negative characteristics of the physical body and consciousness. Some of them are noted in brief below:

(i) A certain inertia is the most common characteristic of the physical body and consciousness: This is the reason why it does not like to learn new tasks and exercises. It will not show readiness to learn new exercises even for regaining health. That is the reason most people prefer medicine to the physiotherapies. And that is why it is not always ready to perform physical exercises regularly daily, but generally desires to skip them often. It will not prefer to sit and work for long hours for work. That is why parents and teachers have a hard time to persuade children to sit for long duration to complete their lessons. Yes, but with assiduous practice this inertia can be minimized. Amma of Kerala and The Mother are two exemplary illustration of persons, who had removed this quality of inertia from their body:

Amma, the mother Amritanadmayee, of Kerala has removed inertia of her body to such an extent that she has been reported to perform her ritual of graceful consciousness exchanging hugging to a large number of international devotes for a full day and thus has given them divine blessings.

The Mother (Sri Aurobindo Ashram) had done away with inertia-force of the body. She never needed the gross physical sleep that the human body needs. Her body needed only two hours of spiritual relaxation in her couch and during those two hours her consciousness

---

[140] SABCL Vol. 22, pp. 347-353; SABCL Vol. 24, pp. 1111, 1429-30, 1445 and 1461; SABCL Vol. 16, pp. 717-19; CWM Vol. 3, pp. 130 and 361; CWM Vol. 4, pp. 50-51; Rishabhchand, *The Integral Yoga of Sri Aurobindo,* (Pondicherry: Sri Aurobindo Memorial Fund Society, 1974), p. 262

was busy visiting her devotee children in the Ashram and out of the Ashram. That proves that she was able to get her body to work continuously. We know marathon runners run hours together and soldier's continue fighting and moving sometimes for more than twenty four hours without sleep. This is possible for them for their training has infused in their body a strong consciousness force and diminished the inertia.

(ii) From inertia follows bodies tendency to sleep: Even while watching cinema, it may feel drowsy and actually sleep. In daily classes some students are prone to sleep. We know, when a person has to go on a long drive, he gets some friend to accompany him so that they may continue to converse and he may avoid sleep and accident.

(iii) Indolence or laziness is the quality of the physical consciousness that prompts persons to be slow in work and leave work half done and not to complete it in a reasonable period.

(iv) Body is unwilling or unable to increase the strength so as to endure long sessions of spiritual effort, such as sessions of concentration, meditation, physical exercises, reading and reflecting, etc.: Almost all sadhaks of yoga experience this difficulty while doing tapasya. Only constant practice of concentration etc. can increase the strength of the physical consciousness and body. Generally every yogi experiences at a certain stage of advancement that his body, mind and vital should develop more strength, endurance, suppleness, peace, concentration, etc., if he is to receive and hold higher consciousness.

(v) The physical consciousness and body has natural resistance to higher consciousness and change demanded by it: When higher knowledge tries to descend in the mind and brain during sadhana or ordinary life, they refuse to admit it and make efforts to learn to express it. When an old person at the age of 80, found his legs have become weak and maybe crippled soon, he embarked upon a regular programme of walking and exercise that would infuse higher energy in legs; the legs resisted lot, but he pursued and then to the surprise of all friends and doctors, his legs re-learnt normal way of walking.

(vi) Hankering after material comforts and wellbeing by the modern man is actually due to these natural qualities of the physical consciousness and body.

(vii) Hankering after physical desires, greeds, lust is also the feverish activity of the modern man, for body demands all these things: Rampant desire for excessive sex, food, greed for money and lust for enjoying sex are common maladies of modern life. For, people do not make efforts to educate their body otherwise, and

(viii) Preference for everything made easy is also a negative quality of the physical consciousness and body: That is why students avoid reading standard but difficult **texts and prefer** easy sub-standard reading material and thus continue to remain ignorant. That is why average people cannot work or keep awake or meditate or read high level spiritual writings for long hours. Physical Consciousness demands that life must be made easy and so man have created many "easing" machines. Now, medical research has found that small and large machines have started "easing out" the body's strength and capacity for work and have decreased its immunity to disease and death. These incapacities of physical consciousness are inherited from the parent Inconscient and so they are constitutional, but the inheritance can be changed and transformed if scientific and yogic spiritual knowledge and practices are applied. Some examples noted in the following paragraph illustrate this fact.

Against all such negative qualities of the physical consciousness, the Nature has given to body certain positive qualities also:

2. Positive Qualities:

(i) The physical consciousness and body is a docile servant of the vital and the mind and the psychic: If the mind, vital and the psychic insist ultimately body puts away its resistance and does as an obedient servant what they demand of it. There are instances of weak bodies becoming great athletes.

(ii) To serve them faithfully even at its own cost is the other self-denying quality of the physical: Some students desire to study for long hours during night and their body co-operates at its own risk, is a well-known fact. The body is such a faithful servant of the mind and the vital that they generally encourage the body to overwork for satisfying their desires, preferences and egos. To win the boxing competition, boxers over-exercise, consume chemicals and ultimately injure the body. To stand first and defeat the rival classmate, a student may burn midnight oil and invite ill health or take anti-sleep medicine and ruin the mental and physical well-being.

(iii) If trained properly, the body becomes an instrument of expression in the outer world and expresses vital force and psychic grace ultimately.

IV. A FEW OTHER CHARACTERISTICS OF PHYSICAL CONSCIOUSNESS

1. IT IS THE MOST OUTWARD GOING CONSCIOUSNESS

Vedic Rishis knew, *Paranchi Khani, which means man's eyes see always outward at surface consciousness of things.* Physical mind judges a person perceiving only his/her outer appearance. For example, a person, named, John, an American, is on his daily morning walk in the nearby park. He meets an unknown person who greets him and starts talking. The person does not have good clothes on his body, does not speak sophisticated language, is a little rustic in behaviour and is black. John judges that he is a bad black American personality and decides that he should not linger to talk to him for long. He cut shorts the talk saying "Nice talking to you, but I am in a little hurry to get back to my home, so please excuse me, we shall continue our talk when we meet again. Thanks for talking to me" and leaves him. The other person was a very good, civil and intelligent personality, which he could not perceive. He notices only surface appearance; he could not perceive his subtle good qualities of candidness, humility and innocence and brilliance of mind behind. For John has only the outward perceiving physical mind that perceives the surface of things and misses to observe what is under the surface; he had not developed the subtle sympathetic mind, that could have observed the subtle graceful gentle behaviours of humility and innocence the other person was displaying. So, he misses to note the poor fellow's bright side of personality. Moreover, because his physical mind is outward going consciousness, his sense of physical eye is also outward going, he could not look inside himself and notice the prejudice he had developed against the black people. He did not perceive his own dark side he had created in his own being. He willingly missed the opportunity to interact with an intelligent person and unknowingly missed the opportunity to increase his knowledge. Physical consciousness cannot appreciate inner beauty of nature, literature and arts. It impoverishes personality.

2. IT IS THE NORMAL CONSCIOUSNESS OF MOST OF THE HUMAN BEINGS

The majority of people are under the active guidance of their physical mind only. That is the reason society at large is still unseemly, ignoble, utilitarian, ugly, rough and non-idealistic.

3. THE PHYSICAL IS GENERALLY AT WAR WITH THE MENTAL AND THE VITAL
(War between Members)

One day friend Ramesh came to see me. He asked me, which author should I read to improve my English. I suggested, "For that purpose, Sri Aurobindo is the best author." And in addition I said, "To read Sri Aurobindo is a Yogic Exercise that uplifts and widens the intellect, strengthens the cells of the brain, increases the power of concentration, and purifies the nature. So, because you have an interest in philosophy, pick up from my library and start reading "The Life Divine". He sat in the armchair and started the exercise of reading. I left for bath room to take shower. When I returned after fifteen minutes, I found him in deep sleep. So, I picked up *The Life Divine* from his lap to read it myself. After about fifteen minutes he wakes up and tells me, "My mind found the thought in the book very interesting, though it was a lot difficult for it to comprehend it. But, my head and brain in it felt crushing pressure and so asserted their desire for ease and confronted the mind's desire for knowledge. But mind's will to read would not submit to the will of the brain and mind tried to continue reading. But, my eye lashes started drooping and I fell into sleep." "Yes", I said, "Will of the mind was defeated by the will of the material brain, the physical mind. Same thing has happened with so many readers at the time of their first reading of Sri Aurobindo's book. What you can do is that you read a few paragraphs only at a time and as the inertia of the brain goes on diminishing, you go on increasing the number of paragraphs to read. Thus you can end the struggle between the brain and the mind and harmonise them." It is a well-known observation of child psychology that an infant is hungry so tries to suckle the milk from the mother's breast but his body falls asleep and so cannot suckle the milk and then goes on weeping and weeping. Here body is opposing baby's vital desire (war between members) and also its own need of nourishment (internecine war).

V. PERFECTION OF THE PHYSICAL

1. THE MUNDANE PERFECTION OF THE PHYSICAL

(i) It can be taught to be automatic in many skills (riding cycle, skating, etc.)

(ii) It can be educated to remain perfectly healthy.

(iii) Qualities of strength, fitness, endurance, dexterity, stability in action can be developed in the body.

(iv) Also skill for different tasks can be taught to it.

(v) It can be made unusually plastic.

(vi) It can learn to be responsive to mental control even in its instinctive automatic action.

These are the qualities of **perfection** that are available to the body in its present nature and in the present limitation of evolution.

These qualities can be developed beyond ordinary imagination by proper physical culture, management of food, sleep, yogasans, meditation, and yoga, which infuse more consciousness into the cells of the body also. We have now a lot of knowledge regarding these matters.

2. THE INNER PERFECTION OF THE PHYSICAL

The inner or subliminal perfection is described *in Ch. IX* and the psychic, the spiritual and the supramental perfection *in Ch. XVI.*

3. THE PSYCHIC PERFECTION OF THE PHYSICAL *(See Ch. XVI)*

4. THE SPIRITUAL PERFECTION OF THE PHYSICAL *(See Ch. XVI)*

5. THE SUPRAMENTAL PERFECTION OF THE PHYSICAL *(See Ch. XVI)*

SUMMARY

1. Our physical consciousness is individual but as a part of the universal consciousness. It is an instrument of our psychic being, which uses it as a support for action in the outside world. It is the most basic and the most important part of human consciousness.

2. The physical consciousness has five sub-parts: (i) The Supramental Physical, (ii) The Spiritual Physical, (iii) The Mental Physical, (iv) The Vital Physical and (v) The Subconscient Body.

3. The material body has three parts: (i) The Gross Body, (ii) the Vital Body and (iii) the Mental Body. It has negative qualities that can be minimized or got rid of. It has positive qualities also that can be augmented. It is the most outward going consciousness. Its different parts are always at dispute with each other and as a whole it is always at cross purposes with the mind and the vital. By proper discipline body can be made perfect on its own level and on Psychic, spiritual and supramental level also.

Suggestions for Further Reading

1. Indra Sen, Integral Psychology (Sri Aurobindo International Centre of Education, Pondicherry, 605 002, India; 1986); pp. 9-29

2. Tulsidas Chatterjee, *Sri Aurobindo's Integral Yoga* (Pondicherry: SABDA, Sri Aurobindo Ashram; 1970), pp. 57-83

3. The Mother (Author) & Georges Van Vrekhem (Editor); *The Mother's Vision* (Publisher: Sri Aurobindo Ashram, Pondicherry, 605002, India; 2005); pp. 81-190, 551-594, 353-384, 431-541: (Ch.3: The Human Species in Evolution, Ch. 4: Plants and Animals, Ch. 5: The Gradations of Existence and Their Expression in the Human Being, Ch. 6: The Psychic Being or Soul, Ch. 14: Day-to-Day Life, Ch. 17: Yoga and Meditation, Ch. 18: The Integral Yoga, Ch. 19: The Supramental)

WORKBOOK: QUESTIONS FOR PREVIEW AND REVIEW

Essay Type Questions

1. Describe the physical consciousness.
2. Describe nature of the human body.
3. State with examples the qualities of the body.

Short Answer Type Questions

1. Name evolutionary steps in ascending order.
2. Behind the Conscient is the _____. And behind it is _____.
3. _____ is the most outgoing consciousness.
4. Majority of people live in the _____ consciousness.
5. There are two types of qualities of the body: 1. _____, 2. _____.
6. What is internecine war in the body?
7. Illustrate body's war with the mind and the vital.
8. List four levels of perfection of the body.

Exercises

1. Construct a table showing positive and negative qualities of the physical mind.

SELF TEST

1. List five planes of the physical consciousness.
2. List three parts of the body.
3. List seven qualities of the gross body.
4. Neurological system is _____ (vital physical or mental physical)
5. Cortex of the brain is _____ (mental physical or vital physical)
6. List 8 negative qualities of the physical.
7. List two positive qualities of the physical.
8. Which is the most outward going consciousness of man.
9. Physical is good friend of mind and the vital. (True or False)
10. List five qualities of perfection of the physical.

CHAPTER VII

THE VITAL CONSCIOUSNESS OF A HUMAN BEING

I. THE NATURE AND FUNCTIONS OF THE VITAL BEING AND CONSCIOUSNESS

II. IMPORTANCE OF THE VITAL

III. PLANES AND PARTS OF THE VITAL

IV. THERE IS ALWAYS WAR AMONG ITS OWN PARTS AND WITH OTHER PLANES OF HUMAN BEING

V. MUNDANE PERFECTION OF THE VITAL

VI. INNER, VII. PSYCHIC, VIII. SPIRITUAL, AND IX. SUPRAMENTAL PERFECTION OF THE VITAL

We have already discussed that the vital being and consciousness plane emerged from the material physical plane due to the process of terrestrial evolution. With it evolved vegetation and animals on earth. In this chapter, we shall examine its nature and ways of its perfection.

I. THE NATURE AND FUNCTION OF THE VITAL BEING AND CONSCIOUSNESS[141]

(i) The vital consciousness is a thing of desires: All our desires emanate from our vital being. Moreover, it has many conflicting desires. It desires for high grades in examination and on the other hand, desires to enjoy partying and movies, etc. Thus it keeps mind confused and distressed.

(ii) It is seat of impulses: Our impulsive behaviours that suddenly occur and difficult to check, such as sexual actions, sudden manifestation of anger, etc., are created by the vital being. When a male impulsively does sex with a woman, he just does it fast and ejects fast, so woman does not achieve orgasm and remains unsatisfied. If he does sex with deliberate will to satisfy woman, he would keep sex impulse under mental control, first make woman ready to have sex by fondling and kissing her and when she is ready, will start with copulation. When any action is done impulsively, it is the impulse that enjoys the action and not the man, but when man does action under mental or psychic control he enjoys the action.

(iii) It is seat of our emotions, such as anger, love, hate, pity, lust, etc. Generally it receives vibrations of emotions from the universal nature and expresses it. It can deny them if it wishes to do so. As soon as an emotion is seen coming to enter the being, a person can stop it from entering inside of him and send it back to the universal nature.

(iv) It is seat of our sensations also. It makes us to go for sensational pleasure of eye, ear, touch and taste. That is why people like to watch good scenes, beautiful persons, cinemas, dances, etc. For example, the vital consciousness of a wife may make her stick to the sofa and watch TV shows for enjoying sensational themes and scenes throughout the day and thus neglect her husband, whose dissatisfied vital would make him lose interest in her and create interest in another

---

[141] SABCL Vol. 22, pp. 334-347; SABCL Vol. 24, pp. 1111-12, 1219

woman to satisfy his vital, mental and physical needs only a woman can satisfy. The vital makes people to enjoy tasty food and drinks. Sexual pleasure is mostly sensational pleasure of touch: the rubbing of penis of man and vagina of woman makes both feel indescribable bliss.

(v) It seeks after life. It seeks after life and its movements for their own sake and would not leave hold of them even if they bring it suffering. Too much of sex makes body weak and sick yet people who have no control over their vital goes on enjoying sex. It can even luxuriate in tears and suffering as part of the drama of life.

(vi) It always seeks for fulfilment. If a desire is not fulfilled it feels dissatisfaction and becomes depressed. If a husband cannot sexually satisfy his wife, wife will either start affair with a man who can satisfy her or seek for divorce.

(vii) Vital makes people to seek after more and more possession. People want more and more money, houses, ornaments, land, power, knowledge, fame, etc. because they have strong vital.

(viii) It is narrow and limited and subject to dualities, such as dualities of transient joys and grief, exultations and depressions.

II. IMPORTANCE OF THE VITAL

1. MEDIATION AND FORCE OF THE VITAL IS INDISPENSABLE FOR ANY MANIFESTATION, EXPRESSION AND PROGRESS, MUNDANE OR SPIRITUAL, AND FOR SUPRAMENTAL TRANSFORMATION OF OUR BEING

(i) **Mediation of vital is a must for any mundane, psychic, spiritual and supramental change:** For example,

(a) If one makes an effort to strengthen his muscles by particular exercise and vital does not take part in the effort, he will not be able to strengthen his muscles. But if vital collaborates, he will succeed.

(b) If one tries to apply psychic force and cure a trouble in an organ of the body, he will succeed only if vital also takes part in his effort. Thus for any psychic change in any parts of personality, vital's collaboration is absolutely necessary.

(c) If one goes within and calls forth hid psychic and requests it to bring down spiritual peace in the body and spiritual love in the heart and spiritual knowledge in the mind, and spiritual light and in the subconscient, the psychic may make the approach of the higher consciousness down to the subconscient possible, but without the vital action would not be complete.

(d) Similarly vital's cooperation is necessary for supramental descent in the physical, vital and mind for any supramental transformation in them.

(ii) Even though it is under control of the mind and limited by the body, if it is unregenerate — enslaved to desire, passion and ego — it may harm the body and the mind:

For example, if vital has a strong desire for food and sex, it can **cloud the better understanding of the mind**, which knows that over-sex and over-eating is injurious for body by giving them false reasoning that the pills of energy and digestion will help the body to perform excessive sex and digest excessive food. Thus to satisfy its own unregenerate desire it may get body to overwork and injure itself. If the vital of an athlete is too much desirous for fame, it will **impel** the athlete to consume medically forbidden energy-boosting drug to perform the best; that will ultimately ruin the health of the body. Thus, to satisfy its own desire, it can cloud the better understanding of mind and body and even compel them to overwork. It is a good servant but a very bad master.

(iii) A strong vital is necessary not only for mundane achievements, but also for the divine work. It is very difficult for a strong vital to surrender, as it has sense of its own power. But if it surrenders, one can achieve any spiritual realisations. The weak vital cannot turn spiritually. Being weak, either it is led away or finds it difficult to attempt at what is beyond its own habitual nature. That is why a Gujarati poet says, "હરિનો મારગ છે શૂરાનો, નહીં કાયરનું કામ જોને." A strong vital may misuse the spiritual power it gets due to sadhana. Many Gurus have fallen prey to sex with their disciple ladies, because their strong vital would misuse the sexual energy received by sadhana. That is why it is always advisable to first realise satvic (सात्विक) nature, and then try to make vital and body strong by making higher consciousness descend in them.

III. PLANES AND PARTS OF THE VITAL[142]

1. THE MENTAL VITAL OR THE VITAL MIND

It gives a mental expression by thought, speech or otherwise to the emotions, desires, passions, sensations and other movements of the vital being: It plans or dreams or imagines what can be done. In man of action this faculty is prominent and a leader of their nature.

2. THE EMOTIONAL VITAL

It is the seat of various feelings, such as love, joy, sorrow, hatred, anger, etc. Patel Chandrakant P.[143] has discussed in detail the nature, control and mundane perfection of the emotional consciousness. Here we shall examine emotion in his light.

(i) An Emotion has three aspects: (a) External behaviour, (b) physiological changes and (c) mental thought. If one feels fear of a coyote, he will **think** it may attack, bite, there will be bleeding from body and I will feel pain. Moreover **inside of his body certain movements** will occur, such as heartbeat will increase, blood will flow

---

[142] SABCL Vol. 22; p. 334

[143] Patel Chandrakant P.; સુખી જીવન માટે મનોવિજ્ઞાન (અખિલ હિન્દ પ્રકાશન, અમદાવાદ, ગુજરાત, ઇન્ડિયા, ૧૯૭૩); pp. 16-48

towards the extremity of the body, mouth may become dry, etc. and he will perform certain **external actions,** such as he may run away from coyote or shout and fire to make coyote run away from him. So emotion is an agitated state of the human consciousness.

(ii) Emotions are very helpful in life:

(a) It makes life interesting and full. Happy **emotions like Love,** joy and excitement of success make our mind joyful, increase our confidence, boost our morale and health and increase our friends and thus enliven our life. While sad emotions like frustration due to failure in the examination, shock of loss in the business, trauma of sudden death of son create worries in the mind, make one feel that life is hopeless, make a person to withdraw from active social life, and thus make man to experience dullness in his life. Mere happiness or mere sadness will make life monotonous and boring, but both together makes life colourful, rich and interesting.

(b) Emotions create unity: A wife sees a beautiful rose in the garden and feels joy, she calls husband to view it who also likes it and feels joy. Both feel the same joy and feel unity between them.

(c) The basis of art is emotion: Poetries, songs, dances, an architectural piece is created by particular emotions and they create similar high emotions in the audience. Thus emotions make life cultured and civilised.

(d) Emotions supply extra energy: In times of crisis a weak becomes brave; a tiny woman can fight a goonda if she sees her child is threatened by him. Love for her child supplies the bravery and guts to her.

(e) Emotions make man to do good deeds: Compassion and love for poors makes people to start charities and establish institutions for them.

But there is opposite side of the emotion also, which is not helpful to life.

(iii) Emotions are Injurious to life also, if uncontrolled

(a) Emotions promote anti-social acts also: As the Islamic State of Pakistan hates The Republic of India and as it covets Kashmir, it sends terrorists in Kashmir.

(b) Emotion can be used to cheat: Social media manipulates emotions of public to misguide the people. Articles advocating use of certain drugs for children are published in newspapers. Naturally they are appealing to the mothers love for child. Mothers, if brainwashed, will buy the injurious drug. Thus public is often cheated.

(c) Our emotions can mislead us: Because a father loves his child, he will overlook his misdeeds. If the neighbours complain that his child has bullied their children, he would say, "Your children must have abused him and he must have acted in self-defense." Father will never advise his naughty child to mend his uncivil habits.

(d) Emotions like anger waste energy of the body: Anger excites adrenal gland to release sugar from the lever in the blood, even though it is not needed for helping limbs to act for defence. So it is wasted, it simply goes out in urine. Sexual enjoyment waste the seminal energy, which if saved and absorbed in the body can make body strong, healthy and beautiful. Sri Aurobindo's body had become golden yellow because he could observe celibacy.

(e) Emotions spoil Health: Habitual anger creates high-blood pressure, heart attack, indigestion and diabetes.

So, it is advisable to control emotions and perfect them.

3. THE CENTRAL VITAL

It is the seat of the stronger vital longings and reactions, e.g. ambition, pride, fear, love of fame, attractions and repulsions, desires and passions of various kinds and the field of many vital energies.

4. THE LOWER VITAL

It is occupied with small desires and feelings, such as make the greater part of daily life, e.g. food desire, sexual desire, small likings, dislikings, vanity, quarrels, love of praise, anger at blame, little wishes of all kinds — and a numberless host of other things.

5. THE PHYSICAL VITAL

It is being of small desires and greeds etc. It is closely connected with the vital physical, the nervous being.

6. THE PSYCHIC VITAL

Sri Aurobindo says,

"There is always a part of ... the vital which is or can be influenced by the psychic, ... can be called the psychic-vital. According to the personality or the degree of evolution of each person, this can be small or large, weak or strong, covered up and inactive or prominent and in action. When it acts the movements of the vital accept the psychic motives or aims, partake of the nature of the psychic or follow its aims but with a modification in the manner which belongs to the mind, vital or physical. The psychic-vital seeks after the Divine, but it has demand in its self-giving, desire, vital eagerness. ... The psychic-vital is subject to pain and suffering."[144] *(See Ch. XVI)*

7. THE SPIRITUAL VITAL *(See Ch. XVI)*

8. THE SUPRAMENTAL VITAL *(See Ch. XVI)*

9. IT HAS POWERFUL EGO

---

[144] SABCL Vol. 24; pp. 1111-1112

IV. THERE IS ALWAYS WAR AMONG ITS OWN PARTS AND WITH OTHER PLANES OF HUMAN BEING

1. THE INTERNECINE WAR

(i) **War between Two Desires**: As has been already seen above the various parts of it go on quarrelling with each other. That is called the internecine war in the vital. Various desires conflict with each other. One wants to study in the evening but friends come and ask him to accompany them to the cinema. He also wants to satisfy desire of companionship. So, there arises a conflict in the mind. Either he studies or goes to cinema. He selects one but he has to dissatisfy the other desire.

(ii) **War among Two Parts:** The higher vital is interested in attending a concert. But the lower vital desires to be with girlfriend to enjoy sex. There is a tug of war between the two parts of the vital. The lower vital wins and he goes to his girlfriend to enjoy petty sex. His higher vital is frustrated and becomes sad. So, he cannot fully enjoy the company of his girlfriend.

2. THE WAR BETWEEN MEMBERS

Vital generally acts at cross purposes with the mind and the body and that is called war between the members (physical, vital and mind) of the individual being; For example, Vital desires to enjoy food that is not good for his body. He wants to eat sweet laddoo, but he has diabetes. Body says no to vital. But vital overpowers the body and makes the person to eat laddoo. Then there is excess sugar in the blood. He has to rush to doctor. He misses his college class. Not only body, but his mind also misses the study. Let us consider another example: Mind wants to relax, but vital wants to visit friends just to chitchat with them. Again there is a war between mind and the vital. Vital persuades the mind that it can relax during night so it should not disagree with it. The mind is persuaded and the person goes to friends. They talk till late in night. The mind does not get rest. It feels tired and frustrated. Vital creates such tug of war often and makes body and mind suffer. One has to put physical, vital and mind under the rule of the psychic, if he wants to establish harmony among members.

So, one has to perform tapasya of control and education of the crude vital and regenerate it and enculture it to respect other members and be in harmony with them. This perfection of the vital can be done at mundane level, psychic level, spiritual level and supramental level.

V. MUNDANE PERFECTION OF THE VITAL

1. EMOTIONAL CONTROL AND MATURITY

We saw above that vital can enrich as well as impoverish our life. So it is so controlled that it enriches the life. Here are discussed few characteristics of the vital control.

(i) To be free from undesirable emotional reaction and to be equipped with desirable healthy emotional reactions is one of the criteria of emotional control: In childhood one fears lizard, cockroach, darkness, lightening, etc. and so one is considered immature and elders try to make him unlearn these emotional reactions. Such things are not harmful is explained to him. He sees adults do not bother about them. This encourages him to remove the fearful emotional reaction to such innocuous stimuli. Not to fear the social gatherings is very necessary for human friendly interaction to develop qualities of love, sympathy, harmony, and it improves health also.

(ii) One should develop the capacity of voluntary happy desirable behaviours for that is one more sign of emotional control: If a wife cannot reciprocate her husband's expression of love and care, they will never be able to live happy married life. If a friend writes a beautiful poetry, you should willingly appreciate his work and feel joy. That will increase mutual bind and joy. Instead if you feel jealous and neglect to provide suitable feedback or provide negative feedback, your mutual relation will not be happy.

(iii) Suitable control of emotional expression is the third characteristic of emotional control: Loud lifter in playground while watching play is proper and will be appreciated but same in the theatre is awkward and will be considered a sign of immaturity.

(iv) To live a balanced full emotional life is also a characteristic of emotional control: One must know to express love when needed and one must be able to spontaneously express anger against a bad action of other. One should be able to enjoy all emotions in life and make life more full and rich and colourful; one need not restrict oneself to a few of them and make life truncated. Like balanced food balanced emotions are healthy.

(v) One must be always aware of one's emotions: During discussion if one notes anger is rising in him against the other group member, he can check it and avoid quarrel. If he is not aware of that rising anger, he will flare up, will quarrel and spoil the discussion and relations with all.

Thus to so control emotional behaviours that one succeed in life, one enjoy life and help others to enjoy life and progress is very much necessary in life. Such a person is considered a mature one. And all would like his company.

2. STRONG AND STEADY AND DURABLE EMOTIONS ARE CONSIDERED PERFECT

If your lover misbehaves with you, even then you love him as before, then your love is strong and durable. But if you lose love for him, it means your love is fickle, temporary, conditional and weak. Strong love will change other's rude behaviour and help him to cultivate love. If a teacher has strong anger against indiscipline in class, students will desist from unruly behaviours and learn how to behave in a civilised manner. If his anger is weak and soft, they will disregard his anger and continue to be indisciplined.

3. TEMPERATENESS AND PEACEFUL EXPRESSION OF EMOTION IS ANOTHER CRITERIA OF EMOTIONAL CONTROL

One must fondle a child or girlfriend with in a graceful, peaceful and measured manner and not so violently that hurts the child or girlfriend. The intemperate fondling is always detested and so the child or girlfriend will avoid him.

4. ONE MUST BE ABLE TO SATISFY EMOTIONS WITHOUT FEELING CONFLICT IN MIND

If a Christian believes that sex is sin, he will never be able to satisfy his and her wife's sexual desire completely. He will always feel he is performing sin, when performing sex, his mind will withhold its participation in sex, and that will make sexual act weak and insincere. It will result in an unhappy married life. Satisfaction of desires and emotions without what is called mental conflict under the rule of moral mind is the perfection of emotion sought after by the modern scientific psychology. But this is merely an ordinary mundane perfection. The modern psychology abounds in methods of achieving it also; but it stops there only. Integral psychology seeks more wide and higher perfection of the vital. That will now be discussed below.

5. PROPERLY DEVELOPED AESTHETIC SENSE IS ONE MORE CHARACTERISTIC OF PERFECT VITAL

One should be able to discern really beautiful scenes, poetry, picture, cinema, speech, dress and behaviour from ugly and dirty ones. For, then only one will expose oneself to real beauty and learn to express real beauty. For, ugliness and baseness is barbaric culture and civilisation.

VI. THE INNER PERFECTION OF THE VITAL *(See Ch. IX)*

VII. THE PSYCHIC PERFECTION OF THE VITAL *(See Ch. XVI)*

VIII. THE SPIRITUAL PERFECTION OF THE VITAL *(See Ch. XVI)*

IX. THE SUPRAMENTAL PERFECTION OF THE VITAL *(See Ch. XVI)*

SUMMARY

I. Above the individual subconscious being, there are the subliminal, the psychic, the conscient and the environmental consciousness of the individual. Outer triple personality, the physical-vital-mental complex of man, is in the front of his being and is the conscient. Behind it is the inner triple being, the inner physical-vital-mental personality. It is also called the subliminal. Behind it is the psychic being. Around the inner and outer beings is the environmental consciousness, and above them is the superconscient. This structure of human consciousness is pictured in Figure 5.1 in this chapter. Human nature is dual and full of multiplicity. Different parts of human being always go on quarreling with each other. Only Psychic can purify and harmonize them and transform them. Psychicisation leads to spiritualisation and Supramentalisation. The vital consciousness is the seat of emotions, passions, impulses and desires. The vital seeks after possessions, power, fulfilment, etc. The vital can be helpful as well as injurious to life. So it must be properly controlled and evolved.

II. Importance of the Vital: Mediation of vital is a must for any mundane, psychic, spiritual and supramental change. Even though it is under control of the mind and limited by the body, if it is unregenerate — enslaved to desire, passion and ego — it may harm the body and the mind. A strong vital is necessary not only for mundane achievements, but also for the divine work. It is very difficult for a strong vital to

225

surrender, as it has sense of its own power. But if it surrenders, one can achieve any spiritual realisations. The weak vital cannot turn spiritually. Being weak, either it is led away or finds it difficult to attempt at what is beyond its own habitual nature.

III. Mental vital, central vital, physical vital, lower vital, psychic vital spiritual vital and supramental vital are planes of the vital consciousness.

IV. The different parts of the vital are always at war with each other. The vital is always at war with the mind and the physical.

V. Emotional control, emotional maturity, awareness of one's emotions, temperateness and gracefulness in expression of emotions, strong emotions and proper aesthetic sense is necessary for mundane perfection of the vital.

VI. Inner, psychic, spiritual and supramental perfection are wider and higher levels of perfection of the vital.

Suggestions for Further Reading

1. Indra Sen, Integral Psychology (Sri Aurobindo International Centre of Education, Pondicherry, 605 002, India; 1986); pp. 9-29

2. Tulsidas Chatterjee, *Sri Aurobindo's Integral Yoga* (Pondicherry: SABDA, Sri Aurobindo Ashram; 1970), pp. 57-83

3. The Mother (Author) & Georges Van Vrekhem (Editor); *The Mother's Vision* (Publisher: Sri Aurobindo Ashram, Pondicherry, 605002, India; 2005); pp. 81-190, 551-594, 353-384, 431-541; (Ch.3: The Human Species in Evolution, Ch. 4: Plants and Animals,

Ch. 5: The Gradations of Existence and Their Expression in the Human Being, Ch. 6: The Psychic Being or Soul, Ch. 14: Day-to-Day Life, Ch. 17: Yoga and Meditation, Ch. 18: The Integral Yoga, Ch. 19: The Supramental)

WORKBOOK: QUESTIONS FOR PREVIEW AND REVIEW

Essay Type Questions

1. Describe the vital consciousness.
2. Is the vital consciousness important for man's progress?
3. Describe different levels of perfection of the vital.
4. Describe criteria of mundane perfection of the vital.

Short Answer Type Questions

1. What is death?
2. There are four types of perfection of nature: 1._____ 2. _____, 3._____.
3. Explain how vital can help man's development.
4. Describe how vital can prove injurious to man.
5. Describe mundane perfection of vital.
6. Describe psychic perfection of vital.
7. Describe spiritual perfection of vital.
8. Describe supramental perfection of vital.
9. Illustrate the internecine war and war between members wedged by the vital.

Exercises

1. Make a list of the functions of the vital.
2. Make a list of Characteristics of mundane perfection of the vital.

SELF TEST

1. The vital is seat of _____, _____, _____, _____.
2. List three importance of the vital.
3. List eight parts of the vital.
4. List three aspects of emotional behaviour.
5. List five benefits of the vital.
6. List five drawbacks of emotions.
7. Illustrate internecine war in the vital.
8. Illustrate war of vital with mind and physical.
9. List five criteria of mundane perfection of emotional life.
10. Mundane perfection of vital is wider than the inner perfection of the vital. (True or False)
11. Psychic perfection of vital is higher than the mundane perfection of the vital. (True or False)

CHAPTER VIII

THE MENTAL CONSCIOUSNESS

I.   THE MENTAL CONSCIOUSNESS

II. PLANES AND PARTS OF MIND

III. THE MENTAL EGO

IV. THE INTERNECINE WAR IN THE MIND AND THE WAR
     AMONG MEMBERS OF PERSONALITY

V.   ORDINARY MUNDANE PERFECTION OF MIND

I. THE MENTAL CONSCIOUSNESS

1. MIND AND BRAIN ARE TWO DIFFERENT THINGS

It can very happily be noted at the outset that neurologist Wilder Penfield's[145] latest crowning conclusion after years of research is that the mind and the brain are two fundamental independent elements of the human being. That he should scientifically arrive at a fact reached by the intuition, by ancient Indian psychology and by Sri Aurobindo, is a pleasant incident of 1975 A.D. Dr. Eben's NDE also proves existence of mind separate from the brain. *See Chapter II Section III-1 The Field of Study is Integral.*

---

[145] Penfield Wilder, "The Mind and the Highest Brain Mechanism", *Mother India,* XXIX, 12 (November, 1977), pp. 858-64

2. WHAT IS MIND?

For Sri Aurobindo[146], the mind means the part of nature which has to do with our certain functions. We shall note and illustrate them one by one.

(i) To cognition outside things and the stimuli inside the body: Mind cognizes or recognises persons as my wife, Ramesh's sister, Piyush, prime minister, driver and so on, objects as plate, table, chair and so on, animals as cow, elephant and so on, trees as champa, neem, eucalyptus, etc. and internal conditions of body pain and hunger in the stomach, breathlessness in the lung, dryness in the mouth, etc.

(ii) Mind itself is the sixth sense: Mind can perceive directly on its own without any instrumentation of senses: It can feel thought currents coming from others directly from distance. It can send messages directly to others. It can act on other persons and objects from distance.

(iii) Mind is our intelligence also, it thinks about problem, work, and all things it cognizes. It writes an essay. It solves a mathematical problem, can write poetry, can provide scientific explanation for a phenomena, can judge if something is good or bad, ugly or beautiful.

(iv) It receives ideas and puts them together as a theory of say gravitation. It can express ideas about what is universe. It can give ideas as to what type of government is best or worst. It can say which is the best method of teaching a child.

(v) It can form particular will: It may make a will that it will study medicine and makes efforts accordingly. It can form a will that stomach should digest properly and send the will to stomach which will receive it and digest properly without any medical help.

---

[146] SABCL, Vol. 22, pp. 320-334 and 370

(vi) It can see vision: It can visualise that unmanned airplane can be made and used for putting out fire in the forest. Wright Brothers saw vision of plane and eventually made a flying airplane.

3. IN ITS ORIGIN, IT IS LIMITED, LIMITING AND A SUBORDINATE POWER OR INSTRUMENT

It has been put forth from the supermind as a subordinate instrument. It is instrument of the psychic being also. It takes its stand in the standpoint of division, is forgetful of the oneness behind, though able to return to it by reillumination from above. For example: It sees parts of a things separately then join them and construct a whole which is an abstract thing, it is not a thing in itself. It sees physical objects and universe, but cannot perceive the One Divine Consciousness behind them. When the higher consciousness descends into it and enlarges and illuminates it, it can see the oneness behind separate things of the world.

4. INTERPERSONAL RELATIONS OF MIND WITH VITAL AND BODY

It is higher power than the body. It can impose its will on the body and force it to work for long hours. But the body will not obey always. The body assails mind with its inertia, dullness and makes it inactive often in ordinary man and sometimes in mentally developed man. Body can make mind to sleep, even if mind wants to work. It can restrain the vital. When vital desires to overwork, mind can subdue it and make it to control itself and moderate its desire. But vital as we have seen before, can abuse mind also. Vital can persuade it to buy wrong things and ideas. As vital would like to eat sweet things, it will explain to mind that sugar is energy and needed for work, so one should consume it as much as he likes. Thus, the vital can persuade it to distort, limit and falsify the truth according to its desires, passions and emotions.

5. MOREOVER, IT HAS ITS OWN DEFECTS

(i) Mind is obstructive, narrow and, unwilling to open to high knowledge. It is so narrow that it cannot read and grasp large philosophical, psychological or scientific knowledge. That is why students avoid to study great authors and difficult subjects.

(ii) Intellectual unscrupulousness in thinking is its another defect. It admits only the Informations it prefers and likes, avoids those that it does not like and then from this half information infers the wrong knowledge, which is not true. Then acts on the basis of this untrue knowledge and fails. Its unscrupulousness thus hamper its actions of knowing and achieving.

(iii) It cannot change the lower nature but as it is the highest faculty of man, at its best it can control it. That is why people say man cannot be changed. Only the psychic being can do the job of changing and transforming the human nature.

6. IT CANNOT KNOW THE ESSENTIAL TRUTH: IT IS AN INSTRUMENT OF IGNORANCE

Even if purified of all these defects and allowed its highest powers, it cannot know the essential truth.

For mind knows by first analysing and then synthesizing, and thus its knowledge is ignorant abstractions, it cannot know the thing in itself, worldly or spiritual; it cannot know the Self or the Reality. To know all these it must transform itself under the Supermind. So, Sri Aurobindo defines it as ignorance seeking for knowledge. Sri Aurobindo vividly describes its ignorant working:

> "Its highest knowledge is often abstract, lacking in a concrete grasp; it has to use expedients and unsure means of arrival, to rely upon reasoning, argumentation and debate, inferences, divinations, set methods of inductive or deductive logic, succeeding only if it is given correct and complete data and even then liable to reach on the same data different results and varying consequences; it has to use means and accept

results of a method which is hazardous even when making a claim to certitude and of which there would be no need if it had a direct or supraintellectual knowledge."[147]

It does not create thoughts, but receives them and gives them forms which are harmful or helpful and which can act over others, over himself or parts of himself.

II. PLANES AND PARTS OF MIND

Mind has five parts below its proper level: The subconscient mind, the cellular mind, the body-mind, the physical mind and the vital mind.

1. THE SUBCONSCIENT OR SUBCONSCIOUS MIND

Sri Aurobindo writes,

"It is not different from the outer mentality, but it only acts below the surface, unknown to the waking man perhaps with a deeper plunge and a larger scope. ... In matter there is a subconscious Mind at work, which is certainly responsible for its own emergence, first in the nervous consciousness of plant-life and the primitive animal and, secondly in the ever-developing mentality of the evolved animal and of man."[148]

Influences of the inconscient come up through this subconscious mind in the mind of man without the conscious knowledge of man.

---

[147] SABCL, Vol. 16; p. 57
[148] SABCL Vol. 18; pp. 86, 173-174, 182-184

2. THE CELLULAR MIND

Sri Aurobindo writes, "There is too an obscure mind of the body, of the very cells, molecules, corpuscles. Haeckel, the German materialist, spoke somewhere of the will in the matter, and recent science dealing with the incalculable variation in the activity of the electrons" has also seen an intelligence at work in matter[149].

The Mother, during the course of her yoga of transformation of cells, had heard cells of her body chanting mantra collectively. She says, "It's strange, the mantras have a cohesive effect on the cells; the entire cellular life becomes one solid and compact mass of incredible concentration – with a single vibration. Instead of the body's many usual vibrations, there is only one single vibration."[150]

3. THE BODY MIND OR THE MECHANICAL MIND

There is the mechanical mental physical or Body-mind which when left to itself simply goes on repeating the past customary thoughts and movements or at the most adds to them such further mechanical reactions to things and reflexes as are in the round of life. Its nature is to go on turning round in a circle on the thoughts that come into it. This sometimes happens when the thinking mind is quiet. This is part of the physical mind and one should not be disturbed or alarmed by its rising up, but see what it is and quiet it down or get control of it.

4. THE PHYSICAL MIND[151]

(i) The physical mind is that part of the mind which can only deal with outward things not inner things — it depends on the sense-mind, sees only objects, external actions, draws its ideas from the data given by external things, infers from them only and knows no other

---

[149] SABCL Vol. 22; p. 340

[150] Satprem; *The Mind of Cells* (Publisher: Institute for Evolutionary Research; 200 Park Avenue, New York, NY, 10116, USA); p. 146

[151] SABCL Vol.22; pp. 327-330

Truth until it is enlightened from above. Only Buddhi or mind proper can deal with our inner or higher world.

(ii) The physical mind has first to open to the higher consciousness — its limitations are then removed and it admits what is supraphysical and begins to see things in harmony with the higher knowledge. It becomes an instrument for externalising that knowledge in the pragmatic perceptions and actions of the physical life. It sees things as they are and deals with them according to the larger Truth with an automatic rightness of perception and will and reaction to impacts.

(iii) The physical mind has no reason except its whims, its habits or an inclination to be tamasic.

(iv) It is the physical mind that would like everything made easy.

(v) The physical mind is in the habit of observing things with or without use.

(vi) Repetition is the habit of the mental physical.

(vii) The true physical mind is the receiving and externalising intelligence which has two functions — first, to work upon external things and give them a mental order with a way of practically dealing with them and, secondly, to be the channel of materializing and putting into effect whatever the thinking and dynamic mind sends down to it for the purpose.

(viii) The mechanical mind is a sort of engine — whatever comes to it it puts into the machine and goes on turning it round and round no matter what it is. That is the nature of the mental physical to go on repeating without use the movement that has happened. It is what we call the mechanical mind — it is strong in childhood because the thinking mind is not developed and has besides a narrow range of interests. Afterwards it becomes an undercurrent in the mental activities.

5. THE VITAL MIND

(i) Sri Aurobindo[152] says, "It lives by imagination, thoughts of desire, will to act and enjoy from its own impulse and this is able to seize on the reason itself and make it its auxiliary and justifying counsel and supplier of pleas and excuses."

(a) All imaginations that we see in science fictions, in movies, in literature and all imaginations a person makes about anything is work of the vital mind,

(b) A person or a nation thinks about how to increase wealth, property and land. It is their vital mind that does this thinking.

(c) It wishes to enjoy from its own impulse sex, love, anger, etc.

(d) It does not only think but create will to act upon its thoughts. A nation may raise large army and invade neighbour to get land.

(e) It can persuade reason to justify its thinking, will and actions. Today we find its desire for unnatural gay-sex has created thoughts in favour of gay-sex, generated activities to spread it on whole earth, and to make laws in the favour of gay-sex.

(ii) The physical mind would like to continue to live in the given physical conditions, in the established material order but the vital mind comes in with it demands of more products, more enjoyments, more varieties of life-activities and disturb the inert physical mind and impel it to think and act for more and more new things. Thus the vital mind is a means of progress.[153]

(iii) The vital mind is more open to the psychic, though obscurely, is capable of first forming frontal formation of vital Purush, which is not the psychic. This vital Purush can sense and contact the things of the life-world and tries to realise them here.[154]

---

[152] SABCL Vol. 22; p. 323
[153] SABCL Vol. 22; p. 414
[154] SABCL Vol. 19; pp. 718-719

6. THE MENTAL MIND OR THE MIND PROPER

Sri Aurobindo[155] writes, the mind proper is divided into three parts: (i) thinking Mind, (ii) dynamic Mind and (iii) externalising Mind.

(i) The Thinking Mind: It is concerned with ideas and knowledge in their own right. Albert Einstein's thinking mind was concentrated on thinking the theory of relativity and splitting of atom. It received ideas which were not garbed in the language of physics. His Dynamic mind then got active.

(ii) The Dynamic Mind: It is concerned with the putting out of mental forces for realisation of the idea. His dynamic mind searched for right words for ideas and used its will to write them in a language that others can understand.

(iii) The Externalising Mind: It is concerned with the expression of them in life (not only by speech, but by any form it can give). Einstein's expressing mind then wrote theory and formulas and published book on it. Later on other scientists and technicians worked on his knowledge and found how to create an atom bomb and explode it.

There are three higher parts of the mind proper that human being can develop by sadhana: (i) the inner mind, (ii) the psychic mind, (iii) the spiritual mind and (iv) the supramental mind.

7. THE INNER MIND

According to Sri Aurobindo, the inner mind is behind the surface mind. When **one** goes inside and widens into cosmic consciousness then the inner mind becomes his field of action. The inner mind is open to cosmic world and receives influences and forces from the cosmic world. It can so act on anything from a distance.

---

[155] SABCL Vol. 22; p. 326

8. THE PSYCHIC MIND

Sri Aurobindo says,

"There is a part of ... the mind which is or can be influenced by the psychic, ... can be called the psychic-mind. According to the personality or the evolution of each person, this can be small or large, weak or strong, covered up and inactive or prominent and in action. When it acts the movements of the mind accept the psychic motives or aims, partake of the nature of the psychic or follow its aims but with a modification in the manner which belongs to the mind."[156]

It means then the mind turns towards the Divine, accepts supra-physical knowledge as valid, makes an effort for the spiritual development of personality, enlarges love to humanity and works for one unified world order. *(See Ch. XVI)*

9. THE SPIRITUAL MIND *(See Ch. XVI)*

10. THE SUPRAMENTAL MIND *(See Ch. XVI)*

III. THE MENTAL EGO

The "I" or the little ego is constituted by nature and is at once a mental, vital and physical formation meant to aid in centralising and individualising the outer consciousness and action."[157] It is three in one formation. It has three aspects: mental ego, vital ego and physical ego.

Vital ego is in the surface vital. When we enter into the inmost of our inner consciousness, we find there our true being: the true mental

---

[156] SABCL Vol. 24; pp. 1111-1112
[157] SABCL, Vol. 22; p. 278

Purush, vital Purush and physical Purush and the ego's utility is over and is replaced by the true being.

IV. THE INTERNECINE WAR IN THE MIND AND WAR AMONG MEMBERS OF PERSONALITY

Mind's parts go on quarrelling among themselves; for example, spiritual mind may quarrel with reason. The physical mind will oppose the vital mind if it is told to think and achieve new things. Vital mind will not accept control of the mental mind over his excessive enjoyment of desires. This is called the internecine war in the mind. The Mother says[158] that an individualized harmonious mind is rare, even learned people hold contradictory ideas without being aware of the contradiction.

Mind even abuses the vital and the body. It may for the pursuit of study force Vital to forgo its legitimate enjoyments and make it weak; it may force body to keep waking for long hours and spoil health. This is called the war among members. Not only man's mind, vital and body are always at war with each other, but each is also a house divided against itself; for example, outer mind, vital and body are always in discord with inner mind, vital and body. The first is also called the war among members of our personality and the second can be called the internal war in each of the members. The ordinary mind cannot resolve it but by going within one can take the first necessary step in the direction of the solution. And if one continues to go within and realises his psychic, the psychic will change belligerent nature of each of the members and make them to stand in harmonious relations with each other and both the wars would cease.

---

[158] CWM, Vol. 9; pp. 43-44

V. ORDINARY MUNDANE PERFECTION OF THE MIND

All the following powers developed to their highest and finest working capacity, is a perfect mind sought after by our ordinary education:

1. At its highest the ordinary mind is free intelligence. It is free from the physical and the vital. And can control them.

2. Perfect mind receives intuitions and intimations from above which it intellectualises. It can think and write philosophy, poetry, etc.

3. Generally, it would be still on the surface and see things from outside, but when helped by intuition and other higher powers will see deeper and higher also.

4. It will be alert and moderately calm and settled.

5. It will be free from vital emotions and feelings of likings and dislikings, vital demands and inertia of the physical.

6. It will have powers of judgement, which means it will have discernment of good and bad, ugly and beautiful and true and false.

7. Its power of imagination will be pretty developed.

8. Its faculty of memory will be strong. It will remember all types of matter for a long time and recall them whenever needed.

9. Its observation power will be perfect.

10. It will be equipped with logical reasoning.

11. It will have power of concentration.

12. It will have capacity to learn as many branches of knowledge as possible.

13. It will have refined aesthetic sense, interest in lofty ideas and ideals.

14. It will have capacity to think on an abstract level.

SUMMARY

1. Brain is not mind. Mind is that part of our conscious that cognizes, thinks, imagines, judges, reasons, discerns wills and vision. It is subordinate power or instrument. It is limited. It is sometimes controlled by the physical and the vital. It is narrow, obstructive, unwilling to open to higher knowledge. It cannot change the lower nature. It is an instrument of ignorance.

2. It has many planes and parts: 1. subconsciousness mind, 2. the cellular mind, 3.the body mind or the mechanical mind, 4. the physical mind, 5. the vital mind, 6.the mental mind, 7. the inner mind, 8. the psychic mind, 9. the spiritual mind and 10. the supramental mind.

3. Mind has ego and it can form inside itself mental Purush.

4. There is always war among its parts, which is called the internecine war. It is always at war with other parts of the consciousness, which is called war between members.

5. Mundane perfect mind will be free intelligence, would receive intuitions from above, will be alert, plastic, strong, will control vital and physical, will have developed imagination, will have powerful memory, strong will power, power of reasoning, power of concentration, capacity to learn many branches of knowledge, and capacity to think on abstract level.

Suggestions for Further Reading

1. Indra Sen, Integral Psychology (Sri Aurobindo International Centre of Education, Pondicherry, 605 002, India; 1986); pp. 9-29

2. Tulsidas Chatterjee, *Sri Aurobindo's Integral Yoga* (Pondicherry: SABDA, Sri Aurobindo Ashram; 1970); pp. 57-83

3. The Mother (Author) & Georges Van Vrekhem (Editor); *The Mother's Vision* (Publisher: Sri Aurobindo Ashram, Pondicherry, 605002, India; 2005); pp. 81-190, 551-594, 353-384, 431-541: (Ch.3: The Human Species in Evolution, Ch. 4: Plants and Animals, Ch. 5: The Gradations of Existence and Their Expression in the Human Being, Ch. 6: The Psychic Being or Soul, Ch. 14: Day-to-Day Life, Ch. 17: Yoga and Meditation, Ch. 18: The Integral Yoga, Ch.19: The Supramental)

WORKBOOK: QUESTIONS FOR PREVIEW AND REVIEW

Essay Type Questions

1. Describe the nature of mental consciousness
2. Describe the planes and parts of the mental consciousness.
3. Enumerate and illustrate criteria of mundane perfection of the mind.
4. Describe the physical and vital mind.

Short Answer Type Questions

1. Describe mundane perfection of the physical Mind.
2. Which the topmost mind level.
3. Brain is mind. (True or False)
4. List a few functions of the mind.
5. Why is mind also called the sixth sense?
6. List a few defects of the mind.
7. It is instrument of ignorance. Explain.
8. Name all planes and parts of the mind.
9. Cellular mind and mind of body are same. (True or false)
10. What is mechanical mind?
11. The vital mind is always helpful to the mind proper. (True or False)
12. Name three parts of the mental mind.
13. Define the inner mind.
14. Define the psychic mind.

15. Describe in short the mental ego.
16. Give an illustration of the internecine war in the mind.
17. Give an illustration of war among body, mind and vital.
18. List a few characteristics of the perfect mundane mind.

Exercises

1. Make a table of types of mind.

SELF-TEST

1. Is brain mind?
2. List functions of mind.
3. List 6 defects of mind.
4. List 10 parts of mind.
5. List 10 perfections of mind.

CHAPTER IX

THE SUBLIMINAL OR INNER CONSCIOUSNESS

I. THE SUBLIMINAL OR THE INNER CONSCIOUSNESS

II. THE ENVIRONMENTAL OR CIRCUMCONSCIENT
CONSCIOUSNESS

Behind the outer mental-vital-physical consciousness there is its extension called the inner mental-vital-physical or subliminal consciousness.

I. THE SUBLIMINAL OR THE INNER CONSCIOUSNESS[159]

1. DEFINITION

The subliminal or inner consciousness means the inner mind, inner vital and inner physical.[160] The subliminal is on the same level but

---

[159] SABCL, Vol. 22, pp. 270, 308, 309-10, 352 and 368; SABCL, Vol. 21, p. 841; CWM, Vol. 4, pp. 63 and 272-74; CWM, Vol. 10, p. 41; CWM, Vol. 9, pp. 345-46; M. P. Pandit, *Dictionary of Sri Attrobindo's Yoga* (Pondicherry: Dipti Publication, Sri Aurobindo Ashram, 1966), pp. 120-21 and *Glossary of Terms in Sri Aurobindo's Writings* (Pondicherry: Sri Aurobindo Ashram, 1978), p. 153

[160] According to Sri Aurobindo, "the inner consciousness means the inner mind, inner vital and inner physical and behind them the psychic which is their inmost being" (refer SABCL, Vol. 22, p. 308). But the researcher has restricted the concept of the inner consciousness to mean the inner mental, vital and physical only. For, the psychic is

behind the outer and veiled from it. Its innermost part is variously called the true physical, true vital and true mind; inmost physical is called the true physical, the inmost vital is called the true vital and inmost mental is called the true mental.

2. WHERE DOES IT RECEIVE FORCES FROM?

This subliminal consciousness receives formations from subconscious below, from the universal from around and from the psychic on the same level and from the higher consciousness from above.

3. WHAT SEPARATES IT FROM UNIVERSAL CONSCIOUSNESS?

It is separated from the universal consciousness and worlds by a fence of its mental, vital and subtle-physical sheaths with extremely fine, subtle and wide ranging senses, just as outer nature's consciousness is walled from the physical world by gross physical body, which has gross and narrow senses.

4. THE MENTAL BODY (MANOMAYA KOSHA)

It houses the inner mind and the true mind and is a window to the universal mental.

5. THE VITAL BODY (PRANMAYA KOSHA)

It houses the inner vital and the true vital and is a window to the universal vital. It is called the nervous envelope also. It is around the gross body radiating from it. It has the same density as the vibrations of heat observable when the day is very hot. It is intermediary between the subtle body and the material body.

---

radically different from them and it was found necessary to do so for the sake of short, clear and easy statement of integral psychology.

It protects the body from everything: all contagion, fatigue, exhaustion and even from accidents. Fatigue, lack of sleep, strong emotions, slackness in consciousness, etc. make holes in it, and then the body becomes vulnerable to illness, and with inattentive mind, to accidents. If one becomes conscious of its slackness, concentrates for a few minutes, calls and establishes force and the inner peace there, it becomes strong and intact and an illness can be pushed off and accidents avoided.

This body actually has vital senses as the physical body has physical senses. Individualised and awakened vital body can perceive, feel and interact on its own level with the vital universal worlds and the vitals of other persons, as physical body does in physical life. Awakened mental body and subtle physical body can do the same on their respective levels with their respective universal worlds and respective corresponding parts of other individuals.

6. THE SUBTLE BODY (ANNAMAYA KOSHA)

It houses inner physical and true physical and is a window to the universal physical. The subtle body has a subtler consciousness and substance than the gross body, and contains, penetrates and is interfused with the gross body. It can go to a distance from the body and can feel and be aware of things in a not merely mental or vital way. There are subtle nerves in it which are connected with the physical nerves in the physical.

7. THE INNER CONSCIOUSNESS IS OF THE SAME ESSENTIAL NATURE OF THE SURFACE CONSCIOUSNESS, AND SO LIKE IT AND OPEN TO ALL DUALITIES

But unlike our outer consciousness the inner can contact, receive and respond to the physical and the universal world directly through the subtle and immensely widely acting senses of its more subtle and supple inner bodies.

If one lives in the outward physical consciousness, one does not usually know illness, a universal force, is to enter him, until it actually declares itself in various symptoms in the body. But when one goes inward, one becomes aware of his subtle environmental consciousness and feels the force of illness coming through it, even at a distance, and if one has learnt, can throw it back. One feels its symptoms, for example, of cold or fever, in his subtle physical, and destroys them there, before they enter the physical body.

One can directly read other people's ideas and wills, feel their emotions and feelings and physical states and forces directly and act upon them beneficially or harmfully by sending his counterparts to them; thus one can consciously handle the intermixture of his being with other people and objects around him, which is a constant fact of the life on the earth.

One can from this part also enter into the universal worlds, have dealings with forces and beings there and call and utilise them here. This explains the extra-sensory perceptions studied by the western psychic researchers; great achievements of great writers, great scientists and great philosophers, great men of ideals, and great men in practical fields and miraculous physical fits of physical culturists. They do have more or less inner life.

8. TRUE MENTAL, VITAL AND PHYSICAL BEINGS ARE STATIONED IN ITS INMOST PART

Through the true mental, vital and physical being one can even know and respond to the Divine directly, when he descends in response of his call. Same is the case with the knowledge of oneself. When one is in the surface consciousness one only knows vaguely and partially, and that too in a constructed figure, of his whole intermixed and conflicting complex unit of the mental, the vital and the physical. The mind cannot disentangle and separately know the three cords of the being, cannot know why they are discordant, and cannot know why there are conflicting elements, ideas, desires, etc. in them; why on surface there is so much of struggle and confusion. The mind can barely and rarely control them effectively, because mind is bogged and dogged down by the vital and the body.

But when a man goes in and gets established in the true mental, vital and physical, he can see his mind, vital and physical as distinct and separate levels, he can see that all sorts of conflicting forces, movements and personalities enter from his inner consciousness as well as from the universal consciousness, and they get mixed up here and so there is war among members and the internal war in each member. The true inner being — the true mental, the true vital and the true physical — answers to the central being, the Jivatma, above; while the whole triple consciousness, especially the outer, does not. In the true vital is an instrumental force for all divine realisations. Ultimately, one can go inside, station himself there in the true inner being with ego absolved.

But in effect, so far ignorance lasts, a man can live in one of these inner beings, and that one becomes his sole inner being with the result that, that part of his nature, gets pre-eminence over the whole triple nature. In any case, it observes the whole triple nature with calm and detachment. Then one has double existence, existence calm, strong and responding to the Divine behind and an obscure existence on the surface. Man's self, being, is liberated from the triple nature. Now, he can gradually increase his receptivity to receive higher forces in a large measure. The outer and the inner consciousness fuse and he has a wide consciousness and nature acting in his life.

At the most, and at its best, that is when the mind is predominating, one can have an outer consciousness or nature that acts very powerfully with a broad scope, a calm mind which has clear and wide vision and peaceful and strong will, a vital very strong, dynamic and in the service of the divine, and a body like a fortress and extremely supple and efficient and all the three responding to the Divine. Such a preliminary or precursory perfection is imperative for a complete psychic spiritual realisation. But as these inner mental, vital and physical beings have also discordant tendencies, they are subject to dualities and disharmony.

9. HIGHER PERFECTION

For perfect harmony and purity in the outer consciousness, the inner being has to look for help to the psychic that is behind it. One thing becomes clear here that the inner consciousness is the link between the inmost psychic and the outer consciousness and also a link between the higher and the lower outer.

II. THE ENVIRONMENTAL OR CIRCUMCONSCIENT CONSCIOUSNESS[161]

The subliminal consciousness of a man has a formation which projects beyond his inner sheaths and is around his gross physical body. It is called the circumconscient or environmental consciousness.

Man may not be aware of it, but by it he is in touch with others and with the universal forces. It is through this that thoughts, feelings, etc. of others and waves of all sorts of the universal forces — desire, sex, etc. — come in and take possession of the mind, vital, and body. Thus, it is full of mobility: it is a field of vibrations or a passage of forces. If someone is conscious of it, he detects the forces and can voluntarily allow or prevent the incoming forces according to his/her choice. Anything thrown out of our consciousness, if it does not go out for good, lingers in the environmental consciousness to get its chance to return. The environmental consciousness can gradually widen more and more and become more and more silent. It can go on widening and a stage comes when it becomes one with the universal consciousness. Then, a man feels a great liberation; he becomes a universal man.

A man without it would be a man insulated from the world.

---

[161] CWM, Vol. 9, pp. 345-46, 541; SABCL, Vol. 16, p. 541; SABCL, Vol. 22, p. 541 and SABCL Vol. 19, p. 960

Suggestions for Further Reading

1. SABCL Vol. 22; pp. 307-313

WORKBOOK: QUESTIONS FOR PREVIEW AND REVIEW

Essay Type Questions

1. Describe the nature of subliminal or inner consciousness.
2. Describe the nature of the true mental, vital and physical.

Short Answer Type Questions

1. What is the relation of subliminal consciousness with the outer consciousness?
2. What is the inmost physical consciousness called?
3. What separates the inner consciousness from the universal consciousness?
4. What kind of senses the subtle physical has?
5. What houses the inner mind?
6. What houses the inner vital?
7. What houses the inner physical?
8. How can one protect oneself from illness?
9. Describe the inner perfection.
10. Write a note on the environmental consciousness or the circumconscient.

SELF TEST

1. Subliminal is _____ the outer consciousness. (Below or Behind)
2. The true mental is the _____ part of the mind. (the innermost or the outermost)

3. The subliminal consciousness receives forces from _____, _____ and _____.
4. _____ houses the mind.
5. _____ houses the vital.
6. _____ houses the physical.
7. The mental body is window to the universal _____.
8. The vital body is window to the universal _____.
9. The subtle body is window to the universal _____.
10. The vital body protects the gross body from _____, _____ and _____.
11. The inner consciousness is smaller than the outer consciousness. (True or False)
12. When can one read other's thoughts?
13. Where is the true physical stationed?
14. When can one see that his vital, mental and physical are distinctly separate from each other?
15. Environmental consciousness is part of the _____.
16. What will happen if one is without the environmental consciousness?

CHAPTER X

THE PSYCHIC BEING AND CONSCIOUSNESS[162]

I. THE SOUL, THE PSYCHIC SPARK (CHAITYA SPHULLING)

II. THE PSYCHIC BEING (CHAITYA PURUSH, ANTARATMA)

III. THE JIVATMA (ADHYATMA)

IV. THE JIVATMA, SPARK SOUL AND PSYCHIC BEING

I. THE SOUL, THE PSYCHIC SPARK
(CHAITYA SPHULLING)

(i) The soul is a "spark-emanation" of the Divine, involved in nature and an evolving divine.

(ii) The soul is not above the manifested being but into the manifestation and yet not subject to it. It is not outside of the human consciousness, but it is inside seated in the heart centre as a divine love, light and bliss, *(See Figure 5.1 in Chapter V).*

(iii) It is man's immortal part, for it is an emanation of the divine. It is always connected with the divine.

(iv) It develops a psychic personality (or consciousness or being) around itself; it develops, broadly speaking, triple states of psychic being or consciousness or personality. For example, the soul puts out psychic physical being, psychic vital being and psychic mental

---

[162] SABCL, Vol. 22, pp. 276, 285, 295-297, 298-99; SABCL, Vol. 24, p. 1093 and CWM, Vol. 3, p. 7

being in increasing order of density. Explaining the difference between the soul and the psychic being, The Mother replied to a sadhak in the letter dated January 2, 1967, "The soul is the eternal essence at the centre of the psychic being. The soul is like a divine spark which puts out many states of being of increasing density." The reply with question is quoted below:

> "Question: In the human being, is the psychic being the entire soul or do both the soul (in its essence as a divine spark in all creatures) and the psychic being exist together?
>
> The Mother's Answer: The soul is the eternal essence at the centre of the psychic being. The soul is in fact like a divine spark which puts on many states of being of increasing density, down to the most material; it is inside the body, within the solar plexus, so to say. These states of being take form and develop, progress, become individualised and perfected in the course of many earthly lives and form the psychic being. When the psychic being is fully formed, it is aware of the consciousness of the soul and manifests it perfectly. (*1 February 1967*)"[163]

(v) The knowledge and force in it are involved and come out only as it develops its psychic consciousness and being, the psychic personality, around itself.

II. THE PSYCHIC BEING (CHAITYA PURUSH, ANTARATMA)

(i) Definition: The psychic being is psychic personality formed by the soul in its evolution, and can be called Chaitya Purush also. The psychic is behind the inner consciousness in the heart centre (See *Figure*

---

[163] CWM Vol. 16; p. 358

14.1: Physiological Topography of the Planes and Parts of Consciousness of Human Being in Chapter XIV).

(ii) Soul, the spark emanation of the Divine, the Psychic spark evolves a growing psychic personality around itself due to experiences in life birth after birth; its wisdom and strength also grows during lives on the Earth.

(iii) The soul with its psychic personality enters into the body at birth and goes out of it at death.

(iv) It supports and uses as its expression the mind, the vital and the physical, grows by their experiences and carries man's triple lower nature from life to life. At first it is veiled by the mind, vital and physical, and it has to depend on them for its expression and cannot use them freely. The man is human and not divine then. But when it comes forward, becomes dominant and freely uses its instruments, then the impulse towards the Divine is complete and the change of the mind, the vital and the body becomes possible. The man starts becoming divine. So, its awakening and its rule over nature is absolutely indispensable for the transformation of the individual and his life and that of the collectivity.

(v) One's psychic can feel affinity, harmony and sympathy and oneness with others, but not union with them.

(vi) The Psychic Being has a power to realise the true mind, the true vital and the true physical.

(vii) The soul, being the spark of the divine, receives help and guidance from the Divine directly.

(viii) Through its psychic elements it acts and imparts its qualities to, and finally psychicises, the triple cord of the being. It opens the lower consciousness to the higher spiritual consciousness above for its descent into a nature prepared to receive it with a complete receptivity and right attitude. For the psychic brings in right thought, right perception, right feeling, and right attitude.

(ix) It can establish unity and homogeneity in the triple being. In other words, it purifies and harmonises our three cords of instrumental being, and tunes it to the celestial musical play, and makes it safely ready for spiritual transmutation or ascension. It is not possible for the inner being to do so. One can rise directly to the spiritual height but that is dangerous, so it is safe and better to go on travelling on the spiritual mountain with the psychic as the guide. The process of psychic purification of triple nature is called Psychicisation.

(x) The evolution of the individual is carried by the central being (the soul and the psychic being, Antaratma) and not by the spirit (the Jivatma-the Adhyatma).

III. THE JIVATMA (ADHYATMA)

The Jivatma is also emanation of the divine. But it does not enter into the birth. It just impartially sits above the human consciousness. The Jivatma is the divine above nature and does not evolve. When the psychic, after growing and rising from below, meets it, man gets a new birth in the Divine.

IV. THE JIVATMA, SPARK SOUL AND PSYCHIC BEING

They are three different forms of the same reality, the multiple Divine. The Jivatma and the soul are two aspects of the same reality, the multiple Divine.

SUMMARY

I.-II. The soul is the eternal essence at the centre of the psychic being. The soul is in fact like a divine spark which puts on many states of being of increasing density down to the most material; the psychic being is psychic personality formed by the soul in its evolution and can be called Chaitya Purush. It enters into body at the time of birth and goes out at the time of death. It develops as it gathers experiences through outer being in life. It can purify and transform the mind, vital and physical. It can establish harmony in the personality and end the internecine war and the war between members. It carries out evolution of a person.

III. The Jivatma is also emanation of the divine. But it does not enter into the birth. It just impartially sits above the human consciousness.

IV. The Jivatma, Spark Soul and Psychic Being are three different forms of the same reality, the multiple Divine. The Jivatma and the soul are two aspects of the same reality, the multiple Divine.

Suggestions for Further Reading

1. Indra Sen, Integral Psychology (Sri Aurobindo International Centre of Education, Pondicherry, 605 002, India; 1986); pp. 9-29

2. Tulsidas Chatterjee, *Sri Aurobindo's Integral Yoga* (Pondicherry: SABDA, Sri Aurobindo Ashram; 1970), pp. 57-83

3. The Mother (Author) & Georges Van Vrekhem (Editor); The Mother's Vision (Publisher: Sri Aurobindo Ashram, Pondicherry, 605002, India; 2005); pp. 81-190, 551-594, 353-384, 431-541: (Ch.3: The Human Species in Evolution, Ch. 4: Plants and Animals, Ch. 5: The Gradations of Existence and Their Expression in the Human Being, Ch. 6: The Psychic Being or Soul, Ch. 14: Day-to-Day Life, Ch. 17: Yoga and Meditation, Ch. 18: The Integral Yoga, Ch.19: The Supramental)

WORKBOOK: QUESTIONS FOR PREVIEW AND REVIEW

Essay Type Questions

1. Describe the psychic consciousness.

Short Answer Type Questions

1. What is the function of the psychic?
2. State relation between soul and psychic.
3. When does psychic enter the body and leave it?
4. How the psychic being grows?
5. Which parts of personality it can transform?
6. Who carries out evolution of an individual?
7. Who can establish harmony in the personality?
8. Is it emanation of the Divine?
9. Compare Jivatma and the psychic being.
10. What is relation of the psychic being with the soul?

SELF TEST

1. Soul and Psychic being are same. (True or False)
2. Soul enters the body at the time of _____.
3. Soul leaves the body at the time of _____.
4. _____ carries out the evolution of the man.
5. State the difference between the psychic and the Jivatma.
6. _____ uses the mind, vital and physical.
7. _____ purifies the personality. (Psychic or Jivatma)
8. If man realises the _____, he starts becoming the Divine.

CHAPTER XI

THE SPIRITUAL CONSCIOUSNESS[164]

I. THE SPIRITUAL CONSCIOUSNESS

II. THE PLANES AND PARTS OF THE SPIRITUAL
CONSCIOUSNESS

III. WHAT IS SPIRITUALISATION?

I. THE SPIRITUAL CONSCIOUSNESS

The process of Psychicisation opens lower triple nature to the higher spiritual consciousness, wherein is stationed the Jivatma *(See Figure 5.1 in Chapter V)*. One gets a new birth in the spiritual consciousness and starts his spiritual growth under the presidentship of the Jivatma and the Prime-ministership of the psychic.

The spiritual domain is a part of our mind, but superconscient to it. It is universal consciousness capable of identifying itself with only the static aspect of the transcendental consciousness but not with its dynamic side.

---

[164] SABCL, Vol. 22, pp. 200, 250, 257, 264-65, 277, 302, 324-25, 331; SABCL Vol. 9, pp. 199-390, 517-61; SABCL, Vol. 26, pp. 221-350; SABCL, Vol. 29, pp. 743-44, 759, 802-16; SABCL, Vol. 19, pp. 939-63; and SABCL, Vol. 23, pp. 1054, 1082, 1084, 1085

II. THE PLANES AND PARTS OF THE
SPIRITUAL CONSCIOUSNESS

The spiritual consciousness consists of the Jivatma and the four mind planes:

1. THE HIGHER MIND

It is above the normal mental consciousness or the mind of reason. It is a luminous thought mind and is full of vast peace. Describing the thought of higher mind Sri Aurobindo writes,

> "We are aware of a sea like downpour of masses of a spontaneous knowledge which assumes the nature of Thought but has a different character from the process of thought to which we are accustomed; for there is nothing here of seeking, no trace of mental construction, no labour of speculation or difficult discovery; it is an automatic and spontaneous knowledge from a Higher Mind that seems to be in possession of Truth and not in search of hidden and withheld realities. One observes that this Thought is much more capable than the mind of including at once a mass of knowledge in a single view; it has a cosmic character, not the stamp of an individual thinking."[165]

2. THE ILLUMINED MIND

It is a mind of the truth sight full of light. What is thought-knowledge in the higher mind becomes illumination in the Illumined Mind. Explaining the illumined nature of illumined thought, Sri Aurobindo says,

> "Beyond this Truth-Thought we can distinguish a greater illumination instinct with an increased power and intensity and driving force, a luminosity of the nature of Truth-

---

[165] SABCL Vol. 18; p. 277

Sight with thought formulation as a minor and dependent activity. If we accept the Vedic image of the Sun of Truth, — an image which in this experience becomes a reality, — we may compare the action of the Higher Mind to a composed and steady sunshine, the energy of the Illumined Mind beyond it to an outpouring of massive lightnings of flaming sun-stuff."[166]

3. THE INTUITIVE MIND

It sees the truth of things by direct inner contact. What is thought-knowledge in the higher mind becomes illumination in the Illumined Mind and direct intimate vision in the Intuition.[167] Regarding this intuitive mind Sri Aurobindo writes,

"Still beyond can be met a yet greater power of the Truth-Force, an intimate and exact Truth-vision, Truth-thought, Truth-sense, Truth-feeling, Truth action, to which we can give in a special sense the name of Intuition; for though we have applied that word for want of a better to any supra-intellectual direct way of knowing, yet what we actually know as intuition is only one special movement of self-existent knowledge. This new range is its origin; it imparts to our intuitions something of its own distinct character and is very clearly an intermediary of a greater Truth-Light with which our mind cannot directly communicate."[168]

4. THE OVERMIND

It is the power of the global knowledge. Sri Aurobindo says,

"At the source of this Intuition we discover a superconscient cosmic Mind in direct contact with the Supramental Truth-Consciousness, an original intensity

---

[166] SABCL Vol. 18; p. 277
[167] SABCL Vol.24; p. 1154
[168] SABCL Vol. 18; 277-278

determinant of all movements below it and all mental energies, — not Mind as we know it, but an Overmind that covers as with the wide wings of some creative Oversoul this whole lower hemisphere of Knowledge-Ignorance, links it with that greater Truth-Consciousness while yet at the same time with its brilliant golden Lid it veils the face of the greater Truth from our sight, intervening with its flood of infinite possibilities as at once an obstacle and a passage in our seeking of the spiritual law of our existence, its highest aim, its secret Reality. This then is the occult link we were looking for; this is the Power that at once connects and divides the supreme Knowledge and cosmic Ignorance."[169]

One can realise the cosmic divine and consciousness when he attains to overmind. Overmind is the golden lid mentioned in the Upanishad. The spiritual domain is still subject to ignorance so it belongs to man's Aparārdha. All genuinely inspired writings, especially poetry, comes from this region. The spiritualisation starts when one ascends to this domain and the spiritual starts coming down into the lower triple being.

III. WHAT IS SPIRITUALISATION?

Spiritualisation means descent of peace, light, knowledge, purity, Anand, etc. from any of the higher planes into the lower members. It establishes the awareness of the self and the Divine and of the higher cosmic consciousness and the change of the whole consciousness to that.

It will be interesting to note the special change that occurs in the physical mind and the physical body. When the physical mind opens to higher consciousness, its limitations are removed and it admits what

[169] SABCL Vol. 18; p. 278

is supraphysical and starts seeing worldly things in harmony with higher knowledge. It becomes an instrument for externalising that knowledge in the pragmatic perceptions and actions of the physical life. It uses things as they are and deals with them according to the larger truth with an automatic rightness of perception and will and reaction to impacts. The higher consciousness brings light, consciousness, force and anand into the cells and all the body's movements. The body becomes conscious and vigilant and performs right movements, as now it obeys the higher will and is automatically guided by the higher consciousness that has come into it. It becomes easier to control its functions and set right anything wrong or illness. One can have more control over happenings to it from outside; for example, one can minimise accidents and small mishaps. The body becomes a more effective instrument. Fatigue can be minimized. Peace, happiness, strength, lightness settle in the whole physical system.

Spiritualisation brings about a subjective change only; the instrumental nature is only so far changed that it becomes instrument for the cosmic Divine — the universal Mother, the cosmic maya — to get some work done. So the spiritualised mind can realise the Sachchidananda fully in its static aspect only and not in its dynamic aspect because of this instrumental imperfection. The Jivatma does not mind the imperfection, as it is quiet, free and united with the Divine. The old yogas used to lead into static One, and the abandonment of the world. The full transformation of the instrumental nature can come only when the supramental change takes place.

Until now the earth life was under the overmind's rule. But on Feb. 29, 1956, the Mother broke the golden lid, brought down and made effective the supramental consciousness into the earth life; now it is man's highest secret guide and controller.

SUMMARY

I. The spiritual domain is a part of our mind, but superconscient to it. It is universal consciousness capable of identifying itself with only the static aspect of the transcendental consciousness but not with its dynamic side.

II. It consists of Jivatma and four mind-planes: the higher mind, the illumined mind, the intuitive mind and the overmind.

III. Spiritualisation means descent of peace, light, knowledge, purity, Anand, etc. from any of the higher planes into the lower members. It establishes the awareness of the self and the Divine and of the higher cosmic consciousness and the change of the whole consciousness to that.

Suggestions for Further Reading

1. Indra Sen, Integral Psychology (Sri Aurobindo International Centre of Education, Pondicherry, 605 002, India; 1986); pp. 9-29

2. Tulsidas Chatterjee, *Sri Aurobindo's Integral Yoga* (Pondicherry: SABDA, Sri Aurobindo Ashram; 1970), pp. 57-83

3. The Mother (Author) & Georges Van Vrekhem (Editor); The Mother's Vision (Publisher: Sri Aurobindo Ashram, Pondicherry, 605002, India; 2005); pp. 81-190, 551-594, 353-384, 431-541: (Ch.3: The Human Species in Evolution, Ch. 4: Plants and Animals, Ch. 5: The Gradations of Existence and Their Expression in the Human Being, Ch. 6: The Psychic Being or Soul, Ch. 14: Day-to-Day Life, Ch. 17 Yoga and Meditation, Ch. 18: The Integral Yoga, Ch.19: The Supramental)

WORKBOOK: QUESTIONS FOR PREVIEW AND REVIEW

Essay Type Questions

1. Describe the spiritual consciousness.
2. What is spiritualisation?

Short Answer Type Questions

1. What does the process of Psychicisation open?
2. The spiritual domain is _____ to mind and is _____ .
3. The spiritual consciousness consists of _____ and four _____.
4. _____, _____, _____ and _____ are four parts of the spiritual consciousness.
5. Describe thought in the higher mind.
6. In the _____ mind, thoughts are illumined thoughts.
7. In which mind direct knowledge is possible?
8. Overmind is called the _____ mind also.
9. Define spiritualisation.
10. Describe spiritualisation of the body.
11. Spiritualisation brings _____ change. (objective or subjective)
12. Does Jivatma mind imperfection?

Exercises

1. Make a table showing the hierarchy of mind from sensational mind to overmind in ascending order.

SELF TEST

1. The spiritual consciousness consists of _____ and _____ .
2. List four mind-parts of the spiritual consciousness.
3. Spiritualisation makes _____ changes in the being. (objective or subjective)
4. List changes in the body due to its spiritualisation.

CHAPTER XII

THE SUPRAMENTAL CONSCIOUSNESS

I. THE SUPRAMENTAL CONSCIOUSNESS

II. THE PLANES AND PARTS OF THE SUPRAMENTAL

III. SUPRAMENTAL WILL TRANSFORM THE PRESENT MAN

IV. THE SUPRAMENTAL NATURE

V. THE SUPRAMENTAL FIRST ESTABLISHES ITSELF IN AN INDIVIDUAL

Picture:
(12.1) The Mother in Her Chair
(12.2) The Mother Playing Piano

I. THE SUPRAMENTAL CONSCIOUSNESS[170]

The supermind is above the overmind *(See Table 4.1 in Chapter IV, Figure 5.1 in chapter V)* and is entirely a different consciousness from the spiritual consciousness. Thus it belongs to man's Parārdha.

It is the Sachchidanand's power of self-awareness and world awareness, the world being known as within itself and not outside. It is

---

[170] SABCL Vol. 16, pp. 36-42, 47, 67; SABCL Vol. 17, p. 26; SABCL, Vol. 21, pp. 768, 781-94, 841; SABCL Vol. 18, pp. 250-51; SABCL Vol. 19, pp. 821-23; SABCL Vol. 22, pp. 34-35; SABCL Vol. 24, pp. 1229-39; CWM Vol. 3, pp. 175-76, 242; CWM Vol. 10, pp. 114-20, 188-95

in its very essence a truth consciousness, a consciousness always free from the ignorance which is the foundation of man's present natural or evolutionary existence and from which nature in man is trying to arrive at self-knowledge and world-knowledge and a right consciousness and right use of his existence in the universe. The supermind, because it is the truth consciousness, has this knowledge inherent in it and this power of true existence. Its course is straight, and goes direct to its aim. It has not to acquire knowledge but it is in possession of knowledge, its knowledge is knowledge by identity. It not only possesses divine omniscience but omnipotence also; knowledge is inherent with effective will and power to realise itself. So, it does not fumble in its handling of things or fumble in its paces. This being its nature, it can change the mind, the vital and the body into divine mould and means of expression of the divine nature, which overmind cannot do. So, this will enable man to possess the Divine in its static as well as in its dynamic aspect. Here only the Mother — the Divine — can be known in her (His) own swarupa.

II. THE PLANES AND PARTS OF THE SUPRAMENTAL

1. The interpretative supermind,
2. The representative supermind,
3. The imperative supermind and
4. The mind of light are supermind's four layers from above downward.

III. SUPRAMENTAL WILL TRANSFORM THE PRESENT MAN

The supermind will transform the present man quite radically and create on earth a transitional species, a race of superman. The superman will have the mind of light as his highest instrument, but still in its external form it will belong to the human being with its animal origin. The Mother had realised this status, as soon as Sri Aurobindo withdrew from the earthly scene in 1950 A.D. The True supramental race will manifest upon the earth later on. Sri Aurobindo and the Mother have written extensively on the nature of the supramental man and society. As it is beyond the scope of the present work, it is not being described here.

IV. THE SUPRAMENTAL NATURE

Showing difference between mind and supermind,
Sri Aurobindo writes,

"Mental nature and mental thought are based on a consciousness of the finite; supramental nature is in its very grain a consciousness and power of the Infinite. Supramental Nature sees everything from the standpoint of oneness and regards all things, even the greatest multiplicity and diversity, even what are to the mind the strongest contradictions, in the light of that oneness; its will, ideas, feelings, sense are made of the stuff of oneness, its actions proceed upon that basis. Mental Nature, on the contrary, thinks, sees, wills, feels, senses with division as a starting-point and has only a constructed understanding of unity; even when it experiences oneness, it has to act from the oneness on a basis of limitation and difference. But the supramental, the divine life is a life of essential, spontaneous and inherent unity. It is impossible for the mind to forecast in detail what the supramental change must be in its parts of life action and outward behaviour or lay down for it what forms it shall create for the individual or the collective existence. For the mind acts by intellectual rule or device or by reasoned choice of will or by mental impulse or in obedience to life impulse; but supramental nature does not act by mental idea or rule or in subjection to any inferior impulse: each of its steps is dictated by an innate spiritual vision, a comprehensive and exact penetration into the truth of all and the truth of each thing; it acts always according to inherent reality, not by the mental idea, not according to an imposed law of conduct or a constructive thought or perceptive contrivance. Its movement is calm, self-possessed, spontaneous, plastic; it arises naturally and inevitably out of a harmonic identity of the truth which is felt in the very substance of the conscious being, a spiritual substance which is universal and therefore intimately one with all that is included in its cognition of existence. A mental description of supramental nature could only express itself either in phrases which are too abstract or in mental figures which might turn it into something quite different from its reality. It would not seem to be possible, therefore, for the mind to anticipate or indicate what a supramental being shall be or how he shall act; for here mental ideas and formulations cannot decide anything or arrive at any precise definition or determination, because they are not near enough to the law and self-vision of supramental Nature. At the same time certain deductions can be made from the very fact of this difference of nature which might be valid at least for a general description of the passage from Overmind to Supermind or might vaguely construct for us an idea of the first status of the evolutionary supramental existence"[171]

So, while mind sees divisions and constructs unity among them, the supramental sees unity and divisions as integral part of unity.

---

[171] SABCL Vol. 19; pp. 965-966

V. THE SUPRAMENTAL ESTABLISHES ITSELF FIRST IN THE INDIVIDUAL

Sri Aurobindo clarifies,

"It is first through the individuals that it [the supramental consciousness] becomes part of the earth-consciousness and afterwards it spreads from the first centre and takes up more and more of the global consciousness till it becomes an established force there."[172]

It has first established itself in Sri Aurobindo and the Mother, the supramental Avatar of the supramental evolution. Below are quoted a couple of illustrations of this fact:

SUPRAMENTAL IN SRI AUROBINDO AND THE MOTHER

1. AMIDHAR'S EXPERIENCE

Here, author would like to note the supramental force of Sri Aurobindo and The Mother experienced by Amidhar Bhatt, an accomplished Tantric. When he was 14 somebody presented him with a copy of the Patanjali Yoga Sutra. By the study and practice of this book, Swami Vivekananda's Rajayoga, Hathayoga Pradipika, Gherand Sanhita and Kundalini yoga, he attained many siddhis by the age of 17. He continued to be with different Gurus and to practice different sadhanas. He had attained Trikal Drishti (knowledge of past, present and future) due to the combined practice of Aghor Sadhana and a Buddhist discipline called Anapan Satti and had experienced the descent of palpable silence. He had experience of Sad Brahmana, which Sri

---

[172] SABCL Vol. 22; p. 15

Aurobindo identified to be an experience of Sad Brahman on the Mental Plane.[173] Below is quoted his story in his own words:

> "...Experimenting with different Sadhanas, I stumbled upon Sri Aurobindo's Bases of Yoga. It indicated to me that individual mind and vital are fragments of universal Mind and Vital which has a constant existence and which gave inherent permanence to individual mind and vital, but that was all.

> "Then, when I was 17 or 18, The Life Divine entered my life. It exploded all previous concepts. ... if Sri Aurobindo was right only the Supreme Supermind which could solve the problems of Life and could resolve the riddles of all the systems of sadhana. But then were the great ancient yogis ... misguided? ... Were the realisation of Raman Maharshi, Ramdas, Narayan Swami, etc. incomplete?

> "Something was wrong somewhere. There was the heavy weight of the past Shastras and sadhanas against what Sri Aurobindo propounded. And it was on these grounds and against the background of personal experiences that I wrote to Sri Aurobindo challenging him to prove himself not in the verbal theory of The Life Divine but by showing experience his Supermind as a realised fact, which he himself had not been able to do to all appearance. And it was on this point that Sri Aurobindo invited me to visit the Ashram and to find for myself whether I, with my Shastras and great practices and experiences was right or whether his unrealised but realisable Supramental Transformation was the ultimate solution."[174]

***

---

[173] Shyam Kumari; "*Amidhar's Story Part I*"; in Collaboration Vol. 38, No. 3; Winter / Spring 2014 (Publisher: Sri Aurobindo Association, 2715 West Kettleman Lane, Ste. 203-174, Lodi CA, 95242, USA); pp. 11-14

[174] Ibid; p. 14

"Bal Krishna Shukla who had given me the book *Bases of Yoga* had told me that during the Darshan nobody could stay in front of Sri Aurobindo for more than a few seconds and that the longest anybody had stayed was 15 seconds. Brimming with self-confidence, I decided to establish a new record. I did not believe in the light of Sri Aurobindo. "Will he give me the experience of Chit-Tapas and Ananda?" I doubted it very much but thought that unexpected things did happen. There was no harm in trying. When I stood before the Lord and The Mother I could not look at Sri Aurobindo and the Mother. Then, fleetingly I looked into the luminous eyes of the Lord and saw two solid indescribable beams of light of Consciousness Force in many colours come out of them. They hit me, even physically, with such a force that my body became hot and within four seconds, against my own will my legs ran out. Nonplussed and crestfallen I was unable to understand how, even if Sri Aurobindo had achieved Sachchidananda, could his gaze affect my body. After all I had done Hatha Yoga and had achieved control over my body. Now I realised that Sri Aurobindo's Force could act as a physical force does. It was a blow to my ego and against Vedantic explanations.

"The next day when I went for offering Pranam to the Mother I was in a chastened frame of mind. People had to take prior permission to speak with the Mother during the Pranam. But I spoke without permission, "Mother, what should be done about my future in sadhana? My difficulty is that I cannot find my psychic being in my heart, so there is no question of bringing it forth to give it charge of my sadhana." Actually, even though I had talked about my psychic being I wanted the Mother to help me realize the Chit-Tapas Force.

"She always responded to the hidden aspiration behind the words of people. She gracefully nodded and smiled. She save me a Champa flower which she has named "Psychological Perfection" and then said, "You are on the right path. You have done what you could and the rest you should leave to the Divine." I asked when I would get the total solution or a premonition about the solution, because at that time I was feeling as if I was facing an impenetrable wall. The Mother replied, "Whatever you want you will realise within six months." ... She acted so powerfully that I had the realisation within 24 hours.

***

"During my travels in the Himalayas, thousands of miles away from Pondicherry I had the realization of the all-pervading infinite and the existence of a divine element everywhere. And there, amongst the snow-clad peaks at last I found my sheet anchor, a firm faith in the Divinity. Also I realized that Pondicherry was the best place for sadhana. The elements that stood in the way of an integral faith, my self-regarding ego and the sense of my own importance vanished, to be replaced by humility and love for the Twin Avatars of Pondicherry.

"In 1947 I again came to the Ashram for the August Darshan. This time I went to the Mother for Pranam with full humility and with a prayer that this time for me the Darshan might be as Sri Aurobindo would want it to be. I tried my best to open myself to receive from the Mother the power to retain the Darshan riches. On the Darshan day I advanced slowly towards Sri Aurobindo. This time I was determined to set a new record by standing in front of Sri Aurobindo for more than 15 seconds. "After all, I have done Vedantin sadhana. I must prove myself", I thought with a 25 -year-old youth's confidence.

"As I advanced towards Sri Aurobindo I saw on the Darshan couch instead of Sri Aurobindo, the Godhead of Gurla Mandhata in all its effulgence. The Lord's eyes encompassed and radiated Sat-Chit light and this effulgent laughter-filled mass of light was like the red pollen in the heart of a beautiful bud of roseate golden hue. From this roseate light a vibration of soft love spread out and touched me. This touch was so sweet that I felt a sort of sensation, till then unknown to my dry Vedantin heart. For the first time a movement of Love touched my heart. I had some feeling that two people, one of them probably Nirodbaran, gestured me to move away but I ignored them. I stood there for one or one and a half minutes still holding in my hands the lotus flowers and garlands I had brought for offering. Two minutes passed. Then Sri Aurobindo shut his eyes. The whole scene of Gurla Mandhata vanished, but still I stood firmly and thought, "When the Lord will open his eyes I will see him again".

"Meanwhile to save each precious second, I hurriedly put the lotus flowers and garlands in the box kept there for this purpose. Sri Aurobindo again opened his eyes and this time I saw him as the Nara-Singha Avatar, effulgent with a golden mane. Since I had practised Tratak for years I gazed at the Lord and saw his beautiful hands, and also noticed the curtain behind the couch. Sri Aurobindo kept looking at me. He neither closed his eyes nor gestured me to move away. But by now the two persons standing guard became thoroughly agitated. The Mother noticed their agitation and she was about to break out into laughter but suppressed the impulse by covering her mouth with her handkerchief for half a second. But her laughter was reflected in her eyes, twinkling with merriment. As my attention was drawn to the Mother I realized that it was not the Darshan of Sri Aurobindo alone but also of the Mother. I bowed to both. Sri Aurobindo lowered his eyelids. Then only after doing Pranam did I move away.

"In 1950 my mother said to me, "You wander all over the country. Take me also on a pilgrimage. All right," I replied. "Let us first go to Pondicherry. From there we will go to other holy places." (Now I could afford to take my mother on a pilgrimage.) We came for August Darshan. I saw Sri Aurobindo and the Mother in their own swaroop but my mother had the Darshan of Shiva and Parvati instead. She told me, "Now that I have seen the living Shiva and Parvati, I have no need to go to Rameshwaram or any other holy place. Let us remain here for some time". So I cancelled all our other pilgrimages. It was an unexpected grace. ... .

***

"In September 1950, after a happy stay in the Ashram, I with my mother boarded a Bombay bound train from Madras. The Razakar movement of Hyderabad was at its height. ... The train suddenly made an unscheduled stop at a small station near Adoni. ... A young Muslim, clad in a black coat, rushed at me with a long dagger ...and occupied my seat . .. and began to abuse me. ... At that time I silently called the Divine Mother for protection and, within my heart, kept repeating her name. Ardent invocation of the Mother's physical presence drew her to our aid. I saw a figure of the Mother appear. She descended into the elderly Muslim sitting there. He looked like a priest or Fakir. Immediately this venerable man began to speak with authority. He told the rowdies to stop abusing me since I had given up my seat and offering no opposition to them. After this the miscreants fell silent.

***

"...I reached Pondicherry on December 9, 1950, a few hours after the Lord's body was laid in the Samadhi. As I bowed at the Samadhi a hand stretched out from the Samadhi and rested on my head. I heard the words, "So, after all, you have arrived, my son!"

***

"The Mother usually appeared on the Balcony between 6 and 6:30 AM.... As she approached the Balcony, the Mother first looked towards the sky. Later she revealed that at first she looked at the gods assembled for her Darshan.

***

"Between 1961 and 1965 ... I had the conscious experience of the vital words described in Book II of Savitri.

***

"Another span of my service required that I do hazardous jobs. There had been at least ten attempts to kill me by violence or poison. Each time the Mother warned me."[175]

Amidhar's story tells us about the supramental powers of Sri Aurobindo and The Mother. Integral yogi of Auroville, Late Georges Van Vrekhem describes beautifully and lucidly The Mother's efforts to transform her body in the following words:

2. THE MOTHER'S ATTEMPT TO SUPRAMENTALISE HER BODY

"After the manifestation of the Supramental Consciousness and the realisation of the intermediary being between man and superman, the Mother embarked on the ultimate phase of her Yoga: the transformation of her physical body. In the past, great yogis have transformed their mental consciousness and even their vital being, but nobody has ever wanted to transform his physical body into the body of a new species. The repercussion of her efforts was immediate and caused serious corporeal trouble. Towards the end of 1959, she

---

[175] Shyam Kumari; "Amidhar's Story Part 2"; in Collaboration Vol. 38, No. 3; Winter/Spring 2014 (Publisher: Sri Aurobindo Association, 2715 West Kettleman Lane, Ste. 203-174, Lodi CA, 95242, USA); pp. 10-19

gradually withdrew to the second floor of the central Ashram building, which she but rarely left anymore.

"What would a supramental body be like? It would resemble what humanity has always dreamed of. It would be light, supple, adaptable, immune to illness and death. People have always dreamed of flying, of knowing what is going on in other places, of being able to lift the heaviest objects, of going to other places in an instant, of being in several places at the same time. They have dreamed of a state in which hunger, illness, infirmity and death would no longer make their life into hell. For the supramental being, these dreams would be reality.

"How to change an ordinary human body into a supramental one? The Mother did not know. The Integral Yoga was absolutely new from the very beginning. It had always been an adventure into the unknown, "hewing a path into a virgin forest", as Sri Aurobindo and the Mother had so often said. But she had accepted to do the job. Her main yogic tool was the basic attitude of the Integral Yoga: surrender to the Divine, the real Master of the Yoga and Guide on the path. Ce que Tu veux, what Thou willest, were the words that cropped up in her conversations time and again, and if she did not pronounce them aloud, she raised both hands with the palms upwards in a gesture of surrender.

"Little by little a new body was forming within her physical body. She sometimes had glimpses of it. This means that she was now living in two bodies at the same time, however bizarre this may seem. Two different bodies meant two different worlds, our visible world and a "subtle" one. This was difficult and dangerous, for in the beginning she had not yet found out how to change from the one to the other, and it happened, in between both worlds, that she suddenly fainted. Besides, organ after organ, or several organs simultaneously, had to be transformed. Because of the transformation process, they did not function normally, and the people around her, the doctors in the first place, thought that she was ill, seriously ill. She had to state so often that her "symptoms" were not a matter of illness but of the yogic transformation of her body.

"In the meantime the outward life continued. She had to receive her secretaries and heads of department, the sadhaks on their birthdays, disciples from the four corners of India and from abroad. She had to receive prominent people from the

Picture 12.1 The Mother in Her Chair

political world, military chiefs, religious leaders, film stars. President V.V. Giri went to see her. So did Indira Gandhi when she was Prime Minister, and the Dalai Lama, and King Mahendra of Nepal.

"In 1968, she founded Auroville, "the City of Dawn". C'est une grande aventure, it is a great adventure. She wrote the charter for this futuristic township which is now known the world over, but which would without her strong protection not be there anymore because of difficulties without number. "Auroville belongs to nobody in particular. Auroville belongs to humanity as a whole ... Auroville will be the place of an unending education, of constant progress, and a youth that never ages. Auroville wants to be the bridge between the past and the future ... Auroville will be a site of spiritual and material researches for a living embodiment of an actual Human Unity." The Mother's Yoga continued with its ups and downs, soaring ever higher, plunging ever deeper into the horrors of the subconscient and the inconscient, of pure Hell. That too had to be transformed. She followed what was going on in the world: May 1968 in France, the first landing on the Moon in 1969, the war with Pakistan and the creation of Bangladesh in 1971. "All the top brass of the HQ Eastern Command, from the Army Commander on down to the other heads of staff and "Arms and Services" like me, all had received the Mother's blessing" (Major General K. K. Tiwari).

"In May 1970, the Mother had already seen her new body, how it would be when externalised — and how she "inwardly" already actually was. Of this, she had the confirmation in March 1972. "For the first time, early in the morning, I saw myself, my [new] body ... Truly a harmonious form ... And I saw that I was like that, I had become like that." Thus she reported her incredible accomplishment in the simplest of words.

"The foundations of the Integral Yoga were laid; the Supramental Consciousness had manifested and had become active on earth; the prototype of the future body had been built. Sri Aurobindo and the Mother's Work was done. The foundations of the New World were ready.

"Towards the end of May 1973, the Mother stopped receiving people. For six more months she continued her Yoga in solitude, assisted by three or four attendants and seeing very few people. What went on in those six months, when she had a supramental body, and when her physical body was steadily "deteriorating" to ordinary human eyes? Nobody knows. She will no doubt have continued working for the world and for humanity with all her Love and Power, as she, the Shakti, had always done.

"The Mother left her physical body on 17 November, 1973. This body now rests together with Sri Aurobindo's in the Samadhi at the central building of Sri Aurobindo Ashram." [176]

---

[176] Georges Van Vrekhem: *The Mother: the Divine Shakti* (Publisher: Rupa & Company, 7/16, Ansari Road, Daryaganj, New Delhi, 110 002, India, 2004); pp. 69-74

Picture 12.2 The Mother Playing Piano

The supramentalised bodies of Sri Aurobindo and The Mother emanate supramental subtle force-waves and those who have consciousness sufficiently subtle and open receive the force and feel change initiated in them. There are hundreds of documented case histories and anecdotes of experiences of integral sadhaks as well as of non-sadhaks that impels us to accept the validity of the foregoing statement. If the rational psychology is to doubt the veracity of this reporting of these experiences, then it will have to disbelieve almost all of its data and findings, for they are all based on introspective reports of some sample of persons. The fact that the potential dynamism of

Samadhi and Auromere's force is inseparable part of the theory and praxis of integral psychology is thus rational.

SUMMARY

The supramental is above the overmental mind and has innate power of self-awareness and world-awareness. It has the Divine's omniscience and omnipotence. It sees unity and sees divisions only as unity's parts. It can divinise human nature. It first establishes itself in an individual and then spreads around in the world. It has established itself in Sri Aurobindo and the Mother.

Suggestions for Further Reading

1. Indra Sen, Integral Psychology (Sri Aurobindo International Centre of Education, Pondicherry, 605 002, India; 1986); pp. 9-29

2. Tulsidas Chatterjee, *Sri Aurobindo's Integral Yoga* (Pondicherry: SABDA, Sri Aurobindo Ashram; 1970), pp. 57-83

3. The Mother (Author) & Georges Van Vrekhem (Editor); The Mother's Vision (Publisher: Sri Aurobindo Ashram, Pondicherry, 605002, India; 2005); pp. 81-190, 551-594, 353-384, 431-541: (Ch.3: The Human Species in Evolution, Ch. 4: Plants and Animals, Ch. 5: The Gradations of Existence and Their Expression in the Human Being, Ch. 6: The Psychic Being or Soul, Ch. 14: Day-to-Day Life, Ch. 17: Yoga and Meditation, Ch. 18: The Integral Yoga, Ch. 19: The Supramental)

WORKBOOK: QUESTIONS FOR PREVIEW AND REVIEW

Essay Type Questions

1. Describe the nature of the supermind.
2. Describe Sri Aurobindo and The Mother as illustration of the supermind.

Short Answer Type Questions

1. The supermind in its very essence is _____ .
2. The supermind can _____ human nature.
3. List four gradations of the supermind.

SELF TEST

1. The supermind is above _____ .
2. The supermind is _____ power of _____ and _____ .
3. The supermind possess the Divine's _____ and _____ .
4. The supramental man will have mind of _____ .
5. _____ sees division and constructs the _____ but _____ sees _____ and sees divisions as part of it.
6. In whom was the supramental established?

CHAPTER XIII

THE SACHCHIDANANDA PLANE[177]

I. THE SACHCHIDANANDA PLANE AND THE
SACHCHIDANANDA

I. THE SACHCHIDANANDA PLANE AND
THE SACHCHIDANANDA

Above the supramental plane are planes of Infinite existence
(Sat), Consciousness and Force (Chit) and Bliss (Anand). Over it the
Mother stands as the eternal Divine power.

All beings there live and move in an ineffable completeness and
unalterable oneness, because she carries them safe in her arms forever.
Beyond this, beyond all manifestation is the Divine, the Supracosmic
Sachchidananda, the Transcendental Mother. There we can have
Anandamaya body.

Sachchidananda is one with a triple aspect. He is above this and
all manifestation, not bound by any, yet from whom all manifestation
proceeds. In its aspect of consciousness and power it is Adya Shakti or
the Divine Mother, the Transcendental Mother. It is through her that
everything is manifested. But she manifests in a different way according
to the plane on which one sees her.

---

[177] SABCL, Vol. 25, pp. 22, 65; SABCL, Vol. 18, p.109; SABCL, Vol. 22, pp. 239, 242

SUMMARY

Above the supramental plane is the Sachchidananda plane and above it is the Sachchidananda. There the Mother stands as the eternal Divine power.

Suggestions for Further Reading

1. Indra Sen, Integral Psychology (Sri Aurobindo International Centre of Education, Pondicherry, 605 002, India; 1986); pp. 9-29

2. Tulsidas Chatterjee, *Sri Aurobindo's Integral Yoga* (Pondicherry: SABDA, Sri Aurobindo Ashram; 1970), pp. 57-83

3. The Mother (Author) & Georges Van Vrekhem (Editor); The Mother's Vision (Publisher: Sri Aurobindo Ashram, Pondicherry, 605002, India; 2005); pp. 81-190, 551-594, 353-384, 431-541: (Ch.3: The Human Species in Evolution, Ch. 4: Plants and Animals, Ch. 5: The Gradations of Existence and Their Expression in the Human Being, Ch. 6: The Psychic Being or Soul, Ch. 14: Day-to-Day Life, Ch. 17: Yoga and Meditation, Ch. 18: The Integral Yoga, Ch. 19: The Supramental)

SELF TEST

1. The Sachchidananda is below the Sachchidananda plane. (True or False)
2. What type of beings live on the Sachchidananda plane?
3. Where does the Mother stand as the eternal divine power?
4. Where can we have Anandamaya body?
5. From where does all manifestation begin?

CHAPTER XIV

OBJECTIVES OF PERSONALITY DEVELOPMENT

I. GENERAL OBJECTIVES OF OVERALL PERSONALITY DEVELOPMENT

    1. Study and Education are Two Different Processes

    2. The Cardinal Aim: Individual's Evolution

    3. The Individualistic, Socialistic and Universal Aim

    4. The Aim of Nationalism and Internationalism

    5. The Attitude of Continuous Lifelong Learning

II. OBJECTIVES OF THE DEVELOPMENT OF SPECIFIC PARTS OF HUMAN CONSCIOUSNESS

    1. Aims of Physical Development

    2. Aims of Vital Development

    3. Aims of Mental Development

    4. Aims of Psychic Development

    5. Aims of Spiritual Development

    6. Aims of Supramental Development

Figure:

(14.1): Physiological Topography of the Planes and Parts of Consciousness of Human Being

Corresponding to the six aspects of the total personality and consciousness of the individual, there are six aspects of integral education – psychological development – physical, vital, mental, psychic, spiritual and supramental education (development), which the Individual and the society must provide to themselves, so as to ultimately evolve into beings with supramental consciousness and beings and thus help the cosmos to evolve into the same. The aspects of development are depicted according to physiological topography of consciousness in *Figure 14.1* in this chapter.

I. GENERAL OBJECTIVES OF PERSONALITY DEVELOPMENT: AIMS COMMON FOR EACH OF THE ASPECTS OF PERSONALITY

1. STUDY AND EDUCATION ARE TWO DIFFERENT PROCESSES

There is widespread confusion about the meanings of the concepts of study and education. Study is an external process of learning a subject, such as Gujarati, English, biology, cooking, dancing, acting, driving, etc. Study is an external process and behaviour. For example, the study of mathematics involves external actions of writing, computation, reading, listening, etc., which develop skills, qualities, abilities and knowledge of the student. The study of mathematics does develop precision, perseverance, concentration, etc. *in* the personality and thus develop, change and educate the personality. This inner development or change in the consciousness or personality that study causes is education. Even other activities done by a person do develop certain qualities of personality and thus they change and educate it. So, activity of study is one of the means of education of human being. Reading and study of this text would be very rewarding, if this difference between study and education is well understood. Education means to bring out and develop the hidden potential abilities of the consciousness of the educand and to develop more the manifest abilities of the person. Education is defined in similar terms by T. Percy Nunn in his book; *Education and Its First Data.*

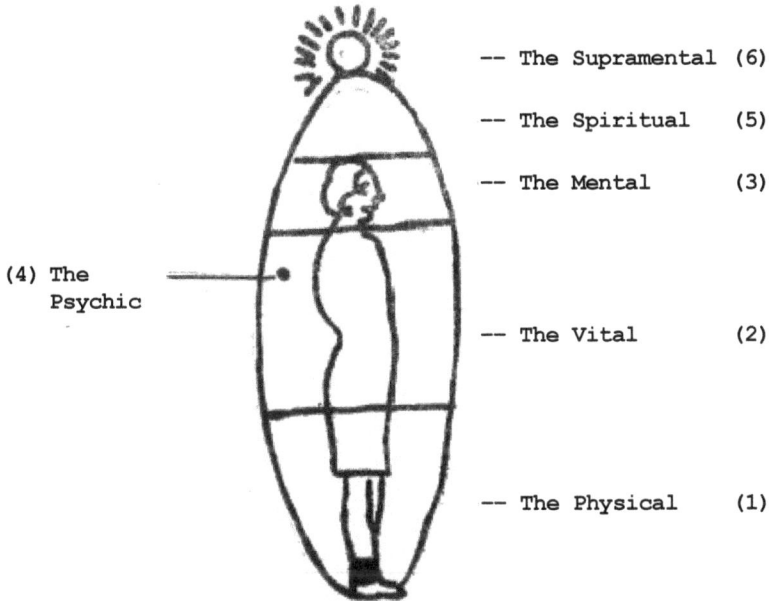

Figure 14.1

Physiological Topography of the Planes and Parts
of Consciousness of Human Being

    The objectives of psychological development of integral
personality and integral education and the free progress system of
education being developed in Sri Aurobindo International Centre of
Education of Sri Aurobindo Ashram, Pondicherry, India are noted
briefly in this chapter and the processes of development of those
objectives are also noted briefly in the next chapter.

2. THE CARDINAL AIM: INDIVIDUAL'S EVOLUTION

The main aim of integral psychology and education is to develop and perfect progressively the human being under the leadership of the psychic being and the influence of the superconscient forces. If one is to be more precise, it can be said that the chief aim of integral educational practice is to help oneself and the society to call forth the psychic and allow the psychic being to gain experience and grow and at the same time to allow it to harmonise, integrate and perfect progressively the physical, vital and mental beings, to develop potentialities of higher consciousness and to achieve ultimately **the realisation of the supramental consciousness.** In short, to evolve the next evolutionary species, the superman, and then the supramental being or in the words of the Mother, "to prepare the man of tomorrow for the new creation"[178] adopting the practice of integral yoga, especially, **Integral Karmayoga** named by Sri Aurobindo as "The Yoga Of Divine Works"[179] is the aim of the life-development. Thus, what one does is not important, but what is important is how he does the work, whether he does the work in the spirit of integral Karmayoga or otherwise.

3. THE INDIVIDUALISTIC, SOCIALISTIC AND UNIVERSAL AIM

The psycho-philosophy of integral education asserts that the above-mentioned individualistic aim carries in itself implicitly, as a corollary, the socialistic aim, because "the individual who develops freely in this manner . . . will have a much greater power for the service of the race."[180] But this does not mean that it solely disregards the other

---

[178] CWM, Vol. 12; p. 366

[179] Sri Aurobindo; *The Mother* (Sri Aurobindo Ashram, Pondicherry, 605 005); Ch. 5; Sri Aurobindo and The Mother; *The Mother with the Mother's Comments* (Sri Aurobindo Ashram Publication Department, Sri Aurobindo Ashram, Pondicherry, 605 002, India, 2002); Part One Ch. 5, Part Two Ch. 5, Part Three Ch. 5; SABCL Vol. 20, pp. 47-270; CWSA Vol. 23, pp. 53-284; SABCL Vol. 25, Part One Ch. 5

[180] SABCL, Vol. 13; p. 500

social aims. For example, to help social groups to develop their general group consciousness and to develop their personality is also one of its socialistic aims. In fact, aim is to lead the whole humanity into the supramental consciousness. And as a natural repercussion to change and transform the universal consciousness into supramental consciousness. Ultimately, to divinise all of them and unite them with the parent creator the Sachchidananda is the crowning objective. *Refer Ch. II; Section I (Definitions 5 &6).*

4. THE AIM OF DEVELOPING NATIONAL AND INTERNATIONAL CONSCIOUSNESS

It also seeks to develop the spirit of nationalism as well as internationalism in the students. By harmoniously blending all that is best in all the cultures, it wants to develop a synthetic world culture, and thus "build a material and real basis for human unity".[181] These are its national and international aims.

5. THE ATTITUDE OF CONTINUOUS LIFELONG LEARNING

Under free progress system, Teacher does not teach the subject to the students but students put up their own efforts to study. Teacher merely helps them to study. Teacher would seat in a corner of the class, students will be reading their book and learning particular portion of the book by their own efforts. If they find some difficulty, they would approach the teacher and then teacher will help them to solve the particular reported difficulty only. Suppose, a student asks meaning of a word. Then teacher would tell him to refer a dictionary that is kept in the class and find out the meaning of the word. Thus, student learns the method of study and the attitude of self-dependency which helps him to

---

[181] Sri Aurobindo and the Mother, *On Education* (Pondicherry: Sri Aurobindo Ashram, 1973), p. 155

continuously teach himself to solve problems that continuously come across him in life.

II. OBJECTIVES OF THE DEVELOPMENT OF SPECIFIC PARTS OF HUMAN CONSCIOUSNESS

1. AIMS OF PHYSICAL DEVELOPMENT

The relative human aims of physical education described by Sri Aurobindo[182] and the Mother can be put in brief thus:

(i) To develop the body's qualities of health, strength and physical fitness, to increase the mastery of the functions of the body's members and organs, to achieve total methodical and harmonious development of all the parts and movements of the body and to develop endurance, dexterity, and stability in all kinds of physical action, skill for different tasks, plasticity or suppleness, perfect responsiveness to enlightened mental and vital will, alertness, agility and resistance to fatigue and illness in the body. This is the aim of resolving the internecine war and the war between the members.

(ii) To realise grace, beauty and harmony in the body.

(iii) To lengthen the life-span of the body as much as possible.[183]

(iv) To develop instinctive body consciousness and total physical consciousness; especially to become conscious of the subtle physical body and to learn to act from there.

---

[182] SABCL, Vol. 16, pp. 1-4, 9-10, 11, 13 and 35-36; Sri Aurobindo and the Mother, *On Education* (Pondicherry: Sri Aurobindo Ashram, 1973), pp. 94-95, 100-103, 105, 108, 135, 139 and CWM, Vol. 8, p. 243

[183] Pranab Kumar Bhattacharya, "The Role of Physical Education in the Sri Aurobindo Ashram", *Mother India*, XX, 10 and 11 (November-December, 1968), pp. 173-74

(v) To develop discipline, morale and sound and strong character; to develop qualities of courage, hardihood, steadiness of will, rapid decision, co-operation, sporting spirit and leadership and obedience to leadership in combined action. These are the qualities indispensable for spiritual life as well as peaceful and harmonious national and international life.

(vi) To rectify the defects and deformities of the body, if there are any.

(vii) Vaidya Bhagawan Dash[184] says, according to Ayurveda healthy body means harmony of mind, vital and physical with the psychic.

2. THE AIMS OF EDUCATION OF THE VITAL

(i) To develop and utilise the sense organs[185]:

(a) To develop their accuracy and sensitivity far greater than what is normally expected of them.

(b) To cultivate discrimination and aesthetic sense, the capacity to choose and take up what is beautiful and harmonious, simple, healthy and pure. In other words, to teach the senses to relish vibrations and stimuli that are nourishing to the vital. Sri Aurobindo[186] insists that aesthetic education need not aim at turning each one into an artist, but it must try to develop in all artistic faculty and sense of appreciation of arts, eastern or western. This is its national and international aim also.

(ii) To become conscious and master of one's character:

By eliminating despair, depression, passions and all other negative and base emotions and impulses and cultivating morally

---

[184] Vaidya Bhagawan Dash; *Massage Therapy in Ayurveda* (Concept Publishing Company, A/15-16 Bali Nagar, New Delhi, 110015, India, 1994)

[185] Sri Aurobindo and the Mother, *On Education* (Pondicherry: Sri Aurobindo Ashram, 1973); pp. 36, 109, 110, 141

[186] SABCL Vol. 17; p. 251

permissible qualities (straightforwardness, unselfishness, generosity, tolerance, etc.), desires, ambitions, and other vital movements to resolve its dualities and contradictions,[187] and to realise a strong, buoyant, bold dynamic and co-operative vital that serves the enlightened demands of the mind and the body. This is the aim of resolving the internecine war and the war among the members.

3. THE AIMS OF MENTAL DEVELOPMENT

The Mother[188] mentions five main primary objectives of mental education:

(i) To develop the power of concentration, the capacity of attention and the capacity of observation, precise recording and faithful memory.

(ii) To develop the capacities of expansion, wideness, complexity and richness. But this does not mean that the child should be made to stuff its brain and mind with lots of subjects. But it does include, as Pavitra, the former Director of the S.A.I.C.E. would like to put it, "the training in acquiring and applying knowledge".[189]

Elaborating on this second aim Pavitra analyses it into three related sub-goals:

"(a) The capacity to gather old knowledge, i.e. how to use the various means of documentation (Text-books, reference books, technical magazines, etc.) to find out what is already known on a subject, how to grade and organize that knowledge so that it can be made available to oneself for ready reference and to others;

---

[187] Kireet, "Research in Education at Sri Aurobindo Ashram", *Mother India*, XX, 10 and 11 (November-December, 1968); p. 82

[188] Sri Aurobindo and the Mother, *On Education* (Pondicherry: Sri Aurobindo Ashram, 1973); pp. 114-15

[189] Pavitra, *Education and the Aim of Human Life*, (Pondicherry: Sri Aurobindo International Centre of Education, 1976); pp. 58-59

"(b) The capability to find out new knowledge, i.e. to engage successfully in research work, how to face a problem, to analyse and get at the core of it, how to use imagination in the search for analogies and structural similarities; how to formulate and test hypothesis;

"(c) The capacity to use and apply knowledge (old and new) to specific cases and to deal with concrete situations; how to reach optimal decisions; how to get on with fellow workers and engage in team work, understand others and make oneself understood."[190]

(iii) To organise ideas around a central idea or a higher ideal or a supremely luminous idea that will serve as a guide in life.

(iv) To control thought, to reject undesirable thoughts (so that one may, in the end, think only what, one wants and when one wants it).

(v) Mental silence, perfect calm and a more and more total receptivity to inspirations coming from the higher regions of the being.

The third and the fourth aims may be summed up as the aim of resolving the internecine war in the mind. If development of its capacity to rule over and co-operate with the vital and physical with enlightened will is added to the fifth aim, it can be called the aim of resolving the war among members on the mental level.

4. THE AIMS OF PSYCHIC DEVELOPMENT

The psychic education endeavours to realise, rather call forth, the psychic and to hand over to it the reins of the chariot of man's outer triple being so as to reach the following goals:

---

[190] Ibid., p. 59

(i) To purify three parts of external personality: to end the internecine war; to develop in the mind right vision, in the vital right impulse and in the physical right movements, discarding all wrong ones.

(ii) To realise the freedom and individuality of each of the three parts of the being: to end the war among members: to make all the three members (physical, vital, mental) of our personality free from each other's unregenerate influence and dominance, to harmonise them under the reins of the psychic being, and thus to impart to them their autonomous individuality in the harmonious whole.

(iii) To start the process of ascent and descent in the outer being; to create in the outer personality complete receptivity and right attitude to receive higher spiritual consciousness and to open it safely to that consciousness.

(iv) To manifest and develop in the outer being new capacities, which actually are not in one's present outer nature.[191]

(v) To feel oneness with all beings and things: to contact the Mother or the Divine within oneself and in others and thus to feel real oneness with all. (It is clear that the psychic can effectively achieve the national and international goals of education.)

(vi) To know and execute the divine will behind one's life and to be the master of one's destiny, and to have the sense of universality and immortality.[192]

(vii) To develop the psychic being fully, so as to enduringly and completely realise the above aims.[193]

---

[191] CWM, Vol. 9; p. 396

[192] Sri Aurobindo and the Mother, *On Education* (Pondicherry: Sri Aurobindo Ashram, 1973); p. 124

[193] SABCL Vol. 19; p. 900

5. TWO AIMS OF SPIRITUAL DEVELOPMENT

(i) TO SPIRITUALISE AND COSMICISE THE LOWER TRIPLE CONSCIOUSNESS: Spiritual education or development means an attempt to rise into consciousness regions above the mental region. One tries to spiritualise and cosmicise the lower triple consciousness and put it under the rule of the cosmic divine or the cosmic Mother. Spiritual education aims at bringing down from the spiritual consciousness, spiritual knowledge, light, power, force, anand, etc. into the lower triple being. For example, it tries to develop progressively the power of intuitions, inspirations and direct knowledge in the mind, spiritual urge in the vital, integral power of divinations in the body, supernatural control over body's functionings and illness and power to minimise mishaps to it from outside, power to deal with other's consciousness directly in a subtle way. At the same time, it also aims at raising the lower consciousness above the mind, cosmicising it, realising the cosmic divine, and making the whole nature to execute the will of the cosmic Divine to the best of its limited ability.

(ii) TO HAVE UNION WITH THE TRANSCENDENTAL DIVINE: The discipline of psychic-spiritual turn gives upward turn to the triple consciousness to receive the descending higher consciousness and helps it to progressively change itself into higher levels of consciousness till it unites with the overmental consciousness, the ultimate goal of spiritualisation. The upward journey is to still continue, until one identifies one's nature with the highest supramental consciousness, which has power to transform human being into divine being.

The students learn this ideal from the social and educational environment of the Sri Aurobindo International Centre of Education and Sri Aurobindo Ashram and are helped by the rising collective consciousness of the teachers and the sadhaks. Moreover they are helped by The Mother's consciousness, which is always operative and also by the developing spiritual consciousness that have been manifested and which is permanently over-arching the Ashram and the Centre.

6. THE GOAL OF SUPRAMENTAL REALISATION

After realisation of psychic and overmind, the highest level of spiritual mind, one may choose to totally psychicise the ego and to raise the consciousness above the spiritual mind into the supramental region of consciousness. The ultimate objective is unite with the transcendental Divine and for that to try for ascending into supramental consciousness, which, has power to transform the lower nature absolutely so as to make it a fit instrument of the supreme will.

By bringing down the supramental consciousness into the man, the supramental education first aims at transforming man into the superman, a transitional species, who has the mind of light as its highest instrument, a vital that has become revealed as the divine power and a body that is progressively transforming itself, so as to hold supramental consciousness into its cells increasingly. Its ultimate aim is to bring down on earth the supramental race with supermind, divine vital and divine body as its instrument.

Suggestions for Further Reading

1. Pavitra; *Education and the Aim of Human Life* (Publisher: Sri Aurobindo Ashram, Pondicherry, 605002, India, 1976); pp. 167

2. The Mother (Author) & Georges Van Vrekhem (Editor); *The Mother's Vision* (Publisher: Sri Aurobindo Ashram, Pondicherry, 605002, India; 2005); Ch. 16: Education; pp. 405-429

WORKBOOK: QUESTIONS FOR PREVIEW AND REVIEW

Essay Type Questions

1. What is the central and main aim of human life according to integral psychology and education?
2. Enumerate goals of physical development.
3. Enumerate goals of vital development.
4. Enumerate goals of mental development.
5. Enumerate goals of psychic development.
6. Enumerate goals of spiritual development
7. Enumerate goals of supramental development.
8. Fill in the gaps: Integral psychology and integral education aims at developing consciousness of Individual, _____, _____ and _____.
9. Name a few cultural aims of integral psychology and integral education.
10. Why ideal of life long study and education is a must ideal?
11. Prepare a list of developmental qualities common to all planes and parts of consciousness.

Exercises

1. Make a presentation of aims of development of the physical, the vital, the mental, the psychic, the spiritual and The Supramental Consciousness of an individual in a tabular form.
2. Construct a table showing goals of development common to all areas of education.
3. Make a table showing the practical and impractical aims of integral education according to your own view-point.
4. Write an essay of less than ten pages but more than two pages on "Important Goals of Human Development" in standard research report style.

SELF TEST

1. List general aims of personality development.
2. List aims of physical development.
3. List aims of vital development
4. List aims of mental development.
5. List aims of psychic development.
6. List aims of spiritual development
7. List aims of supramental development

CHAPTER XV

INTEGRAL YOGIC METHOD AND PRINCIPLES OF THE DEVELOPMENT OF HUMAN CONSCIOUSNESS

I.   THE METHOD OF PRACTICE OF INTEGRAL PSYCHOLOGY

II. THE CARDINAL PRINCIPLE OF SPIRITUAL EVOLUTION

III. THE GENERAL PRINCIPLES OF PERSONALITY DEVELOPMENT

IV. THE SPECIFIC PRINCIPLES APPLIED IN THE AREA OF PHYSICAL DEVELOPMENT

V.   THE SPECIFIC PRINCIPLES APPLIED IN THE AREA OF VITAL DEVELOPMENT

VI. THE SPECIFIC PRINCIPLES APPLIED IN THE AREA OF MENTAL DEVELOPMENT

VII. THE SPECIFIC PRINCIPLES APPLIED IN THE AREA OF PSYCHIC DEVELOPMENT

VIII. THE SPECIFIC PRINCIPLES APPLIED IN THE AREA OF SPIRITUAL DEVELOPMENT

IX. THE SPECIFIC PRINCIPLES APPLIED IN THE AREA OF SUPRAMENTAL DEVELOPMENT

X.   THE PRINCIPLES OF DEVELOPMENT OF NATIONALISM AND INTERNATIONALISM

XI. THE PRINCIPLES INVOLVED IN THE EFFORTS FOR LIFELONG CONTINUOUS DEVELOPMENT AND THE DEVELOPMENT OF THE PUBLIC

XII. THE PRINCIPLES BEHIND THE ROLE OF THE TEACHER AND HIS EDUCATION

XIII. THE PRINCIPLES OF DISCIPLINE

> *Table:*
> *(15.1) Elements of practice (sadhana) of Purnayoga*
>
> *Appendix:*
> *(15.1) A Talk of The Mother with the Students during her Weekly Class on 4 August 1954 on The Upanishadic Method of Teaching*

I. THE METHOD OF PRACTICE OF INTEGRAL PSYCHOLOGY

Sri Aurobindo says that for the effective practice of this psychology it is absolutely necessary to remember that

> "While this classification is indispensable for psychological self-knowledge and discipline and practice it can be used best when it is not made too rigid and cutting a formula. For things run very much into each other and a synthetical sense of these powers (these planes) is as necessary as the analysis. Mind, for instance, is everywhere."[194]

---

[194] SABCL VOL. 22; pp. 339-340

In the analysis of consciousness, in this chapter, the fact of interpenetration of planes and the fact that each determines each, that is, the higher imposes itself on the lower, but the lower disobeys or puts limitations on the higher also, is hinted clearly here and there. One should never lose sight of this synthetic fact when practicing this psychology.

Sri Aurobindo[195] has declared that the practice of integral psychology, that is the Sadhana of this Yoga, does not proceed through any set mental teaching or prescribed forms of meditation, mantras, etc.; but by **aspiration**, by a **self-concentration inward or upward**, by **self-opening to the divine Power above and its workings and to the divine Presence in the heart and by the rejection of all that is foreign to these things**. It is only by faith, aspiration and surrender that this self-opening can come. **By opening to the Mother within or above, practice of Sri Aurobindo's Yoga can be done, and siddhi can be achieved**. All has to be done by the working of the Mother's force aided by one's aspiration, devotion and surrender. By the Mother is meant the embodied Mother of Sri Aurobindo Ashram, who was one with all aspects of the Mother. And so it is she who is to be accepted and followed as Guru and Guide if someone wants to pursue fully the Purna Yoga. As the Yoga accepts the whole life, one can proceed on the way, doing whatever work that is his lot, with the above attitude and reach the goal, the goal of Supramentalising the nature and the life around. If the student takes up the work of studying and the teacher that of teaching in that spirit, they both can very well be on the way to the supramental as equal comrades. *If the members of any group, including group of business people, work and live in this spirit, each individual member and the group-collectivity will be on the way to the supramental world, the future Golden World of Golden Age.* Nine elements of sadhana of Purnayoga are listed in the *Table 15.1* below. **Aspiration and opening to the Mother within or above are the two elements that include all others.**

---

[195] SABCL Vol. 23, p. 505; SABCL Vol. 25, p. 132

Table 15.1

Elements of Practice (sadhana) of Purnayoga

1. **Aspiration**
2. Self-concentration inward and upward
3. Self-opening to the divine Power above and its workings
4. Self-opening to the divine Presence in the heart
5. The rejection of all that is foreign to all the above things
6. **Opening to the Mother within or above**
7. Devotion
8. Surrender
9. Faith

We shall consider an illustration here: Suppose one wants to do away with the impulse to perform sex. He can proceed by (i) constantly aspiring for not to have impulse of sex. Then (ii) he should continue to concentrate inward and upward. Then (iii) keep his consciousness open towards the divine Power within and above. Next (iv) he should open to the divine Presence in the heart. After that (v) he should keep rejecting whatever is contrary to these things. Next (vi) he has to open to the Mother within or above. Then (vii) he should cultivate and maintain devotion to the Mother and the cause. Following this (viii) he should surrender to the Mother and (ix) keep faith. For developing endurance and for curing an organ of the body similar practice must be adopted.

II. THE CARDINAL PRINCIPLE OF DEVELOPMENT AND EDUCATION: THE PRINCIPLE OF SPIRITUAL EVOLUTION

The main general principle of the practice of integral psychology is the principle of spiritual evolution. Sri Aurobindo has stated this in one of his letters to a disciple. The letter titled by the editors as "Sri Aurobindo's Teaching"[196] follows:

"The teaching of Sri Aurobindo starts from that of the ancient sages of India that behind the appearances of the universe there is the reality of a Being and Consciousness, a Self of all things, one and eternal. All beings are united in that One Self and Spirit but divided by a certain separativity of consciousness, an ignorance of their true Self and Reality in the mind, life and body. It is possible by a certain psychological discipline to remove this veil of separative consciousness and become aware of the true Self, the Divinity within us and all.

"Sri Aurobindo's teaching states that this one Being and Consciousness is involved here in Matter. Evolution is the method by which it liberates itself; Life is the first step of this release of consciousness; mind is the second; but the evolution does not finish with mind, it awaits a release into something greater, a consciousness which is spiritual and supramental. The next step of the evolution must be towards the development of Supermind and Spirit as the dominant power in the conscious being. For only then will the involved Divinity in things release itself entirely and it will become possible for life to manifest perfection.

---

[196] *This statement was published along with "Sri Aurobindo's Asram" (see pages 530 –31 [of CWSA Vol 36]) in the* Hindu *of Madras on 20 February 1934 and in pamphlets entitled "The Teaching and the Asram of Sri Aurobindo" in March and August 1934. It has been reproduced many times since then.—Ed.*

"But while the former steps in evolution were taken by Nature without a conscious will in the plant and animal life, in man Nature becomes able to evolve by a conscious will in the instrument. It is not, however, by the mental will in man that this can be wholly done, for the mind goes only to a certain point and after that, can only move in a circle. A conversion has to be made, a turning of the consciousness by which mind has to change into the higher principle. This method is to be found through the ancient psychological discipline and practice of Yoga. In the past it has been attempted by a drawing away from the world and a disappearance into the height of the Self or Spirit. Sri Aurobindo teaches that a descent of the higher principle is possible which will replace the mind's ignorance or its very limited knowledge by a supramental Truth-Consciousness which will make it possible for the human being to grow out of his still animal humanity into a divine race. The psychological discipline of Yoga can be used to that end by opening all the parts of the being to a conversion or transformation through the descent and working of the higher still concealed supramental principle.

"This however cannot be done at once or in a short time or by any rapid or miraculous transformation. Many steps have to be taken by the seeker before the supramental descent is possible. Man lives mostly in his surface mind, life and body but there is an inner being within him with greater possibilities to which he has to awake – for it is only a very restricted influence from it that he receives now and that pushes him to a constant pursuit of a greater beauty, harmony, power and knowledge. The first process of Yoga is therefore to open the ranges of inner being and to live from there outward, governing his outward life by an inner light and force. In doing so he discovers in himself his true soul which is not this outer mixture of mental, vital and physical elements but something of the Reality behind them, a spark from the one Divine Fire. He has

306

to learn to live in his soul and purify and orientate by its drive towards the Truth the rest of the nature. There can follow afterwards an opening upward and descent of a higher principle of the Being. But even then it is not at once the full supramental Light and Force. For there are several ranges of consciousness between the ordinary human mind and the supramental Truth-consciousness. These intervening ranges have to be opened and their power brought down into the mind, life and body. Only afterwards can the full power of the Truth-consciousness work in the nature. The process of this self-discipline or sadhana is therefore long and difficult, but even a little of it is so much gained because it makes the ultimate release and perfection more possible.

"There are many things belonging to older systems that are necessary on the way — an opening of the mind to a greater wideness and to the sense of the Self and the Infinite, an emergence into what has been called the cosmic consciousness, mastery over the desires and passions; an outward asceticism is not essential, but the conquest of desire and attachment and a control over the body and its needs, greeds and instincts is indispensable. There is a combination of the old systems: the way of knowledge through the mind's discernment between Reality and the appearance, the heart's way of devotion, love and surrender and the way of works turning the will away from motives of self-interest to the Truth and the service of a greater Reality than the ego. For the whole being has to be trained so that it can respond and be transformed when it is possible for that greater Light and Force to work in the nature.

"In this discipline, the inspiration of the Master, and in the difficult stages his control and his presence are indispensable — for it would be impossible otherwise to go through it without much stumbling and error which would prevent all chance of success. The Master is one who has risen to a higher consciousness and being and he is often regarded as its manifestation or representative. He not only helps by his teaching and still more by his influence and example but by a power to communicate his own experience to others.

"This is Sri Aurobindo's teaching and method of practice. It is not his object to develop any one religion or to amalgamate the older religions or to found any new religion, for any of these things would lead away from his central purpose. The one aim of his Yoga is an inner self-development by which each one who follows it can in time discover the one Self in all and evolve a higher consciousness than the mental, a spiritual and supramental consciousness which will transform and divinise human nature. (February 1934)".[197]

It is to apply this principle that all aspects of life and education have to be subjected to the discipline of inward and upward turn (psychic-spiritual turn) along with the application of conscious will to all learning efforts and efforts of one's development. This cardinal principle of development is served by other several principles that are described next.

III. THE GENERAL PRINCIPLES OF PERSONALITY DEVELOPMENT

The cardinal principle of development and education is in fact the principle of human life and terrestrial evolution. So, naturally it has to be mentioned in the beginning. All other principles, practices and aims of human development and education converge around and serve this cardinal and central principle of development. Hereunder, general

---

[197] Sri Aurobindo, "Sri Aurobindo's teaching and Method of Practice", *Bulletin of Sri Aurobindo International Centre of Education*, XXXI, 1 (February, 1979), pp. 4-6; CWSA Vol. 36, pp. 547-550

ones are described and then will follow principles specific to each of the aspects of personality and consciousness.

1. THE PRINCIPLE OF FOUR STAGES OF PERFECTION

"The being has first **to be conscious**, then **to acquire control**, then **to achieve mastery** and finally **to effect transformation**."[198] This is the principle of conscious process of growth, the principle of four stages of perfection, behind the integral education being worked out by the free progress system in the SAICE. And this is the principle one has to apply to one's own living for one's own evolution.

The Mother has explained in language of psychology how this four stages are to be effected in Her articles on The Science of Living."[199]

In case of getting rid of the sex impulse illustrated above, one will have to be immediately conscious of the sex impulse as soon as it appears. Then he should deny it to proceed to do its work and fail it. After repeated such actions he will acquire mastery over sex-impulse; the impulse will keep itself in check. The last stage will be the sex impulse will be out of the vital forever. The vital's sex will be transformed into peace and anand.

2. THE PRINCIPLE OF THE UNIQUE NATURE OF THE CHILD

Describing the new principle and conception of the nature of the child that is behind the modern education, Sri Aurobindo writes:

"We have travelled to another conception of the child as a soul with a being, a nature and capacities of his own who must be helped to find them, to find himself, to grow into their

---

[198] Pranab Kumar Bhattacharya, "The Role of Physical Education in Sri Aurobindo Ashram", *Mother India*, XX 10-11 (Nov.-Dec. 1968), p. 176
[199] CWM Vol. 12; pp. 1-108

maturity, into a fullness of physical and vital energy and the utmost breadth, depth and height of his emotional, his intellectual and his spiritual being."[200]

Sri Aurobindo[201] also advises that the child should not be kneaded and pressured into a form like an inert plastic material.

3. THE PRINCIPLE OF INTERDEPENDENCE OF THE PARTS OF THE BEING

The physical, vital, mental, psychic, spiritual and supramental parts of human being are interdependent and interpenetrative, though they are not intermixed. So, for the perfection of each of them the perfection of all the others is indispensable, and for the perfection of the whole being, the perfection of each is imperative.

This is the principle behind the care that is taken to, perfect the body materially in Sri Aurobindo Ashram. The physical is the base for all other parts of human consciousness. If the body is imperfect, the perfection of the higher parts is held up to the extent it is imperfect. Sri Aurobindo and The Mother[202] insist that a body is needed that can respond to all the higher parts, can co-operate with them and not be a drag on them; a body that does not impose its spirit of inertia, forgetfulness, etc. on the higher planes is necessary, if one wants to have integral perfection. On the other side, for realising beauty in the body, development of other inner and higher parts of the being is a must. The development of the vital also depends on the development of the other parts of the being. For example, accuracy and sensitiveness of the senses depends on anatomically perfect and healthy organs, calm and clear (pure) nervous system and purified, calm and non-interfering vital and

---

[200] SABCL, Vol. 15, p. 605; CWSA, Vol. 25, p. 631

[201] SABCL, Vol.15, pp. 27-28, p. 38; SABCL, Vol. 13, pp. 499-500

[202] The Mother, "Physical Education and Yoga", *Mother India*, XX, 10-11 (Nov.-Dec., 1968), p. 53; Pranab Kumar Bhattacharya, *Op. Cit,.* p. 174; Sri Aurobindo and The Mother, *On Education* (Pondicherry: Sri Aurobindo Ashram, Nov., 1973), pp. 36-37, 39-40, 41, 105; SABCL, Vol. 16, p. 15

calm and attentive mind. Similarly, if the mind is not perfectly cultivated, it would not be able to command the vital and the physical in the right direction, nor would it be able to receive, contain and express the higher light and energy when they descend into it. On the top of this, the principle states that if psychic, spiritual and supramental perfection is not achieved right down up to the physical, all the achievements in these areas are precarious and not enduring and final. It is for this reason that an all-round balanced programme of holistic education is followed at the S.A.I.C.E.. Strictly adhering to this holistic principle, the Mother once vehemently opposed a move to belittle and curtail other educations for the sake of mental one. She declared:

> "They should have sufficient time for their physical exercises. I don't want them to be very good students, yet pale, thin, anemic. Perhaps you will say that in this way they will not have sufficient time for their studies, but that can be made up by expanding the course over a longer period. Instead of finishing a course in four years, you can take six years."[203]

4. THE PRINCIPLE OF THE GOVERNMENT OF REASON

Within the limit of human consciousness, reason is the highest faculty of man, and it should reign till the rule of the psychic is established.

Gymnastic exercises in comparison with sports are not in themselves sensational and thrilling, but dry and monotonous. The Mother[204] maintains that, unlike sports when they are done, gymnastic exercises teach the body and the physical consciousness to obey the reason instead of the vital. The S.A.I.C.E. has also developed on a gigantic scale guiding facility for students to observe their vital movements and select and eliminate them as the reason dictates, and

---

[203] CWM, Vol. 12, p. 170

[204] The Mother, *Op. Cit.,* pp. 55-57; CWM, Vol. 9, pp. 81, 96-7, 98-9

thus try to make the mind the leader of the vital movements. In the area of mental education also there is a conscious attempt to develop all the aspects of reason. While teaching subjects, the teachers, when it is possible, try to so teach that the faculty of reason of students gets cultivated. At the same time by giving psychic-spiritual turn to all the educational activities, the student is also prepared for ushering into the kingdom of the psychic in future, so as to transcend the reason ultimately.

5. THE PRINCIPLE OF ENDING INTERNECINE WAR AND WAR BETWEEN MEMBERS

All-round development of the body is a must for integral and harmonious perfection of the body and to end the internecine war on its level. Keeping with this principle, the S.A.I.C.E. provides compulsorily a general comprehensive training in all sorts of physical activities and shuns specialization. For, as Bhattacharya[205] points out, different activities develop different skills in the body. Similarly for realising a vital free of all conflicts, there is an effort at the S.A.I.C.E.. The vital can serve the whole of our being. But the vital also can eat away the physical by excessively using it for its own passions, desires, vehemences, etc. and can debase mind by making it think and act in terms of justifying itself. Thus "The vital can be a good instrument, but it is a bad master."[206] In other words, it is at war with other members. To end this war, by harmonising it with the mind and the physical, its control by reason is a must, and so the students are instructed and helped into the art of emotional control—into the technique of self-observation and control of lower members by the reason. For ending internecine war on mental level a homogeneous mind is to be realised, and for that all practices of mental purifications and synthesising are a must. So, through personal guidance, the free progress system puts the student on

---

[205] Pranab Kumar Bhattacharya, *Op. Cit.,* p. 175
[206] SABCL, Vol. 22, p. 346

the road of mental purification leading to the reign of reason, which goes a long way towards ending war between members even.

It is for having harmonised and pure outer being and descent of higher mental, psychic, spiritual and supramental forces in the nature that inward and upward psychic-spiritual turn is given to physical, vital and mental education. The psychic is the pure being beyond dualities in its nature and only it can end the internecine war and war among members and effect an enduring true harmony in the outer nature. In keeping with this principle students are advised to pursue their triple education from within before realisation of the psychic and perfect their outer person by it after its realisation. Thus, they are led in the direction of the true integration of the personality.

6. THE PRINCIPLE OF STARTING EDUCATION AS EARLY AS POSSIBLE

Sri Aurobindo and the Mother[207] have stressed at various places in their writings the; need of starting education as early as possible. The earlier the physical training starts the better. The later one begins, the more cone must be prepared to meet bad habits that have to be corrected, rigidities to be made supple and malformations to be rectified. That is why physical education is started in the S.A.I.C.E. from nursery, and parents are advised to start it from the very birth. The education of the vital also must begin, indeed, as soon as the child is able to use his senses. In this way many bad habits will be avoided and harmful influences will be eliminated. If it is started in later age, all these things have to be fought with and that causes a lot of wastage of energy and time. That is why parents are educated about the need of this training and its methods: Parents are generally Sri Aurobindo's disciples and are guided to study the relevant literature by lectures, magazines, etc. Similarly parents are advised to start mental and psychic education as early as possible. The psychic is in front in the: being in infancy and

---

[207] Sri Aurobindo and the Mother, *Op. Cit.,* pp. 100, 106, 109; CWM, Vol. 9, pp. 160-61; CWM, Vol. 4, pp. 25, 27; CWM, Vol. 6, pp. 151-53

childhood, so the psychic education must start right from the infancy. The free progress system allows all the students to study and govern their life as far as possible from within for this purpose only. Moreover, it educates the parent in how to allow the psychic of their child to act at home even during pre-school stage, so that, psychic education may start as early as possible.

7. THE PRINCIPLE OF INWARD AND UPWARD TURN: THE PRINCIPLE OF PSYCHIC-SPIRITUAL TURN

The intervention of the deeper psychic and the higher spiritual and supramental forces is a must for integral perfection and the divine transformation of the physical, the vital and the mental.

This is the psychological principle that operates behind the practice of mass concentration in the beginning and the end of each physical activity. This opens the physical to the psychic and the higher forces and enables the psychic to come forward and the higher forces to descend into the physical and work for its psychic and spiritual transformation. Asserting this principle, Sri Aurobindo wrote:

"Even in its fullest strength and greatest glory of beauty, it (the body) is still a flower of the material inconscience: It is not that the action from the two ends cannot meet and the higher take into itself and uplift the lower perfection; but this can usually be done by a transition from the lower to a higher outlook, aspiration and motive; this we shall have to do if our aim is to transform the human into divine life."[208]

Dwelling on the Body's divine destiny Sri Aurobindo further commented:

"The body ... is a creation of the Inconscient and itself inconscient or at least subconscient in parts of itself and much

---

[208] SABCL, Vol. 16, pp. 7-8, also see pp. 17 and 21

of its hidden action; but what we call the Inconscient is an appearance, a dwelling place, and instrument of secret consciousness or super-conscient which created the miracle we call the universe.... It (the Superconscience) is there in the body... and its emergence in our consciousness is the secret aim of evolution and key to the mystery of our existence."[209]

Pointing to the indispensability of giving the psychic and the spiritual turn to the physical culture for breaking the limits of the body and its higher perfection he further observes:

"The most we can do in the physical field by physical means is necessarily insecure as well as bound by limits; even what seems a perfect health and strength of the body is precarious and can be broken down at any moment by fluctuations from within or by a strong attack or shock from outside: only by the breaking of our limitations can a higher and more enduring perfection come. One direction in which our consciousness must grow is an increasing hold from within or from above on the body and its powers and its more conscious response to the higher parts of our being."[210]

That is why the Mother[211] took care to give psychic-spiritual turn to physical education at the S.A.I.C.E.. For radical and enduring change of the vital also psychic-spiritual turn to vital education is necessary. The Mind can control the vital, but cannot change it, because both are blind-ignorant-parts. How can a blind lead another blind? So the vital is to be placed ultimately under the psychic, spiritual and supramental leadership. Only then the real vital transformation is possible, only then the divine vital can be realised. The psychic-spiritual turn is imperative for radical improvement of the study and the change

---

[209] Ibid., pp. 10-11

[210] Ibid., p. 13

[211] CWM, Vol. 9, pp. 86-87

of mind. If the divine help and inspiration arc called and a student guides his effort at study with these divine factors, the study may become of a higher grade. Following this injunction of The Mother[212] the students are advised to study for the divine and with the divine's help.

8. THE PRINCIPLE OF NECESSITY OF CONSCIOUS WILL IN ANY KIND OF PROGRESS

The Mother[213] has maintained that generally it is not known that physical culture infuses new consciousness, light and life into the body in a general way. It is, of course, known that each physical activity causes specific developments. Even if one goes through physical culture without mental awareness and conscious will as regards its aims and results, he gets the results. But if he goes deliberately and consciously, the results are much better, quicker and general. For these reasons the theoretical instructions from captains and the library have been made an integral part of physical education.

Conscious will can be cultivated and by applying conscious will speedy vital transformation can be achieved. The Mother has advised in this connection:

> "Once the resolution is firmly established, there is nothing more to do than to proceed with strictness and persistence, never to accept defeat as final. If you are to avoid all weakening and withdrawing, there is one important point you must know and never forget: The will can be cultivated and developed even like the muscles by methodical and progressive exercise. You must not shrink from demanding of your will the maximum effort even for a thing that appears to be of no importance; for it is by effort that capacity grows, acquiring

---

[212] CWM, Vol. 5, pp. 47-48

[213] CWM, Vol. 9, pp. 152-53; CWM, Vol. 10, pp. 30-31; S. K. Banerji, "The Demand of the Mother", *Mother India.* XXX, 1 (January, 1978), pp. 20-21

little by little the power to apply itself even to the most difficult things."[214]

Hence the students are guided and counseled to do what once they have decided to do and to pursue it repeatedly even after repeated failures. The above advice applies to the mental education and the psychic education also. For psychic education, "There is need of a special factor, the personal will. ... The discovery is a personal matter and a great resolution, a strong will and an untiring perseverance are indispensable to reach the goal."[215] Along with this Guru is helpful on the way. So, the free progress system gives mental knowledge about the psychic to its students, provides them with protective free environment, and tries in various ways to turn their consciousness towards the Mother.

9. THE PRINCIPLE OF MOVEMENT FROM WITHIN OUTWARD

All transformation that is radical and durable proceeds from within outwards.[216] For example, all sex impulses and desires are to be eliminated first from the mental and the vital consciousness as well as from the physical will and then one should strive for the outward abstinence from sexual act. For the supramental transformation celibacy is inevitable, declared Sri Aurobindo.[217] But keeping in view the above principle, the students are not forced from without to abstain from sex, neither are they looked down on, if they transgress the rule. For the outward abstinence from sexual act must be an inevitable result of the inner renunciation. The students are not subjected to the external impositions and coercion but led to rely more on the inner conscious

---

[214] Sri Aurobindo and the Mother, *On Education* (Pondicherry: Sri Aurobindo Ashram, Nov., 1973), p. 112

[215] Ibid., pp. 123-24

[216] Ibid., p. 139

[217] SABCL, Vol. 3, pp. 331-36, 338, 339

powers and promptings, similarly vital, mental, psychic, spiritual and supramental education is not imposed at the S.A.I.C.E..

10. THE PRINCIPLE OF INDIVIDUAL DIFFERENCE

The Mother[218] was very keen about fixing the physical programme in accordance with the needs of the body of the students and about it being followed regularly and compulsorily. The trainee's mental and vital preference and whims are not allowed to have any say in fixing up the programme. Only on medical grounds the students are allowed to have a change in their programme. But, once the programme is fixed, they are to adhere to it compulsorily. For physical education discipline is a must.

To follow the above principle, regular medical checkups are made and the programmes are adjusted. Of course, on organisational grounds, the choice for the individual is to be restricted.

In the area of vital education also teachers guide and counsel each student according to his or her unique individual need and personality. For example, they employ different methods for awakening the will for the vital control in different students. The students are free to choose their subjects of study, but once they choose a subject, the Mother[219] expected them to attend the class without fail even if they found it difficult or not interesting for the sake of vital training.

To put the principle of individual difference in practice, the free progress class never expects all in the class to be at the same stage of achievement and to learn the same course. Aptly the Mother remarked, "And indeed I do not see any necessity for everybody knowing the same thing."[220]

---

[218] Sri Aurobindo and the Mother, *On Education* (Pondicherry: Sri Aurobindo Ashram, Nov., 1973), pp. 135-38

[219] CWM, Vol. 8, pp. 356-57

[220] CWM, Vol. 5, p. 107

11. THE PRINCIPLE OF TRANSFER

Transfer is the most when practice is undergone with understanding and will to transfer the skill in other fields. Mass exercises, games and group activities develop qualities of co-operation, promote collective spirit and habits needed in the combined action for developing sportsman spirit. These qualities get transferred into the social life of the students and thus physical education caters to social peace and well-being. Combative sports build up courage, strong will and fighting spirit, and they become useful in achievements of any ideal, in efforts towards success in studies, commercial enterprises, constructive projects and for conquering any weakness and difficulty. The students are mentally made aware as to which activities develop which qualities and are encouraged to develop them applying conscious will and to strive to transfer them in other fields. The physical education library is also set up with the eye on this principle by the Department of Physical Education.[221]

The principle also states that the general and basic habits, attitudes, capacities and knowledge have the greatest transfer value. So, it is better to develop them. In the area of mental education also the free progress system establishes itself on this principle according to Pavitra.[222] The free progress system using worksheets and research way of study tries to perfect the mind's capacity to gather old knowledge, its capability to find out new knowledge and its capacity to apply the knowledge. For such a mental formation is a valuable asset in any of the hundred branches of knowledge and jobs that are open to a student, irrespective of his graduation subjects.

---

[221] Department of Physical Education, Sri Aurobindo Ashram, "Running Commentary during the Physical demonstrations, 2nd December, 1962", *Mother India,* XX, 10-11 (Nov.-Dec., 1958), pp. 179, 181; SABCL, Vol. 16, pp. 2-3

[222] Pavitra, *Education and the Aim of Human Life* (Pondicherry: Sri Aurobindo International Centre of Education, 1976), pp. 57-59

12. THE PRINCIPLE OF CELIBACY

According to Sri Aurobindo,[223] celibacy conserves and provides energy for utmost mental development, just as it is necessary for vital and physical education. So the free progress system does not allow the freedom of sex. Sri Aurobindo puts a bar against any kind of vital exchange between persons in the name of love and sex, because that dissipates energy and binds oneself to lower life. So, in the S.A.I.C.E. vital and mental celibacy is a sought after goal and students are fully helped, guided and instructed in that Art. But care is taken as noted earlier in a different context that sex is not suppressed to avoid aberrations in the personality of the student.

13. THE PRINCIPLE THAT ENVIRONMENT IS A VERY IMPORTANT FACTOR THAT DEVELOPS PERSONALITY IN INTERACTION WITH HEREDITY

Perfect hygienic environment is maintained in the Ashram. Hygienic and nourishing diet is provided to the students. All-round physical education is provided to them. Consequently their bodies achieve the maximum development possible to them. Guided by this principle and the psychological principle that plants and flowers have powers to nourish, soothe and calm vital and develop aesthetic sense in the man, the S.A.I.C.E. and Sri Aurobindo Ashram have brought nature to the very doors of the class-room by developing gardens in a big way in every nook and corner of the Ashram and the S.A.I.C.E.. Rich, higher and constantly progressive social and spiritual environment also has been made dynamic in the Ashram and the S.A.I.C.E.. Describing the nature of this environment, Indra Sen notes:

"It consists of essentially the presence of a Higher Consciousness as also of the collective aspiration of the community. And what is more important is that it admits of a

---

[223] SABCL, Vol. 3, pp. 327-40

positive and a systematic cultivation. An individual can nurse and cultivate his own proper air, through conscious aspiration and the invocation of the Higher."[224]

The above principle is stated in an alternate expression in these words: "An ideal community and an ideal individual depend upon each other for the attainment of perfection."[225] Indra Sen asserts the importance of the atmosphere in these words: "Integral Education has yet to elaborate its psychological principles, but the fact of the atmosphere is its basic contribution. It is a powerful educational influence."[226]

Dr. Aster Patel, the daughter of Indra Sen, having doctorate degree in psychology from Sorbonne University of France and who is a former student of the S.A.I.C.E., stressed during her two-hour long interview that the spiritual atmosphere built by Sri Aurobindo and the Mother was the central single factor behind the free progress system and that other principles were only offshoots of this central factor.

14. THE PRINCIPLE OF FREEDOM OF LEARNING AND LEARNING FOR JOY

During one of the talks with the researcher, Jugal Kishore Mukherjee, the Director of Department of the Higher Studies of the S.A.I.C.E., stressed the importance of this principle. Conventions and rules belong to the domain of reason and can lead the man to reason and socially good personality only. The free progress system aims at the psychic, spiritual and supramental perfection of the nature. So, it relegates in the background the fixed conventions. A free atmosphere is a must for the emergence of the psychic. Hence, it provides the maximum freedom possible to the students. Consequently, the child

---

[224] Indra Sen, "The Search for a National System of Education for India", *Mother India,* XVII, 9 (October, 1965), p. 60

[225] Pranab Kumar Bhattacharya, *Op. Cit.,* p. 173

[226] Indra Sen, "The Role of the Teacher", *Mother India,* XXXIII, 8 (Aug., 1981), p. 470

feels that the work of learning is not imposed from without but is freely self-chosen; and he learns joyfully. Ultimately, the child gets into the habit of learning for joy of learning only and not for any other motive or incentive. Of course, in the area of physical education, the freedom is much restricted, but it increases gradually, as one moves to the education of higher parts of the being. A student is free to abstain from any physical activity if and only if his physical instinct suggests him to do so. In the area of vital education, the child is not to be forced into an error-proof discipline. He is allowed; the freedom to stumble and learn. For effective and enduring character education punishment for any stumbling is injurious; it is better to allow the child to stumble and make him realise what was wrong in his movement, so that he may not repeat it. Elaborating on this principle the Mother advises to parents:

> "When a child has made a mistake, see that he confesses it to you spontaneously and frankly; and when he has confessed, make him understand with kindness and affection what was wrong in his movement, so that he should not repeat it. In any case, never scold him, a fault confessed must be forgiven. You should not allow any fear to slip between you and your child; fear is a disastrous way to education; invariably it gives birth to dissimulation and falsehood. An affection that sees clear, that is firm yet gentle and a sufficient practical knowledge will create bonds of trust that are indispensable for you to make the education of your child effective."[227]

Pointing to the efficacy and necessity of this attitude Sri Aurobindo notes:

> "All experience shows that man must be given a certain freedom to stumble in action as well as to err in knowledge so long as he does not get from within himself his freedom from

---

[227] Sri Aurobindo and the Mother, *On Education* (Pondicherry: Sri Aurobindo Ashram, Nov., 1973), pp. 135-38

wrong movement and error; otherwise he cannot grow, society for its own sake has to coerce the dynamic and the vital man, but coercion only chains up the devil, and alters at best his form of action into more mitigated and civilised movements; it does not and cannot eliminate him. The real virtue of the dynamic and vital being, the Life Purush, can only come by his finding a higher law and spirit for his activity within himself; to give him that, to illuminate and transform and not to destroy his impulse is the true spiritual means of regeneration."[228]

In the area of mental education, the child is free to select his subjects and the teachers. He is free to progress in his study at his own pace. He is free even not to study after fourteen years. In the area of the psychic, spiritual and supramental education, he is absolutely free. No formal training is given in these areas.

15. THE PRINCIPLE OF MOTIVATION

For effective learning and teaching appeal to lower as well as higher order motives is very necessary. This is the reason why the use of the gross outer incentives like competitions, prizes, etc. have been considered necessary by the Mother[229] in the free progress system. They are indispensable also because the children are not *yogins* and their consciousness is still infant, mostly mental-vital-physical with vital predominant. Yet, they are also encouraged to depend on higher order motives of the need of self-progress and the need of self-control as far as possible, so that ultimately they may be led even in their physical pursuit by the reason and the psychic, spiritual and supramental forces.

---

[228] SABCL, Vol. 15, p. 216

[229] The Mother, "Physical Education and Yoga", *Mother India*, XX, 10-11 (Nov.-Dec., 1968), pp. 54-56; CWM, Vol. 9, pp. 96-97: Sri Aurobindo and the Mother, *On Education* (Pondicherry: Sri Aurobindo Ashram, Nov., 1973), p. 138

16. THE PRINCIPLE OF INTEREST

In the area of physical education, to apply this principle, captains try to make physical activities of serious nature interesting by bringing in an element of novelty, if possible. At the same time interest is created by allowing the children to make ingenious suggestions and partly to organise their activities themselves. Moreover, according to the Mother's[230] advice, they are instructed to cultivate the will for progress and thus be self-motivated.

In the area of mental education the students are allowed to choose, as far as possible, their subject of study and the teachers. Moreover, they are not spoon-fed but they have to work, learn and study in a research way and at every step they are guided and helped in such a manner that they see themselves successfully progressing in their study. These are some of the general techniques that work out the principle of interest in the area of mental education.

The students are guided to observe, note and cultivate the positive developments in their vital nature and not to worry about their shortcomings so as to maintain interest in their vital education.

They are to pursue psychic and spiritual education, only if they are interested in them. Thus, the free progress system has worked out the principle of interest thoroughly.

17. THE PRINCIPLE OF EQUALITY OF SEX

The girls are provided with equal opportunities in all the areas of education. The uniqueness of the system is in applying the principle in the area of physical education thoroughly.

The Mother[231] asserts that the man's and woman's bodies are equal as far as the capacity to take physical education is concerned. So, it is a prejudice to believe that the woman needs a different programme

---

[230] The Mother, Ibid., p. 52
[231] CWM Vol. 8, pp. 240-243

of education. Guided by this principle the S.A.I.C.E. provides equal opportunities to both the sexes. The woman has no holiday, even, during the monthly menstrual period.

18. THE PRINCIPLE OF INNER DEVELOPMENT

Physical activities if done with higher motives are occasions for the inner development. Students are encouraged to play and do other activities in the best way to express their inner consciousness and not out of base motives of strife, competitions, and jealousy. Moreover, the psychic spiritual turn[232] and musical accompaniment to certain exercises are for causing the inner development. Music[233] makes younger children express their inner feelings through physical movements. Similarly, they are encouraged to pursue their education in other areas with higher motives. Moreover, the psychic spiritual turn given to all activities of education brings into play the inner and the higher consciousness and ensures their inner developments in the physical, vital and mental consciousness.

These are the principles operating generally in all the areas of education. Now, the principles working more or less exclusively behind each of the areas of development and education will be mentioned in brief.

---

[232] The Mother, "Physical Education and Yoga", *Mother India*, XX, 10-11 (Nov.-Dec., 1968), p. 57
[233] Department of Physical Education, Sri Aurobindo Ashram, *Op. Cit.*, p. 179

IV. THE SPECIFIC PRINCIPLES APPLIED IN THE AREA OF PHYSICAL EDUCATION AND DEVELOPMENT

1. PRINCIPLE OF APPEAL TO THE POSITIVE FEELINGS ONLY

Negative emotions (motives) should never have any say; only the positive motives should have their play. So, following the Mother's[234] directive, while teaching hygiene and hygienic habits as a part of physical education, utmost care is taken that fear of germs and disease does not get instilled into the students, as fear is a negative emotion.

2. THE PRINCIPLE OF DEVELOPING AUTOMATION

The body is a material machine and if enough automation is developed in it side by side with plasticity, much conscious energy and will may be harnessed, for higher pursuits. The body is predominantly inconscient and inert in nature and tendency. Regular food, sleep, habits and physical exercises will make it run well automatically without much use of conscious attention and application of will. Thus, our energies can be saved and directed to higher pursuits. Yet, one must create enough plasticity in the body also, so as to adjust to any accidental changes and demands. It is for these reasons that utmost regularity is demanded of each student in his physical culture by the Mother.[235]

3. THE PRINCIPLE OF PHYSICAL INSTINCT

The body has its own consciousness and its own sure instinct, which can most correctly guide it in all its matters. The Mother[236] had

---

[234] Sri Aurobindo and the Mother, *On Education* (Pondicherry: Sri Aurobindo Ashram, Nov., 1973); p. 103

[235] Ibid., p. 100

[236] Sri Aurobindo and the Mother, *On Education* (Pondicherry: Sri Aurobindo Ashram, Nov., 1973); pp. 101-2

advised to listen to the physical instinct in all matters about the body (food, sleep, exercises, etc.) for the instinct of the body is a very sure thing, if it has not been disturbed by thought or vital will. The student is free not to take part in any activity if his instinct, and not desire, dictates him to do so.

4. THE PRINCIPLE OF NECESSITY OF ACHIEVING AS MUCH AS POSSIBLE DURING THIS LIFE ONLY

To accomplish the psychic, spiritual and supramental transformation is a very difficult task and it takes several lives. So by proper physical education the body must be made fit to live as long as possible, so that one can have more time in a single life for more achievements. Though the progress made in one life does not perish, it is also true that in the next life things are to be started from the beginning. The gains of the previous life make achievements comparatively easy. The students may opt for sadhana in future, and so the physical training for the body's longevity is necessary for them, so that in future they may not be handicapped. This is what can be inferred from Pranab's[237] argument for the need of physical education for completion of Sri Aurobindo's Yoga.

V. THE SPECIFIC PRINCIPLES APPLIED IN THE AREA OF VITAL EDUCATION

1. THE PRINCIPLE OF INDISPENSABILITY OF THE VITAL

Pointing to the importance of educating the vital the Mother asserts that the vital is indispensable for any achievement on any plane, for it holds within itself power, energy, enthusiasm and effective

---

[237] Pranab Kumar Bhattacharya, *Op. Cit.,* p. 174

dynamics.[238] Emphasising this fact Sri Aurobindo has advised to perfect it. He has maintained that,

> "The vital is necessary force and nothing can be done or created in the bodily existence, if the vital is not there as an instrument. Even sadhana needs the vital force.

***   ***   ***

> "The vital has not to be killed or destroyed, but purified and transformed by the psychic and spiritual control and perfected and made strong."[239]

Following this principle, much care is being taken to nourish, purify and strengthen the vital of the students in all aspects of the free progress education.

2. THE PRINCIPLE THAT THE SENSATIONS ARE THE NOURISHMENTS AND THE MEANS OF EDUCATION OF THE VITAL

Sensations are to be allowed with discrimination and discernment. Sensations are the excellent instruments for knowledge and education. So they must be used for this purpose and not for entertainment, amusement, pleasure or self-satisfaction. It is very necessary, on the above grounds, to reject and avoid sensations and vital vibrations that are not favourable to harmony and poise of the vital. And so in the S.A.I.C.E. the choicest aesthetic environment described in the previous chapter is maintained.

3. THE PRINCIPLE THAT AESTHETIC EDUCATION DEVELOPS THE CHARACTER ALSO

Explaining this psychological principle the Mother wrote:

---

[238] CWM, Vol. 3, pp. 72-75
[239] SABCL, Vol. 22, p. 346 and also refer SABCL, Vol. 24, 1219

"A methodical and enlightened cultivation of the senses can, little by little, eliminate from the child whatever is by contagion vulgar, commonplace and crude. This education will have very happy effects even on his character. For one who has developed a truly refined taste will, because of this very refinement, feel incapable of acting in a crude, brutal or vulgar manner. This refinement will protect him from many base and perverse movements."[240]

It is to effect this principle that the S.A.I.C.E. in collaboration with Sri Aurobindo Ashram, provides rich aesthetic environment and ample opportunities for learning of arts and crafts.

4. THE PRINCIPLE THAT THE VITAL IS SATISFIED BY NOTHING AND ITS DEMANDS HAVE NO LIMITS[241]

This psychological principle is always brought to the notice of the students, and they are encouraged not to fall prey to the usual practice of trying to please it by indulging in it.

5. THE PRINCIPLE THAT EVERYONE POSSESSES TWO OPPOSITE TENDENCIES IN THE CHARACTER[242]

Everybody has opposite tendencies in his vital, for example, generosity and meanness, selfishness and unselfishness. This psychological fact is at the basis of initial exercise in changing the vital (character) by self-observing one's opposite tendencies and concentrating on cultivation of positive ones only with no botheration with negative ones. It means that not much stress is to be put to eliminate

---

[240] Sri Aurobindo and the Mother, *On Education* (Pondicherry: Sri Aurobindo Ashram, Nov., 1973), p. 111; also refer CWM, Vol. 6, pp. 79-90

[241] Sri Aurobindo and the Mother, *On Education* (Pondicherry: Sri Aurobindo Ashram, Nov., 1973), p. 107

[242] Ibid., p. 108

the negative ones actively, but they are to be crowded out by good ones. Thus is to begin the move for ending the internecine war in the vital.

6. THE PRINCIPLE OF REFRACTORINESS OF THE VITAL

The vital is strongly refractory to any attempt to its reformation, so the "education of the vital is very difficult and to be successful in it one must have endurance, endless persistence and an inflexible will."[243] Conceding to this psychological principle, the free progress system enjoins upon the educators to have extreme patience. If students do not fall in line easily as regards general discipline and personal good behaviour and do not show enough regularity, keenness and speed in study, they are not forced by the teachers into discipline but are helped to bridle the vital by their own rational will gradually, however long time it may take.

7. THE PRINCIPLE THAT THE CHARACTER CAN BE CHANGED

For the change of the character intervention of deeper psychic forces and higher spiritual and supramental conscious powers is inevitable. If the supramental consciousness can be brought down into the subconscient and its control is established there a fundamental change in the character (vital) can be achieved. And that is why the psychic spiritual turn is given to vital education even. Students are advised to depend on the Mother's powers only ultimately for changing their vital and not on their own imperfect mental will.

8. THE PRINCIPLE OF TRIPLE SOURCES OF SUBSISTENCE OF THE VITAL

The Mother[244] has stated that the vital gets its subsistence from three sources: (i) physical energies coming through sensations, (ii) from

---

[243] Ibid., p. 107
[244] Ibid., p. 140

its own plane, when it is sufficiently wide, receptive, and in contact with the universal forces, and (iii) spiritual forces and inspirations from above. That is why the students are provided with various aesthetic sensations in abundance and are advised to open the vital to higher domains. As the aspiration for progress opens the vital to higher spiritual forces, they are advised to have that aspiration too.

9. THE PRINCIPLES OF CHARACTER TRAINING

Principles behind the practice of not using moral textbooks or instructions for character training are these: "The danger of moral textbooks is that they make the thinking of high thing mechanical and artificial and whatever is mechanical and artificial is inoperative for good."[245] Apart from this objection, Sri Aurobindo put forward one other objection on the psychological grounds too: The heart is not the mind and to instruct the mind does not necessarily improve the heart. That is why moral teaching is not done in the S.A.I.C.E.. But the teacher and social life of the S.A.I.C.E. are examples of morality and the students imbibe morality unconsciously from them. Moreover, there is one more objection raised by Dowsett:

> "Today the authorities that 'enforce' education glibly enjoin upon us the urgent need for moral instruction which they sometimes concede, must come from religious instruction. Have we yet to learn that such moral and religious states of consciousness do not come from instruction but emanate from a basic spiritual experience."[246]

10. THE PRINCIPLE OF INTERNALIZATION

No forceful imposition of moral rules is resorted to, because the conformity to the imposed rules becomes hypocritical and temporal. As soon as the force of imposition is absent, the suppressed unregenerate

---

[245] Ibid., p. 27

[246] Norman Dowsett, *Psychology for Future Education*, (Pondicherry: D.F.R.A.D., Sri Aurobindo Society, 1977); p. 82

character will raise its head. Instead, if the norm is internalised, it guides one's behaviours from within, and for all times. So, in the free progress system students are helped to appreciate the need of rules in life and accept, respect and obey them with their own conscious understanding and will through elaborate guidance, which is available everywhere and always in the S.A.I.C.E..

11. THE PRINCIPLE THAT THE SO-CALLED MISCHIEVOUS CHARACTER IS THE PRODUCT OF THE UNUSED EXCESSIVE VITAL ENERGY

Commenting on this principle Sri Aurobindo cautioned:

"Great care will have to be taken that unformed virtues are not rejected as faults. The wildness and recklessness of many young natures are only the over-flowing of an excessive strength, greatness and nobility. They should be purified, not discouraged.[247]

The Mother has given a predominant place to arts and crafts in the educational programme, so that the excessive vital energy may be channelised into healthy behaviours and activities.

VI. THE SPECIFIC PRINCIPLES APPLIED IN THE AREA OF MENTAL EDUCATION

As far as the mental education is concerned, the free progress system in its full-fledged form is introduced from the third standard onwards only, because by that time a student has sufficient knowledge of reading and writing to learn by himself using worksheets.

---

[247] Sri Aurobindo and the Mother, *On Education* (Pondicherry: Sri Aurobindo Ashram, Nov., 1973); p. 30

1. THE PRINCIPLE OF FREEDOM OF NOT TO STUDY

Free progress system makes education compulsory for the student up to his age of 14 only, following the Mother's following assertions:

"Until the child becomes at least a little conscious of itself, it must be subjected to a certain rule, for it has not yet capacity of choosing for itself.

"That age is very variable. . . . But still, it is understood that in the seven-year period between the age of seven and fourteen, one begins to reach the age of reason. If one is helped, one can become a reasoning being between seven and fourteen.

***   ***   ***

"And so I say: if at about that age (fourteen years) some children declare categorically,"Intellectual growth does not interest me at all, I don't want to learn", I don't see by what right one could impose studies on them nor why it should be necessary to standardise them.

***   ***   ***

"One can't make knowledge and intelligence compulsory. That's all".[248]

2. THE PRINCIPLE THAT STUDY IS THE MENTAL GYMNASTIC

Students are encouraged to study as many subjects as possible; because according to the Mother[249] studies of different subjects is nothing but mental gymnastics, which develop the brain and different mental faculties and make the mind supple. Such a mind is necessary

---

[248] CWM, Vol. 8, pp. 180-81
[249] Ibid., pp. 181-84, 364-66; CWM, Vol. 4, p .203; CWM, Vol. 9, p. 402

for expressing multifaceted divine reality which is the final aim of Sri Aurobindo's integral education.

3. THE PRINCIPLE THAT STUDY CAN MAKE THE THE MIND SUPPLE AND COMPREHENSIVE

The students are encouraged to study many subjects and the same subject from various approaches. The principle behind this practice is enunciated by the Mother aptly in these words:

> "In order to increase the suppleness and comprehensiveness of his mind, one should not only look to the number and variety of subjects for study, but particularly to the diverse approaches to the same subject."[250]

4. THE PRINCIPLE OF TIME FACTOR IN UNDERSTANDING

The Mother[251] advised the students to be patient enough with the difficult subject keeping in mind the principle of time factor and understanding: A new difficult idea makes a convolution in the brain and works on the brain incessantly without one's conscious participation. "The way the human being is at present constituted, the time factor must always be taken into account."[252] That is why in the free progress system students have the liberty to study at their own pace.

5. THE PRINCIPLE OF CONCENTRATION

Concentration on what a student is doing, saves his time and him from the vital influences and vibrations of illness. That is why very packed up routine is there for the student and all facility for developing concentration. The Mother clarifies this principle of concentration thus:

---

[250] Sri Aurobindo and the Mother, *On Education* (Pondicherry: Sri Aurobindo Ashram, Nov., 1973), p. 117; CWM, Vol. 6, pp. 18-20

[251] CWM, Vol. 4, pp. 198-99

[252] Ibid., p. 199

"When you work, if you are able to concentrate, you can do absolutely in ten minutes what would otherwise take you one hour. When you have much to do, you must learn, how to concentrate exclusively on what you are doing, with an intensity in your attention."[253]

6. THE PRINCIPLE THAT INTEREST AND WILL FOR PROGRESS DEVELOP CONCENTRATION

The Mother[254] asserted that concentration is indispensable for mental progress, and interest and the will for progress are two dynamic forces helping to develop concentration. That is why all good means from games up to rewards are used in the free progress classes, so that students may progressively develop their concentration. For that there is guidance for meditation also.

7. THE PRINCIPLE OF ATTENDING THE NEED OF THE STUDENT

The material of the course and duration of a course must be according to the need of the class. Following this principle the Mother[255] advised the teacher to prepare and write down his own course and fix up the duration of the course for the class himself, and no other authority should interfere in this work. Thus, the teacher has to produce special material and the books.

8. THE PRINCIPLE OF TURNING THE MIND UPWARD FOR ARTS AND LITERATURE AND ON THE SUBJECT FOR STUDY OF SCIENCE

It is the same instrument of mind that can achieve significant achievements in science as well as arts and imagination, if with a fixed

---

[253] CWM, Vol. 5, p. 125; CWM; Vol. 4, pp. 364-65

[254] Sri Aurobindo and the Mother, *On Education* (Pondicherry: Sri Aurobindo Ashram, Nov., 1973); pp. 115-16

[255] CWM Vol. 5, pp. 106-7, 416

will to know, the mind is concentrated towards the details of matter for studying science and concentrated upward for inspiration for artistic and literary studies. The Mother[256] has assured that with this discipline one could be a genius in both the fields. That is why the students are guided to practice this discipline while studying.

9. THE PRINCIPLE OF EDUCATION FOR MENTAL HEALTH

Glean, Myers, Blair and others[257] insist that for the sake of mental health the student must be free to progress at his pace with calm mind under an environment of protected freedom and with no subjection to competition, frustration and tension. If the student studies in the above conditions, his adrenal glands wouldn't over-secrete and thus his mental as well as physical health wouldn't be jeopardized.

The free progress class provides all the facilities enumerated in the above principle, and thus, it meets the requirements of the students' mental health.

10. THE PRINCIPLE OF EDUCATION FOR UNDERSTANDING

The teacher of a free progress class gives answers and/or shows where the answers can be found to all the questions of a student. He takes pains to ensure that a student understands the things, and not merely mugs them up. This practice is based on the principle that, "One knows only what one Understands."[258]

---

[256] Ibid, pp. 128-29

[257] Glean, Myers, Blair el. al., Educational Psychology, 2nd Edition (New York: The Macmillan Company, 1966); pp. 15-47

[258] Sri Aurobindo and the Mother, On Education (Pondicherry: Sri Aurobindo Ashram, Nov., 1973); p. 116

11. THE PRINCIPLE THAT NOTHING CAN BE TAUGHT

According to Sri Aurobindo[259] a principle of true teaching is that nothing can be taught. The teacher is not an instructor or a task-master, he is a helper and a guide. That is why in the free progress system the teacher has to be in the background and the student is to learn and work himself guided by worksheet and helped by the teacher. The Teacher's task is to educe knowledge that is in the student. That is why there are very few lectures and less of formal collective teaching.

12. THE PRINCIPLE THAT EDUCATION MUST BE ACCORDING TO THE NATURE OF THE CHILD

Sri Aurobindo[260] has insisted that the mind has to be consulted in its growth. The idea of hammering the child into the shape desired by the parent or the teacher is a barbarous and ignorant superstition. That is why the free progress system gives full freedom to the student to choose his subject of study and his career himself and allows him to progress freely in his study.

13. THE PRINCIPLE OF KNOWN TO UNKNOWN

The learning material is presented before the child in the following order as far as possible: local, national and international and past, present and future. For a "principle of education is to work from the near to the far, from that which is to that which shall be."[261] This principle completely finds its application in the worksheet method of teaching and learning: A student goes on to the next topic only after he has sufficiently grasped the previous unit.

---

[259] Ibid., p. 20

[260] Ibid., pp. 20-21

[261] Ibid., pp. 21-22

14. THE PRINCIPLE OF MEMORY BY THE CONSCIOUSNESS

"Consciousness is a much higher memory than the mechanical brain. ... The mechanical brain memory can forget — can confuse and deform—but if you are able to establish in you once again the state of consciousness in which you were at a given moment, you have exactly the same experience. And this depends entirely on the development of your consciousness."[262]

That is why in the free progress system initially there is no stress on learning by heart by the student, but there is emphasis on conscious self-activity with the help of the worksheets and ultimately the stress on guiding the students to widen the consciousness by the inward movements in their mental study.

15. THE PRINCIPLE OF SYNTHESIS OF THOUGHTS

A progressively developing synthesis around only a very high idea is necessary if the thought structure is to prove to be a stable, dynamic and constructive force, and if the mind is to keep its youth always.[263] That is why the students are taught to synthesise their ideas and they are made familiar with the highest central idea of "spiritual evolution" of Sri Aurobindo.

16. THE PRINCIPLE OF TIME-BIAS

Describing the principle of time-bias, Sri Norman Dowsett writes,

"Each individual has his own time-consciousness, his own relation to time importance, his own time harmony, and his own time-synthesis.

---

[262] CWM, Vol. 5, pp. 270, 290-91

[263] Sri Aurobindo and the Mother, *On Education* (Pondicherry: Sri Aurobindo Ashram, Nov., 1973); p. 118

"It is extremely frustrating . . . for a student to have to leave a particular problem or study in which he is fully absorbed because the bell is sounded for the end of the period and he has to go on to some other subject, often for which he has little interest."[264]

The collective work is the innovation introduced in education by the free progress system to practice this principle.

17. THE PRINCIPLE OF HEURISTIC APPROACH OF LEARNING

Research and invention by self-activity develops creativity and harnesses natural creative energy of a student to a good end, affirms Sri Pavitra.[265] So the free progress system employs worksheets as far as possible and library work and question-answer and discussion as methods of learning and teaching, so that the student is not spoon-fed by the teacher, but he has to invent or discover the knowledge. Pavitra[266] has put forward a new definition of research: "For a student every unknown knowledge when found by himself is a research."

18. THE PRINCIPLE OF CLASS CONTROL

For controlling the class the teachers are dissuaded to resort to reward and punishment by the Mother. Vibrations of calm and humility are the only sure means of class control. This is the principle she has put forward for the class discipline. She has asserted this principle by asking the following question.

" ... You have an indisciplined, disobedient, insolent pupil; well, that represents a certain vibration ... but if you yourself do not have within you the opposite vibration, the vibration of discipline, humility, of a quietude and peace, which

---

[264] Norman Dowsett, *Op. Cit.,* p. 89

[265] Pavitra, *Op. Cit.,* pp. 60-61

[266] Ibid.

nothing can disturb, how do you expect to have any influence?"[267]

19. THE PRINCIPLE THAT SILENCE OF MIND GIVES IT REST AND PROVIDES KNOWLEDGE

The Mother[268] prescribes that silence is the best way of giving rest to the mind; and the receptive silence is the best key for unlocking any enigma of any problem. The students have guidance and facility for developing this silence in the form of Silence Room and the sessions of mass meditations.

VII. THE SPECIFIC PRINCIPLES APPLIED IN THE AREA OF PSYCHIC EDUCATION

1. THE PRINCIPLE THAT THE PSYCHIC DEVELOPS NEW POWERS IN THE OUTER BEING

By giving some instances the Mother[269] has advanced the principle that the psychic being can manifest new powers of mind, vital and physical beings. For example, psychic influence can make a man a good artist or a poet or anything else.

2. THE PRINCIPLE OF THE NEED OF THE SILENT OUTER BEING FOR THE PSYCHIC MANIFESTATION

The silent and calm outer being is a necessary condition for the psychic realisation and for making it dynamic in life. Hence, the

---

[267] CWM, Vol. 8, p. 353

[268] Sri Aurobindo and the Mother, *On Education* (Pondicherry: Sri Aurobindo Ashram, Nov., 1973); p. 120

[269] CWM, Vol. 9, pp. 395-97

Mother[270] has prescribed unlearning everything that one has learnt so carefully throughout his life, when one wants his psychic to have its say.

3. THE PRINCIPLE OF THE MIND'S INCAPACITY TO KNOW THE THINGS SPIRITUAL

Mind cannot know the things spiritual, so the Mother[271] insisted that one undergoing psychic education should abstain from all mental opinion and reaction. The system teaches this practice to the students: The students are advised and encouraged not to try to interpret their inner experiences.

4. THE PRINCIPLE THAT PSYCHIC EDUCATION MUST PRECEDE SPIRITUAL EDUCATION

The psychic, being individual divine in the life, can safely open outer nature to higher spiritual forces. That is why the students are advised to open within first before opening upward. This principle is to be followed also for the reason that a person may not opt for Nirvana after spiritual realisation, but remains in the worldly life and continues to perfect it till the divine life on earth is realised.

5. THE PRINCIPLE OF NON-PREFERENCE

The Mother[272] has prescribed that if the students want to study for the Divine and not for themselves, they should not have preference for any subjects.

---

[270] CWM, Vol. 4, p. 203

[271] Sri Aurobindo and The Mother, *Op. Cit.*, p. 125

[272] CWM, Vol. 6, pp. 153-55

VIII. THE SPECIFIC PRINCIPLES APPLIED IN THE AREA OF SPIRITUAL EDUCATION

1. THE PRINCIPLE OF POSTERIORITY OF SPIRITUAL EDUCATION TO PSYCHIC EDUCATION

After sufficient Psychicisation of the outer nature, it is safe to open the being to the higher levels of the mental consciousness. By doing so premature descents of the higher forces are avoided and the external nature is not subjected to unnecessary turmoil. The free progress system instructs its pupils into this principle for their safe spiritual journey, which they may undertake in future. The students are made to study relevant literature.

2. THE PRINCIPLE OF SURRENDER

For spiritual education — for Spiritual change of nature — total surrender to the Higher Forces, the Divine above, is a must. So, the pupils are instructed to act upon whatever comes from above and allow the descended higher forces to have their say in life, when they take up this education.

3. THE PRINCIPLE OF INADEQUACY OF SPIRITUAL EDUCATION FOR TRANSFORMATION

Spiritual education can cosmicise the personality, but cannot radically transform the nature and ensure the divine immortal nature. For that supramental force is necessary. So, the students are informed mentally that a spiritual adventurer should not stop short at spiritual realisation only, but should shoot forth to the Supramental domain also.

IX. THE SPECIFIC PRINCIPLES APPLIED IN THE AREA OF SUPRAMENTAL EDUCATION

1. THE PRINCIPLE OF 'FROM ABOVE DOWNWARD'

The movement of supramental education is from above downwards. So the aspirants are made aware that they must start supramentalising, from mind to vital and to physical in turn.

2. THE PRINCIPLE THAT ONLY THE SUPRAMENTAL CAN DIVINISE THE OUTER PERSONALITY

The pupils are made aware of this fact through the study of relevant literature, so that, they may not stop short at the spiritual education which is partial and feel frustrated at partial realisation.

3. THE PRINCIPLE OF NECESSITY OF LONG LIFE SPAN FOR SUPRAMENTALISATION

Supramentalisation may need a long life, that is why the best type of physical education ensuring fit and long living physical is a must. The students are encouraged to undergo the physical education keeping in view this principle of supramental education also.

4. THE PRINCIPLE THAT FIRST THE INNER NATURE IS SUPRAMENTALISED AND THEN THE OUTER GRADUALLY

Looking to this principle, the students are warned not to judge the presence of the supramental in anybody on the basis of his outer appearances; that would be quite unreasonable.

X. THE PRINCIPLES OF EDUCATION OF NATIONALISM AND INTERNATIONALISM

1. THE PRINCIPLE THAT THE EXTERNAL ENVIRONMENT DOES EDUCATE A PERSON

Following this principle a multinational and international culture is provided to all the students. They may acquire international and national consciousness.

True international spirit can develop only when one realises the psychic, as the psychic in each one is the Divine's own portion. One, who has realised it, can feel oneness with all. That is the principle behind the practice of stress on inward movement in all activities in the S.A.I.C.E..

XI. THE PRINCIPLES INVOLVED IN THE EFFORTS FOR LIFELONG CONTINUOUS EDUCATION AND THE EDUCATION OF THE PUBLIC

1. THE PRINCIPLE THAT TOTAL TRANSFORMATION IS POSSIBLE AFTER A LONG TIME, SOMETIMES AFTER SEVERAL LIVES

Man's psychic spiritual perfection and supramental transformation can be accomplished after several lives. Following this principle, the S.A.I.C.E. encourages and provides means, facilities and attitudes for lifelong education to students and to all adults.

2. THE PRINCIPLE THAT EDUCATION MUST START AT BOTH THE INDIVIDUAL AND THE SOCIAL ENDS AT A TIME, IF IT IS TO BE ENDURING

This principle is behind the S.A.I.C.E.'s concern with public education. If public is properly educated, they will at least be able to appreciate and accept the spirituality and psychicised or spiritualized human beings, and not act as a soap washing away their spirituality. The spiritual man thus can have conducive society around him at least.

XII. THE PRINCIPLES BEHIND THE ROLE OF THE TEACHER AND HIS EDUCATION

1. THE PRINCIPLE THAT THE STUDENT'S TRUE LEADER IS HIS PSYCHIC

True Leader and guide of the student in his education is and must be his psychic. Following this principle free progress system has restricted the role of a teacher. The teacher is to act as merely a friend, philosopher, guide and helper to a fellow student travelling on the same way, and not to replace the leadership of the student's own psychic: He is to encourage the students to act from within only. He is merely one element among many in the environment, and so he is expected to try to be a good example to his student in all matters.

XIII. THE PRINCIPLES OF DISCIPLINE

1. THE FIRST PRINCIPLE OF DISCIPLINE IS THE PRINCIPLE OF THE MIDDLE ROAD

The Mother has made it clear that to lay down any fixed categorical theory about the method of maintaining discipline is very difficult, because each case of indiscipline is absolutely different and asks for a different procedure. So she maintained,

> "Probably, one needs to find a middle term between the two, between the two extremes: that of watching over him all the time and that of leaving him absolutely free to do what he

likes, without even warning him against the accidents which are likely to occur."[273]

2. AN INNER SPONTANEOUS GOVERNING OF LIFE IS THE ONLY EFFECTIVE MEANS OF DISCIPLINE

This is the principle which throbs behind the system of discipline at the S.A.I.C.E.. Too much of external imposition of discipline by the teachers is a taboo in the free progress system.

3. THE REASON SHOULD GOVERN THE BEING BEFORE THE PSYCHIC IS REALISED

Following this principle, the students are encouraged and helped by way of non-directive guidance to obey their own reason and not to lower impulses by the teachers.

4. AFTER THE REALISATION OF THE PSYCHIC, THE STUDENT IS NOT TO FOLLOW ANY DISCIPLINE OTHER THAN DICTATED BY IT

The psychic is really and truly the free part of the human being and once a student realises his psychic, he is not to be subjected to arbitrary external discipline. Perhaps, the system has not to worry about putting into practice this principle, as the teaching of students having the psychic realisation is a matter of the future. But it can be said that the maximum freedom allowed to the students at the S.A.I.C.E. is in a way remote and indirect working out of the principle.

The S.A.I.C.E. has guidance facility and it has built up an environment that works out these principles more or less spontaneously.

---

[273] CWM, Vol. 6, p. 415

SUMMARY

1-2. Human being is an evolved being on the earth and in essence consciousness of man and that of The Divine Being is same, but due to a certain separative consciousness of man, this sameness is not perceived or experienced. If one lives life from within with an upward look, one's outer consciousness unites with one's psychic centre and ascends gradually to supramental consciousness. Concurrently with this human process higher divine consciousness descends helping the ascending evolution and one would ultimately unite with the supramental consciousness, where that separative consciousness can no longer exist. One now knows one is not separate from the divine. This is the central evolutionary principle of human development and integral education.

3. There are several principles for the development of total personality: Such as (i) four stages of perfection, (ii) unique nature of a person, (iii) interdependence of parts of being, (iv) government of reason and then psychic, etc.

4. (i) Appeal to the positive feelings only, (ii) principle of physical instinct, (iii) Developing automation, (iv) achieving as much as possible in this life only are principles of physical development.

5. (i) Indispensability of the vital, (ii) sensations nourish the vital, (iii) refractoriness of the vital, (iv) vital is insatiable, etc. are the principles of vital development.

6. (i) Freedom of not to study, (ii) study is mental gymnastics, (iii) study can make mind supple and plastic, (iv) concentration, etc. are principles of mental development.

7. (i) Psychic develops new powers in the outer being, (ii) education of psychic must precede education of the spirit. (iii) non-preference, etc. are principles of psychic development and education.

8. (i) Posteriority of spiritual education, (ii) surrender, (iii) inadequacy of spiritual education for transformation are a few principles of spiritual development.

9. (i) Only supramental can transform and divinise, (ii) necessity of increasing the life-span are few important principles of supramental development.

WORKBOOK: QUESTIONS FOR PREVIEW AND REVIEW

Essay Type Questions

1. Describe the cardinal principle of integral development and applied integral psychology.
2. Describe a few general principles of personality development.
3. Describe a few principles of physical development.
4. Describe a few principles of vital development.
5. Describe a few principles of mental development.
6. Describe a few principles of psychic development.
7. Describe a few principles of spiritual development.
8. Describe a few principles of supramental development.
9. Discuss the need of equal opportunity to woman and man in terms of personal benefit and social benefit?
10. Humanity is still animal. Discuss a few examples of human behaviour that demonstrate this fact in family situation, social situations, national situations and international situations.
11. Write an essay on effective and ineffective means of character development.
12. Describe three sources of subsistence of the vital.
13. What is principle of internalization? How can it be applied to refine and to evolve the character of the vital being?
14. Mischievous children are not good for families or societies, their unruly energies should be should be suppressed by force and they should be tamed. Discuss this traditional norm.

15. Vedic Psycho-Philosophy and Sri Auromere's integral psychology advises that compulsory standardized study should not be imposed on the children after they attain to age of 14.
16. Write an essay on the principles of discipline that the free progress system of education follows.
17. What type of life should be provided by the society to 14 years old children, if they declare they are not interested in studies?

Short Answer Type Questions and Fill in the Gap Type Questions

I-III
1. After man there are two steps of evolution. They are 1. _____ 2. _____.
2. Former steps of evolution were taken by Nature _____ a conscious will, but the steps after the advent of man are taken by nature _____ a conscious will. [with, without]
3. 1. _____, 2. _____, 3. _____, 4. _____, 5. _____ are the evolutionary steps.
4. Divinity is not involved in the matter. [True or False].
5. Yogic discipline and psychological discipline are two different things. [True or false]
6. Define conversion of consciousness.
7. What is transformation?
8. Humanity is still animal. List a few examples of human behaviour that demonstrate this fact.
9. Are there intervening ranges of consciousness between the mind and the supramental?
10. 1. _____, 2. _____, 3. _____, 4. _____ are the four stages of perfection.
11. What is a child?
12. Parts of consciousness of man are _____, _____, and _____.
13. Why should the mind, the vital and the physical be perfected?
14. Rule of _____ should not end till rule of ____ is established. [reason, psychic]
15. Can the body be divinised?

16. Which parts of human being are always at war with each other? Which part of human consciousness can harmonise them?
17. Psychic education should start in old age only. Discuss.
18. Describe the process of psychic-spiritual turn.
19. It is always better to know and remember the specific developments an exercise accomplishes when a particular exercise is done. Explain.
20. Changing outer behaviour before changing corresponding inner impulses and motives and interest is a quick way to change one's nature. Discuss.
21. How can interest be created?
22. Why, in every field of life and in every activity of life, man and woman should be partner to one another and nowhere, including military, segregation on the ground of sex should be allowed?

IV. THE SPECIFIC PRINCIPLES FOUND APPLIED IN THE AREA OF PHYSICAL EDUCATION

1. _____ and _____ are the two types of feelings.
2. Give example of developed automation in the body.
3. What is meant by plasticity in the physical culture?
4. Why is maintenance of daily routine of life good?
5. What is body instinct?
6. Why it is necessary to achieve as much as possible in existent life?

V. THE SPECIFIC PRINCIPLES FOUND APPLIED IN THE AREA OF VITAL EDUCATION

1. Ascetic disciplines generally prescribes that the vital consciousness should be restricted, bridled and allowed minimum play. What is your opinion?
2. Which activities nourish the vital?
3. How are sensations related to the vital?
4. Why beauty should be the ideal for material organisation?
5. Why sense training is very important, especially for Indians?
6. What is unformed virtues?

VI. THE SPECIFIC PRINCIPLES FOUND APPLIED IN THE AREA OF MENTAL EDUCATION

1. Study is merely mental Gymnastic. Explain this principle enumerating the powers of mind that study develops.
2. Explain the principle of the time factor of study.
3. Discuss in a paragraph of less than 600 words the interdependence of interest and concentration.
4. A parent has graduate degree in child psychology with the first Grade in child psychology. He is not able to persuade his child to do homework given by school. He beats his child and forces him to complete the home work. Give psychological explanation of the incidence.
5. Explain difference between memory of brain and consciousness.
6. Explain principle of time bias given by Norman Dowsett.
7. The Mother says _____ and _____ are the only sure means of education.
8. Why schools should create facilities of silent room for silent readings or relaxation?

VII. THE SPECIFIC PRINCIPLES INVOLVED IN PSYCHIC EDUCATION

1. Psychic develops new powers. Give two or more illustration.
2. If one wants that his psychic should manifest and perfect his outer being made up of mental-vital-physical beings, what should one do with his outer being?
3. It is better not to try to attempt to explain inner spiritual experiences mentally. Why?
4. Which type of student should not make condition not to study a subject that he does not prefer to study?

VIII. THE PRINCIPLES INVOLVED IN SPIRITUAL EDUCATION

1. Efforts for _____ development must precede the efforts for _____ development.

2. For transformation of human nature that ensures the birth into the next stage of evolution, _____ force is not sufficient but _____ force is the only force that is adequate.

IX. THE PRINCIPLES OF SUPRAMENTAL EDUCATION

1. Individual and the collectivity needs to follow a discipline in life that helps to lengthen the life span if supramental human being and supramental world is wanted by them. Explain this statement with proper reasons.

X. THE PRINCIPLES OF EDUCATION OF NATIONALISM AND INTERNATIONALISM

1. How to create international environment around the child in home, in school and in society?
2. Which inner realisation ensures permanent international sprit?

XI. THE PRINCIPLES INVOLVED IN THE EFFORTS FOR LIFELONG CONTINUOUS EDUCATION AND THE EDUCATION OF THE PUBLIC

1. Enumerate the principles involved in the efforts for continuous post school education and the education of the public.

XII. THE PRINCIPLES BEHIND THE ROLE OF THE TEACHER AND HIS EDUCATION

1. Describe in a short paragraph why teacher should play role of a senior peer.

XIII. THE PRINCIPLE OF DISCIPLINE

1. Describe the principle of the middle road in five lines.
2. What is the effective means of governance?
3. What should guide the life before the psychic is realised?
4. Should a person submit to social rules or submit to psychic he/she realises?

Exercises

1. Illustrate how quality of Love can be developed by using nine elements listed in the Table 15.1.
2. Illustrate the four stages of the anger-control and the development of peace.
3. State relation between study and education.

SELF TEST

1. List two most important elements of the practice of integral psychology.
2. There are definite steps of the practice of the integral psychology. (True or False)
3. Can animal evolve? Why?
4. What is the effect of the old Yoga?
5. Master is necessary in integral yoga. (True or False)
6. List four stages of perfection.
7. _____ should follow _____ education. (psychic, spiritual)
8. Why should one try to lengthen the life-span?
9. Write a short note on equality of sex.

Appendix 15.1

A TALK OF THE MOTHER WITH THE STUDENTS DURING HER WEEKLY CLASS ON 4 AUGUST 1954 ON THE UPANISHADIC METHOD OF TEACHING

[THE TEXT OF THE CHAPTER CAN BE FOUND IN COLLECTED WORKS OF THE MOTHER, VOL. 6, *'QUESTIONS AND ANSWERS 1954'*, ON PAGES 266-272]

4 August 1954

Q. Sweet Mother, what is the difference between a servant and a worker?

Ans. I don't think there is much difference; it is almost the same thing. Perhaps the attitude is not quite the same, but there is not much of a difference. In "servant" there seems to be something more: it is the joy of serving. The worker — he has only the joy of the work. But the work that is done as a service brings still greater joy.

Q. What does "self-love" mean?

Ans. I think self-love is a pleasant word for vanity. Self-love means that one loves oneself more than anything else; and what he implies by this, you see, are exactly those reactions of a vanity which is vexed when one is not appreciated at one's true worth, when one does not receive the praise one thinks one deserves, or the reward one believes one has earned, and when one is not complimented for everything one does. Indeed, all these movements come from dissatisfaction, because one doesn't receive what one hoped to, what one thought one deserved to receive!

Q. Sweet Mother, what is a "dynamic identification"?

Ans. It is the opposite of a passive or inert identification. It is an identification that is full of energy, will, action, enthusiasm; whereas one can be identified also in a kind of torpor.

Q. You have written in Words of Long Ago *that we justify all our weaknesses when we lack self-confidence. Why do we do this?*

Ans. Um! So! We justify all our weaknesses? It is not a positive want of self-confidence; it is a lack of confidence in what the divine Grace can do for us. To justify one's weaknesses is a kind of laziness and inertia.

Well, when one doesn't want to make an effort to correct oneself, one says, "Oh, it is impossible, I can't do it, I don't have the strength, I am not made of that stuff, I don't have the necessary qualities, I could never do it." It is absolute laziness, it is in order to avoid the required effort. When you are asked to make progress: "Oh, it is beyond my capacity, I am a poor creature, I can do nothing!" That's all. It is almost ill-will. It is extreme laziness, a refusal to make any effort. One accepts all one's defects and incapacities in order not to have to make the necessary effort to overcome them. One says, "I am like that, I can't be otherwise!" It is a refusal to let the divine Grace work in you. It is a justification of your own ill-will.

Has someone there a question? Or isn't there any?

Q. Sweet Mother, here Sri Aurobindo writes: "You will know and see and feel that you are a person and power formed by her out of herself, put out from her for the play...." What play?

Ans. The universe is called the play of the Divine!

Why?

Ans. Why? That's a way of speaking! You feel that it is not an amusing game? There are many who don't (*laughter*), who find that the play is not amusing. But still, it's a way of speaking.... One speaks of—without thinking that it is joyful — one speaks of "the play of forces"; it is the movement, the interaction. All activities are the play of forces. So one can take it in that sense. But, you see, it means that the divine Force, the divine Consciousness, has exteriorised itself to create the universe and all the play of forces in the universe. That's what it means, nothing else. I don't mean necessarily playing in the Playground! It can mean many other things!

(*Turning to the other children to induce them to ask questions*) Nothing? You don't have anything either?

Q. What is the meaning of "keep yourself free from all taint of the perversions of the ego"?

Ans. Perversions of the ego?

(*After a silence*) Perversion is something that goes astray from the divine truth and purity. The moment you start living in ignorance and falsehood, you live in perversion; and the whole world is made of ignorance and falsehood at present. So this means that if you remain in the ordinary consciousness, you are necessarily in the perversion of the ego.

Q. Mother, here it is said: "Even if the idea of the separate worker is strong in you and you feel that it is you who do the act, yet it must be done for her." For example, our study of sports — we must think that it is for the Divine?

Ans. But surely...

Q. How?

Ans. It is not even very difficult. You can first do it as a preparation so as to become capable of receiving the divine forces, and then, as a service, so that you may help in constructing the whole organisation of the Ashram. You can do it not with any personal gain in view, but with the intention of making yourselves ready to accomplish the divine work! This seems to me even quite indispensable if you want to profit fully from the situation. If you keep the ordinary point of view, well, you will always find yourselves in conditions which are not quite satisfactory, and incapable of receiving all the forces you can receive.

Q. Mother, if for instance in the long jump one makes an effort to jump a greater and greater distance, how does one do the divine work?

Ans. Eh? Excuse me, it is not for the pleasure of doing the long jump, it is to make your body more perfect in its functioning, and, therefore, a more suitable instrument for receiving the divine forces and manifesting them.

Why, everything, everything one does in this place must be done in this spirit, otherwise you do not even profit by the opportunity given to you, the circumstances given to you. I explained to you the other day, didn't I, that the Consciousness is here, penetrating all things and trying to manifest in all movements? But if you, on your side, tell yourself that the effort you are making, the progress you are making, you make in order to become more capable of receiving this Consciousness and of manifesting it, the work will naturally be much better and much quicker. And this seems to me even quite elementary, to tell you the truth; I am surprised that it could be otherwise! Because your presence in an Ashram organised as it is organised would have no meaning if it were not that! Of what use would it be? There are any number of universities, schools in the world which are very well organised!

But if you are here, it is for *a special reason*! It is because here there is a possibility of absorbing consciousness and progress which is not found elsewhere. And if you don't prepare yourselves to receive this, well, you will lose the chance that's given to you!

Why, I have never spoken of this before, because it seemed so obvious to me that it was not at all necessary to say it.

Q. Like that, Mother, one knows one must do all that! But when one does it, then the intention is different!

Ans. No, but... (*Silence*) What do you think, in a general way? It is by some kind of chance or luck — or just because your parents are here — that by chance you happen to be here, or what? I don't know! (*Laughing*) That you could as well be here as anywhere else, or what?

You are all old enough to have thought a little, and reflected a little. You have never asked yourselves, "Why am I here?" Have you asked yourselves this? Or is it something which... I indeed thought that you ought to take it as something quite... that it was understood, quite natural! So, I never spoke to you about it. Why, I would be interested in knowing... (*To a child*) Have you thought of this, you there?

Q. I told you, Sweet Mother, the other day!

Ans. That's right, but you can repeat it. (*To another child*) And you? Have you thought about it? Or do you take it like that... because papa and mamma are here, so I am here? (*Laughter*) (*To another*) And you?

Q. When you gave us "To the Children of the Ashram" — after that I understood.

Ans. Ah, you understood! Not before that?

Q. I did not think about it before.

Ans. But how old are you all, on an average, here? Fifteen or sixteen? Seventeen? Twenty? No? It is not like that? The Red Group is between fifteen and twenty, isn't it? Are there some here who are younger?

A. Child: No!

The Mother: But one begins to think at thirteen. One begins to think, to ask oneself questions, one even wonders, "What is life, and why do we live?" And still more when one finds oneself in a place like

358

this, which is not quite an ordinary place: "Why am I here?" and "What is the use of being here?" and "What is the reason for being here?" Eh?— You do not think? You do not think? I know two or three of you who think about it because you have told me. But (*laughing*) the others? You have never asked yourselves these questions, no?... Nobody is saying a word! (*Laughter*)

(*To a child*) So you, you have never thought about it? You have. (*Nobody replies.*) Ah! They don't want to say anything. All right, let's not talk any more about it then. (*Laughter*)

That's all? Is that enough?

Q. Mother, what's interesting is this: What is there in us that has made us come here?

Ans. Ah, that is interesting! What is the reason of your being here? Well, it's for each one to find it. Have you found it, you? No, not yet? Why, that's another very interesting question!

If you... (*Silence*) If you asked yourselves this, you would be obliged to seek the answer somewhere, within — because it is *within* you, the answer. "What is there in us that has made us come here?" The answer is within. There is nothing outside. And if you go deep enough, you will find a very clear answer... (*silence*) and an interesting answer. If you go deep enough, into a sufficiently complete silence from all outer things, you will find within you that flame about which I often speak, and in this flame you will see *your destiny*. You will see the aspiration of centuries which has been concentrated gradually, to lead you through countless births *to the great day of realisation* — that preparation which has been made through thousands of years, and is reaching its culmination.

And as you will have gone very deep to find this, all your incapacities, all your weaknesses, everything in you that denies and does not understand, all that — you will feel that it is not yourself, it is just like a garment which serves in some way and which you have put on for the time being. But you will understand that in order to be truly capable of profiting fully by the opportunity to do what you wanted to do, what you have aspired to do for such a long time, you must gradually bring the light, the consciousness, the truth into all these obscure elements of the external garment, so that you may be able to understand integrally *why you are here*! And not only that you may understand it, but that you may be able to do it. For centuries this has been prepared in you, not in this... (*Mother pinches the skin of her forearm*) this is quite recent, isn't it?... but in your true self. And *for centuries* it has been awaiting *this opportunity.*

And then you enter *immediately* into the marvellous. You see to what an extent it is extraordinary... that things which one has so long hoped for, things for which one has prayed so much, made so many efforts, suddenly a moment comes when *they are realised.*

It is the moment when great things are done. One must not miss the opportunity.

(*Long silence*)

On the 15th of August I shall give you something written by Sri Aurobindo which is precisely on this subject — it is called *The Hour of God.*

You will read it carefully and you will understand.

There we are.

CHAPTER XVI

THE PSYCHIC, SPIRITUAL AND SUPRAMENTAL PERFECTION OF THE TRIPLE BEING

I. THE PSYCHIC PERFECTION OF THE TRIPLE BEING

II. THE SPIRITUAL PERFECTION OF THE TRIPLE BEING

III. THE SUPRAMENTAL PERFECTION OF THE TRIPLE BEING

Picture:
(16.1) THE MOTHER (1969)

I. THE PSYCHIC PERFECTION OF THE TRIPLE BEING

1. DIFFERENCE BETWEEN THE PSYCHIC AND THE SPIRITUAL PERFECTION

Psychicisation and spiritualisation are two different things. Psychic change is from within, but the spiritual changes from above. Explaining this Sri Aurobindo writes,

"Between psychicisation and spiritualisation there is a difference. The spiritual is the change that descends from above, the psychic is the change that comes from within by the psychic dominating the mind, vital and physical.

* * *

361

Psychicisation means the change of the lower nature, bringing right vision into the mind, right impulse and feeling into the vital, right movement and habit into the physical — all turned towards the Divine, all based on love, adoration, bhakti — finally, the vision and sense of the Mother everywhere in all as well as in the heart, her Force working in the being etc., faith, consecration, surrender."[274]

Thus, psychicisation

(i)   brings right attitude in the physical, vital and mind,

(ii) makes the physical, vital and mind to turn to the Divine,

(iii) makes the physical, vital and mind to love, adore and offer bhakti to the Divine and finally imparts to them vision of the Mother everywhere and makes heart to feel the Force of the Mother working in the triple being and have faith in the Mother and consecrate and surrender to the Mother.

2. PSYCHICISATION AND SPIRITUALISATION ARE COMPLIMENTARY TO EACH OTHER

Explaining interdependence and simultaneousness of the psychic perfection and the spiritual perfection, Sri Aurobindo clarifies to a disciple that

"The two feelings are both of them right — they indicate the two necessities of the sadhana. One is to go inward and open fully the connection between the psychic being and the outer nature. The other is to open upward to the Divine Peace, Force, Light, Ananda above, to rise up into it and bring it down into the nature and the body. Neither of these two movements, the psychic and the spiritual, is complete without the other. If the spiritual ascent and descent are not made, the spiritual transformation of the nature cannot happen; if the full

---

[274] SABCL Vol. 24; p.1093

psychic opening and connection is not made, the transformation cannot be complete.

There is no incompatibility between the two movements; some begin the psychic first, others the spiritual first, some carry on both together. The best way is to aspire for both and let the Mother's Force work it out according to the need and turn of the nature.

* * *

The psychic is the first of two transformations necessary — if you have the psychic transformation it facilitates immensely the other, i.e., the transformation of the ordinary human into the higher spiritual consciousness — otherwise one is likely to have either a slow and dull or exciting but perilous journey.... I have never said anything about a "transformation of the psychic"; I have always written about a "psychic transformation" of the nature, which is a very different matter. I have sometimes written of it as a psychicisation of the nature. The psychic is in the evolution, part of the human being, its divine part — so a psychicisation will not carry one beyond the present evolution but will make the being ready to respond to all that comes from the Divine or Higher Nature and unwilling to respond to the Asura, Rakshasa, Pishacha or Animal in the being or to any resistance of the lower nature which stands in the way of the divine change."[275]

---

[275] SABCL Vol. 24; pp.1093-1094

II. THE SPIRITUAL PERFECTION OF
THE TRIPLE BEING

Sri Aurobindo defines the spiritualisation in the following terms,

> "The spiritual change is the established descent of the peace, light, knowledge, power, bliss from above, the awareness of the Self and the Divine and of a higher cosmic consciousness and the change of the whole consciousness to that."[276]

The inward movement opens the triple being to the overhead spiritual plane of consciousness and makes the peace, light, knowledge, power and bliss descend in the lower triple being. It will be a temporary achievement; they may stay and go and this may continue to happen for long, till they are permanently established in the physical-vial-mental complex. When they are established for good in the triple being, its spiritualisation is complete and supramentalisation may follow.

III. THE SUPRAMENTAL PERFECTION OF
THE TRIPLE BEING

1. SUPRAMENTALISATION CAN START ONLY AFTER THE SPIRITUALISATION IS COMPLETE

After the spiritualisation one has to continue to rise upward and not stop at the lid of the overmind. One has to break this luminous lid and enter into the realm of the supramental world. Regarding this stipulation of sadhana, Sri Aurobindo writes,

> "The supramental transformation can only come when the lid between the lower and higher hemispheres or halves of

---

[276] SABCL Vol. 24; p. 1093

existence is removed and the supermind instead of the overmind becomes the governing power of the existence — but of that nothing can be spoken now."[277]

2. THE EFFECTS OF THE SUPRAMENTALISATION ON THE BODY

(i) Describing the supramental change in the body: Sri Aurobindo writes,

"The supramental perfection means that the body becomes conscious, is filled with consciousness and that as this is the Truth-consciousness all its actions, functioning etc. become by the power of the consciousness within it harmonious, luminous, right and true – without ignorance or disorder."[278]

(ii) The Supramental Body of The Mother

During her last years, The Mother started the yoga of supramentalising of her body. She used to report her experiences as they came. Here is one of her experience on March 24, 1972:

"24 March 1972

For the first time, early in the morning, I saw myself, my body – I do not know whether it is the supramental body or... (how to say it?) a body in transition, but I had a body altogether new, in the sense that it was sexless – it was not a women nor was it a man.

It was very white. But it is because my skin is white, I believe, I do not know.

---

[277] SABCL Vol. 24, p. 1093; CWSA Vol. 28, p.305
[278] SABCL Vo. 24; p. 1236

It was very slim *(gesture indicating slenderness)* – it was pretty. Truly a harmonious form.

So it was the first time. I did not know at all. I had no idea of what it would be like, none at all, and I saw – I *was* like that, I had become like that."[279]

The most unique aspect of her sadhana was that she made her mental and vital to retire so as to leave her body completely do sadhana freely on its own. Her lengthy talk of her this effort and achievement is quoted below:

Picture 16.1 THE MOTHER (1969)

---

[279] CWM Vol. 11; p.301

THE MOTHER'S TALK OF 21 DECEMBER 1968[280]

Key Words of the talk:
Mind and vital eliminated
The body left to itself
Rapid reversal of consciousness in the body
Can one body be transformed alone?
Time needed for collective change
Possibility of sudden change
Fragility simultaneous with feeling of eternity
Wonderful moments, hours of suffering

"21 December 1968

> *A question has been put. I translate it: "While describing her experiences of last August and September, the Mother spoke of the exclusion of the mind and the vital. Why must they be eliminated for a rapid and effective transformation of the body? Does not the supramental consciousness act upon them also?"*

Certainly it acts, it has *already* acted for a long time. It is because the body is accustomed — was accustomed — to obeying the vital and particularly the mind, and therefore this was in order to change its habit, so that it would obey only the higher consciousness. It is for that, so that the thing would go faster. In people it is through the mind and the vital that That acts, but I have said it was also more sure. As an experience this is rather risky. But it increases the tempo considerably, for normally one has to act upon the body through the other two, whereas in this way, when the two are not there, That acts directly. That's all.

The procedure is not recommended! Each time the occasion arises, I repeat it; people should not imagine that they should try it (they

---

[280] CWM Vol. 11; pp. 143-147

would not be able to do so, but that does not matter), it is not recommended. One must take the necessary time. It was only because of the mounting years... so that it would go quicker.

(*Silence*)

What is curious is that there are, as it were, demonstrations of the natural tendency of the body (I suppose it is not the same for all bodies: it depends upon how the body has been built, that is to say, father, mother, antecedents, etc.) a demonstration of the body left to itself. For example, this one has a kind of imagination (it is something queer), a dramatic imagination: all the time it has the feeling that it is living through catastrophes; and then, with the faith it always has, the catastrophe is transformed into a realisation — absurd things like that. So for a time, it is left to this imagination (this is what has happened these days) and when it is completely tired of this stupid activity, it prays, yes, with all its intensity, so that the thing may stop. Immediately, just that, hop! It does this (*gesture*), it turns around straightaway and goes into a contemplation — not distant, but quite close — of this wonderful Presence that is everywhere.

It is like this, like this (*Mother quickly turns two fingers*), it does not take time, there is no preparation or anything; it is hop! hop! in this way (*same gesture*), as though to show the stupidity of the body. It is something altogether idiotic, like a demonstration through evidence of the stupidity of the body left to itself, and then of this wonderful Consciousness that comes, in which all that vanishes... like something which has no consistency, no reality, and which vanishes. And like a proof that it is not merely in the imagination, but that it is in the *fact*: proof of the power so that all this... vain dream of life as it is (which has become for the consciousness of this body something so frightful) can be changed into a wonder, like this, simply by the reversal of the consciousness.

The experience is repeated in all the details, in all the domains, as a demonstration through fact. And it is not a "long process" of transformation, it is as though something is reversed all of a sudden

(*Mother turns two fingers*), and instead of seeing ugliness, falsehood, suffering and all that, suddenly it lives in bliss. And all the things are the same, nothing has moved, except the consciousness.

And so there remains (it is what lies in front, what is probably coming): how is the experience to be translated materially? For the body itself, it is quite evident: during, say, one hour, or two or three, it suffered much, it was quite miserable (not a moral suffering, an altogether physical suffering), and then all of a sudden, brrff! all gone!... The body apparently has remained the same (*Mother looks at her hands*) in its appearance, but in place of an inner disorder which makes it suffer, everything is going well and there is a great peace, a great calm, and everything is going well. But this, it is for *one* body — how does it act upon others? It begins to notice the possibility in other consciousnesses. From the moral point of view (that is to say, in respect to attitudes and character and reactions), it is quite visible; even from the physical point of view sometimes: all of a sudden something disappears — as we had the experience when Sri Aurobindo removed a pain (*gesture as if a hand comes and takes away the pain*): one wondered... "Ah! gone, vanished, like that." But it is not constant, not general, it is only to show that it can be so, by the fact that it is so in one case or another, to show that it can be like that.

One might say it in this way: the body has the feeling that it is imprisoned within something — yes, imprisoned — imprisoned as though in a box, but it sees through; it sees and it can also act (in a limited way) through something which is still there and which must disappear. This "something" gives the feeling of an imprisonment. How is it to disappear? That I do not know yet.

One has to find the relation between the consciousness in *one* body and the consciousness of all. And to what extent there is dependence and to what extent there is independence, that is to say, up to what point the body can be transformed in its consciousness (and as a result, necessarily, in its appearance) without... without the transformation of all — up to what point? And to what extent the transformation of all is necessary for the transformation of one body. This remains to be discovered.

(*Silence*)

If one were to tell everything, it would take hours....

But this "box" you spoke of, it is a universal box...

Yes!

I have often had the feeling that all these so-called human laws or "natural" laws are merely an immense morbid imagination collectively fixed — that is the box.

Yes, exactly so, exactly so.

Then, how...

Yes, to what extent can an individual light act upon that?... There is the problem.... I do not know.

(*Silence*)

The vision is very clear, of the collective progress (our field of experience is the earth) that has taken place upon earth; but considering the past, it would seem that a formidable time is still needed for all to be ready to change.... And yet, it is almost a promise that... there is going to be a sudden change (which is translated in our consciousness as a "descent", an action that "happens", something that was not acting till now and which has begun to act — in our consciousness, it is translated in that way) .

We shall see.

For the body itself, there is a growing experience, that is to say, a more and more precise experience *at the same time* of its fragility (extreme fragility: just a little movement could stop the present existence), and at the same time, at the same time, simultaneously, the sense of an eternity! — that there is an eternal existence. The two at the same time.

370

It is truly a period of transition!

(*Silence*)

Once or twice, when the body's... what one might call its agony to know, was very intense, when it had the full sense of the Presence, this sense of the Presence everywhere, inside, everywhere (*Mother touches her face, her hands*), it asked how (not even why, it had no such curiosity), how could there be the present disorder? Well, when it was very intense, very intense, once or twice it had the feeling: once this is found out, it is immortality. Then it begins thus to push, to push in order to catch the secret, it has the feeling that it is going to be found.... And then there is a kind of lull in the aspiration: "Peace, peace, peace..." Yes, once or twice the impression: "Oh! It is about to be understood" ("understood", that is to say, *lived*; it is not "understood" with the thought: lived) and then... (*gesture of escape*). And a Peace which comes down.

But the feeling: it will be tomorrow. But tomorrow, which tomorrow? Not tomorrow according to our measure.

We shall see.

But the experiences are innumerable, with all the aspects. It would take hours and still one always has the feeling that the word, well, falsifies something. It is no longer so simple, no longer so beautiful, and no longer so clear. It becomes complicated.

The body has absolutely wonderful moments; it has *hours* of agony. And all of a sudden, a wonderful moment. But that moment cannot be explained.... If one is to judge the degree of growth by the proportion of time, well... the wonderful moment lasts a few minutes, and there are hours of agony. There are even hours of suffering. And then if one judged the proportion accordingly, it is still very, very, very, extremely far away....

But what is to be done? One has to go on, that is all."

371

3. THE SUPRAMENTAL VITAL

The ordinary vital will be changed by the supramental as described by Sri Aurobindo in the following passage,

"The supermind in its descent into the physical being awakens, if not already wakened by previous yogic sadhana, the consciousness — veiled or obscure in most of us — which supports and forms there the vital sheath, the *prāṇa koṣa*. When this is awakened, we no longer live in the physical body alone, but also in a vital body which penetrates and envelops the physical and is sensitive to impacts of another kind, to the play of the vital forces around us and coming in on us from the universe or from particular persons or group lives or from things or else from the vital planes and worlds which are behind the material universe. These impacts we feel even now in their result and in certain touches and affectations, but not at all or very little in their source and their coming. An awakened consciousness in the pranic body immediately feels them, is aware of a pervading vital force other than the physical energy, and can draw upon it to increase the vital strength and support the physical energies, can deal directly with the phenomena and causes of health and disease by means of this vital influx or by directing pranic currents, can be aware of the vital and the vital-emotional atmosphere of others and deal with its interchanges, along with a host of other phenomena which are unfelt by or obscure to our outward consciousness but here become conscient and sensible. It is acutely aware of the life soul and life body in ourself and others. The supermind takes up this vital consciousness and vital sense, puts it on its right foundation and transforms it by revealing the life-force here as the very power of the spirit dynamised for a near and direct operation on and through subtle and gross matter and for formation and action in the material universe.

The first result is that the limitations of our individual life being break down and we live no longer with a personal life force, or not with that ordinarily, but in and by the universal life energy. It is all the universal Prana that comes consciently streaming into and through us, keeps up there a dynamic constant eddy, an unseparated centre of its power, a vibrant station of storage and communication, constantly fills it with its forces and pours them out in activity upon the world around us. This life energy, again, is felt by us not merely as a vital ocean and its streams, but as the vital way and form and body and outpouring of a conscious universal Shakti, and that conscient Shakti reveals itself as the Chit Shakti of the Divine, the Energy of the transcendent and universal Self and Purusha of which — or rather of whom — our universalised individuality becomes an instrument and channel. As a result we feel ourselves one in life with all others and one with the life of all Nature and of all things in the universe. There is a free and conscious communication of the vital energy working in us with the same energy working in others. We are aware of their life as of our own or, at the least, of the touch and pressure and communicated movements of our life being on them and theirs upon us. The vital sense in us becomes powerful, intense, and capable of bearing all the small or large, minute or immense vibrations of this life world on all its planes physical and supraphysical, vital and supravital, thrills with all its movement and Ananda and is aware of and open to all forces. The supermind takes possession of all this great range of experience, and makes it all luminous, harmonious, experienced not obscurely and fragmentarily and subject to the limitations and errors of its handling by the mental ignorance, but revealed, it and each movement of it, in its truth and totality of power and delight, and directs the great and now hardly limitable powers and capacities of the life dynamis on all its ranges according to the simple and yet complex, the sheer and spontaneous and yet unfalteringly intricate will of the Divine in our life. It makes the vital sense a perfect means of the knowledge of the life forces around us, as the physical of the forms and sensations of the physical universe, and a perfect channel too of the reactions of the active life force through us working as an instrument of self-manifestation."[281]

4. THE SUPERMIND OR SUPRAMENTALISED MIND

Sri Aurobindo says,

"The gnosis is the effective principle of the Spirit, a **highest dynamis of the spiritual existence.** The gnostic individual would be the consummation of the spiritual man; his whole way of being, thinking, living, acting would be governed by the power of a vast universal spirituality. All the trinities of the Spirit would be real to his self-awareness and realised in his inner life. All his existence would be fused into oneness with the transcendent and universal Self and Spirit; all his action would originate from and obey the supreme Self and Spirit's divine governance of Nature. All life would have to him the sense of the Conscious Being, the Purusha within, finding its self-expression in Nature; his life and all its thoughts, feelings, acts would be filled for him with that significance and built upon that foundation of its reality. He would feel the presence of the Divine in every centre of his consciousness, in every vibration of his life-force, in every cell of his body. In all the workings of his force of Nature he would be aware of the workings of the supreme World-Mother, the Supernature; he would see his natural being as the becoming and manifestation of the power of the World-Mother. In this consciousness he would live and act in an entire transcendent freedom, a complete joy of the spirit, an entire identity with the cosmic self and a spontaneous sympathy with all in the universe. All beings would be to him his own selves, all ways and powers of consciousness would be felt as the ways and powers of his own universality. But in that inclusive universality there would be no bondage to inferior forces, no deflection from his own highest truth: for this truth would envelop all truth of things and keep each in its own place, in a relation of diversified harmony, — it would not admit any

---

[281] SABCL Vol. 21; pp. 841-842

confusion, clash, infringing of boundaries, any distortion of the different harmonies that constitute the total harmony. His own life and the world life would be to him like a perfect work of art; it would be as if the creation of a cosmic and spontaneous genius infallible in its working out of a multitudinous order. The gnostic individual would be in the world and of the world, but would also exceed it in his consciousness and live in his self of transcendence above it; he would be universal but free in the universe, individual but not limited by a separative individuality. The true Person is not an isolated entity, his individuality is universal; for he individualises the universe: it is at the same time divinely emergent in a spiritual air of transcendental infinity, like a high cloud-surpassing summit; for he individualises the divine Transcendence."[282]

SUMMARY

I. Psychicisation and spiritualisation are two different things, though they are complimentary to each other. Psychic change comes from within, but spiritual change comes from above. Psychicisation must precede the spiritualisation. Psychicisation establishes right movements in the triple being.

II. Spiritualisation establishes spiritual peace, love, power and knowledge in the outer being.

III. Supramentalisation makes activities of the triple being harmonious, true and right. The Mother has visioned her supramental body, which was sexless and luminous and very white. Supramental vital is moved by the Divine vital force and not by personal vital force. The supramental mind will see the Divine everywhere. The supramental mind moves by the Truth-consciousness.

---

[282] SABCL Vol. 19; pp. 971-973

Suggestions for Further Reading

1. SABCL Vol. 24; pp. 1091-1242
2. SABCL Vol. 21; Chapters XXI-XXV
3. SABCL Vol. 19; Chapters XXIII-XXVIII
4. K. D. Acharya; Guide to Sri Aurobindo's Philosophy (Divya Jivan Sahitya Prakashan, Pondicherry, 005002, India; 1968)
5. Sri Aurobindo and The Mother; On Education (Sri Aurobindo Ashram, Pondicherry, 605002, India): pages 121-131 are on Psychic and Spiritual Transformation.
6. CWM Vol. 12; pp. 28-36

WORKBOOK: QUESTIONS FOR PREVIEW AND REVIEW

Essay Type Questions

1. Describe the psychicisation of the triple being.
2. Describe the spiritualisation of the triple being.
3. Describe the supramentalisation of the triple being.

Short Answer Type Questions

1. Compare psychicisation and spiritualisation.
2. What are the effects of supramental transformation on the body?
3. State a few characteristics of supramentalised vital.
4. State a few characteristics of supramentalised mental-vital.

SELF TEST

1. What is the difference between psychicisation and spiritualisation?
2. State two changes that psychicisation can make in the personality.
3. Define spiritualisation.
4. _____ should precede _____. (psychicisation, spiritualisation)
5. The supramental is _____ consciousness.

CHAPTER XVII

INTEGRAL PSYCHOLOGY OF HOTEL MANAGEMENT: HOTEL BUSINESS FOR INTEGRAL DEVELOPMENT: A FUTURISTIC IDEAL AND PROJECT FOR LIFE DIVINE ON EARTH

Auromere's unitary theory of consciousness explains and is practicable in all areas of life. Here an attempt is made to suggest how it can be practiced in the social field of hotel business.

I. THE AIM AND FOUR DEVELOPMENTAL PROCESSES OF INTEGRAL PSYCHOLOGY

We have noted in previous chapters **that integral psychology aims** not only at the liberation of the soul from the triple nature but also at the liberation of nature, a physical-vital-mental complex, from the clutches of its own imperfection, the ignorance. The cardinal and ultimate aim of Integral Psychology is to help human nature to progressively transform itself into divine nature ultimately and realise a divine society on the divine earth in the divine universe. **Four developmental processes** of the Rationalization, Psychicisation, Spiritualisation and Supramentalisation of nature are the four significant and basic wheels that have to be gradually more and more developed, realised and fixed in the chariot of life for the journey towards divinisation that ends at the Gate of the Resort of The Divine Kingdom; The Heavenly Divine Being will also become the Earthly Divine Being. God and human both thus will cancel the debt that they owe to each other, the debt that Sri Aurobindo has referred to in his magnum Opus, the epic poem, Savitri.

II. THE SYNTHETIC PRACTICE OF RATIONAL KNOWLEDGE AND PSYCHIC-SPIRITUAL WISDOM IS NECESSARY FOR REALISATION OF THE SUPREME LIGHT

Reason is the highest manifest consciousness force of the human in his present make up. And it must be the controller of life, until the **psychic** is realised and assumes the leadership of life. Sri Aurobindo has cautioned that a sadhak of integral discipline should not end the rule of reason till the psychic takes over the reins of life in its own hand. So, scientific wisdom, which is the product of the logical mind, must also be practiced along with the psychic-spiritual knowledge by the individual and all organised groups of which he is a member. Our ancient forefathers of Vedic times knew this paramount truth of psychological development. Rishi of Upanishad says, those who practice spiritual science [*Vidya*] *only*, enter into the darkness and those who practice *only Avidya*, walk into greater darkness; both need to be synthesised and practiced. **This is the psychology of the Upanishads.**

III. A HOTEL CAN BE A VENUE FOR INTEGRAL DEVELOPMENT OF THE CONSCIOUSNESS

1. An Environment of Beauty and Development of Vital Consciousness

(i) **Material, Social and Psychic-Spiritual Beauty and harmony in the environment:** A hotel must not neglect the science in its physical and social organisation. Its structure, apartments, departments and all other aspects should reflect the ideals of science of architecture and aesthesis. Beauty and harmony are attributes of Mahalakshmi Mother and these forces must be made to exist in the business precincts, for they have appeal to the inner heart and soul and all niceties in the nature of man. Consciousness of a guest would perceive and feel *the beauty and harmony in the physical structure* and the deeper soul qualities will be aroused in him. It will be an occasion for education of the senses and refinement of the emotions and nourishment of the vital being, for as The **Upanishad** says, *art and beauty are food for Prana, the vital, ideas are food for mind and Anna, Eatables, are food for the body...* The *material beauty must be* *augmented by ornamenting it with green and flowery living beauties.* The organisational group of a hotel, including the entrepreneur, the owner/s, must try constantly to be a harmonious cohesive inward and upward looking happy and relaxed yet diligent collective force, that would be a positive dynamic social atmosphere, a **social environmental beauty**[283] influencing the shifting aggregated collectivity of customers. These beauties must be topped and crowned with the enculturing **environment of psychic and spiritual beauty**, discussion about which follows after a few paragraphs.

(ii) Vegetation and Garden and Pots of Flowers: Flower has generally psychic consciousness. Its fragrance and colours and shapes and psychic aura around it create soft feelings, feeling of peace, love and goodwill for all, generosity, forgiveness, gratitude and attitude of inwardness and upwardness. All these influences gradually sublimate the gross vulgar aspects of the emotional vital and soften and refine grossness and aggressiveness of desires and the behaviours of sexual love and need of sensational pleasures by infusing psychic and spiritual colours in the physical-vital-mental consciousness. These influences of the consciousness of flowers thus enhance beauty and harmony of the human consciousness and of the environmental social and of the universal consciousness. Thus, it has a driving force that pushes towards Psychicisation and spiritualisation of the persons working in the hotel and the customers or guests that visit it and the overall general atmosphere.

A hotel and a business must be set into a sort of "Forest Garden: *Udyan Van* – as it is called in Bangalore, Karnataka, India". For evolved greenery and flowers have a definite beneficial evolutionary influence on evolving human consciousness and universal consciousness and vice versa. The interior should also accommodate suitable pots of flowers and herbs at suitable spots in every nook and corner and passage and in

---

[283] Ms. Joanna Zweig CEO, Ph.D., PMP; Organises Workshop for Developing Collective Consciousness in the Organisational Groups that enables them to put up team work harmoniously. [Email: hodajsz@gmail.com]

all rooms and halls. Even the exterior of the building, terraces and walls must be adorned with suitable green and colourful ornamentation of herbs, creepers and flowers.

According to The Mother, greeneries not only provide pure vital nourishment but also refine and strengthen the vital and physical of the man, for the flowers have very subtle effects.

The fragrance, beauty and tenderness of flowers do have nourishing effects on the consciousness of man. The beauty of their colour, shape, aura and fragrance have relaxing effects on the nerves and mind, soothing effects on emotion, and refining effects on sensational consciousness. This induces a gentle calm and almost imperceptible blissfulness in the heart and psychicises and diminishes the pathetic feeling of sadness by infusing soothing tenderness in it. The fragrances and extracted essences of flowers are now used for therapeutic purposes also. The medical science of Aromatherapy has been developed. Apart from its psychological and medicinal physical significance flowers have psychic and spiritual significances also. Ancient wise people had this knowledge and it was passed on by each generation to following generation. But the knowledge was restricted to limited number of flowers. Now, The Mother has identified, using her power of direct knowledge, significances of flowers and her knowledge is documented in books and visual media. For example, flower Black Bean [botanical name: *Castanospermum australe*], according to her knowledge, signifies "Mind of Light Acting in Matter, a powerful aid to progress;"[284] cream white *Leucaena leucocephala* signifies "Knowledge": It is conversant with all sides of a question, whatever it may be[285]. They do have transforming influence on perceiving human consciousness depending on their significance and receptivity of the perceiver.

---

[284] Anand K. C. (Editor); What is Light, Reprint of All India Magazine (Pradeep Narang, Sri Aurobindo Society, Puducherry, 605 002); p. 10

[285] Anand K. C. (Editor); The Four Austerities and Four Liberations, Reprint of All India Magazine (Pradeep Narang , Sri Aurobindo Society, Puducherry, 605 002); p. 16

Dr. Vandana[286] has developed flower remedies based on the significances given to flowers by The Mother; she is busy doing systematic researches in the field for over more than fifteen years. She has experimented upon herself and others. Some of her findings are noted here in her own words, "I started using …four drops four times a day… Peace in the cell *Ixora thwaitesii (white)*. A few days later I noticed a change within me. The mucus in the stomach had increased and my mind was free of conflicting thoughts…The sleep had increased and was more restful….Then someone came with arthritis. He said his joint pains were severe. There was the impression that he had lost enthusiasm in life. I gave him Integral Immortality (*Gomphrena globosa*). He came back a week later; no joint pains and full of life."

Statues, pictures, photos, hanging chandeliers, chairs, tables, sofas and all other articles should be pieces of beauty and not merely utility materials devoid of grace and beauty of the form and should have a suitable reasonable placement so as to blend into a pageant of beauty. Music and entertainment programmes of arts are nourishments for the vital; they must be judiciously integrated in the spread of the hotel life.

2. An Environment for Development of Physical Consciousness

Healthy food [Anna], Gymnasium, swimming pool, workshops and guidance for aquatics, exercises and other physical exercises are the facilities for physical development. Workshops like "Body Bliss: Anandamaya Kosha"[287], that aims at infusing and developing higher body-consciousness, may be given priority for the physical education of the staff, guests as well as the public on payment.

---

[286] Vandana Gupta (Dr.); "Flower remedies based on the significances given to flowers by The Mother"; N*amah (Medical Research Magazine published by Sri Aurobindo International Institute for Integral Health and Research (SAIIIHR), Sri Aurobindo Ashram, Puducherry, 605 002)*

[287] "Body Bliss" exercises are findings of Ms. Gaia Mitra, Sri Aurobindo Sadhana Peetham, 2621 West Highway 12, Lodi, CA, 95242, USA; Phone: +1-209-339-1342 Ext. 103; Website: sasp.collaboration.org

3. An Environment for Development of Mental Consciousness

Mini library cum reading room cum silence room that serves as a place for reflection and mediation and for sitting with oneself and with the divine may help residents to develop their mind and soul, the psychic being. The hotel may have a bookshop, like the "Nalanda" bookshop of the Taj Mahal Palace hotel in Colaba, Mumbai, India, for the sale of books about high level culture and civilization. A Visitor room or front lobby, where people can seat for a while, may have good magazines on the tables.

4. An Environment for Developing Interest in the Ideal of Psychic-spiritual and supramental consciousness and life

A few selected books may be placed in the drawers of the rooms. Magazines published by Sri Aurobindo Ashram and other Sri Aurobindo and The Mother's organisations may be placed in the waiting areas and in the silent room library. Educational programmes may be made available on payment to guests and the public. An atmosphere of peace and calm must be maintained. Selection of staff may be made keeping in mind these criteria also.

5. An Environment for Developing International Consciousness and International Spirit

All aspects of a hotel must be an assortment of international elements. Workshops like the one called "Awakening to the Soul of Your Country and The World"[288] may be made available to the guests, the public and the staff.

Let us hope that the entrepreneurs and managers will act in right earnest and with due speed and will not keep the future waiting long.

---

[288] Organised by Soleil and Wolfgang J. Schmidt-Reinecke; Email: wjsr@gmx.net; Websites: sunwolfcreations.com; www.soulofnations.com/soul-of-nations---workshop

SUMMARY

Hotel business may organise its physical, vital, mental and psychic-spiritual consciousness and provide an environment rich in beauty, love, light, joy, and harmony for its own profit and for the benefit of the society and higher evolution of itself and the society. It should aim at nothing less than progressive upward evolution and ultimate divinization of the individual, the society and the universe.

WORKBOOK: QUESTIONS FOR PREVIEW AND REVIEW

Essay Type Questions

1. Hotels provide comfort to physical and vital. The general belief is that. How far is this true? Discuss in the light of the integral hotel psychology and the current state of hotels.
2. Write one essay on each of the following subjects:
   - (i) Organisation of a room that provides an integral environment for the integral enculturation of the guest.
   - (ii) How can international culture be created in the kitchen, dining hall, and social life of the guests?

Exercises

Observe a hotel and find out and write a short report on how it meets the various needs of the guests and what improvements are needed according to your judgement.

SELF TEST

1. Only spiritual knowledge is needed for perfection of man and society. (True or false)
2. A nice garden around a hotel is very necessary. Why?
3. For development of _____ of the guests a _____ hall is necessary in a hotel.

Chapter XVIII

SUMMARY AND CONCLUSION

I. SUMMARY OF THE FINDINGS

[Sri Aurobindo's Integral Psychology of Human Being]

The Free Progress System of education is based on Sri Aurobindo's integral psychology of human being. Sri Aurobindo's psychology can be deemed as a science of consciousness. In nature, it is a compound of science and metaphysical knowledge. Its method is that of his integral *yoga*. His psychology is called integral, because its field, aim and method are integral and it is all-inclusive. According to the researcher, it can be called a global psychology also.

According to Sri Aurobindo, consciousness is fundamental to existence, and it has many grades. Man is also a form of consciousness and his consciousness has many planes. According to Sri Aurobindo's theory of terrestrial evolution, out of the inconscient (nescient), the subconscient and the matter first appeared. From the matter the vital and living physical beings have evolved, and from the vital, the mind and the thinking living being, the man has evolved. From the mind, the supramental should be manifested. Thus, the man as a man is a transitional being.

The Inconscient: The Inconscient is thus the basis of the man and his world. The lowest part of man's consciousness is the subconscient. Above the subconscient is the conscient, the subliminal, the psychic, and the environmental consciousness. Above this is the spiritual consciousness. Above the spiritual consciousness is the supramental consciousness and then the *Sachchidananda* consciousness.

385

The Sub-conscient: The sub-conscient of man is automatic, obscure, incoherent and a half-consciousness realm. It stores every conscious experience as obscure impressions and everything rejected by the conscient. It sends out of its stuff anything in disguised manner into the conscient and the subliminal.

The Conscient: The conscient part of man consists of three levels: the physical, the vital and the mental. Inertia, indolence, resistance to higher consciousness, greed for physical comforts are the negative qualities of the physical. But it can also be a docile servant of the mind and the vital. The body is a part of it. The body has its sure instinct which can guide it in all its matters perfectly, if the mind and the vital do not interfere. The body is prone to illness, decay and death, but it can be made strong, fit, dexterous, plastic and responsive to higher consciousness by education. It can be perfected beyond imagination. The vital consciousness is the seat of sensations, feelings, emotions and impulses. Meditation and the force of the vital is indispensable for any work and progress, including spiritual progress. So, it should be perfected and put under the control of the mind and the higher consciousness. The mental consciousness has to do with ideas, reasoning, judgments, cognitions, etc. These three parts of man are always at war with one another. There is a constant conflict in each of these planes also. To harmonise them is the first main problem for man. The reason, at the most, can establish a precarious state of peace among them and control them but cannot establish lasting harmony. For that, one has to turn inward.

The Inner Consciousness: The Subliminal: The subliminal consists of the inner physical, the inner vital and the inner mental. They are far more wide and powerful than their outer counterparts. When one opens to them, the outer parts get enlarged. By going there one can develop subtle senses. But the subliminal cannot establish harmony among the outer physical, vital and mental complex. For that one has to reach the psychic.

The Psychic: It is the real "I" and direct representative of the Divine in man. If it is allowed to come forward or allowed to work, it can harmonise the outer physical, vital and mental and can open them to the spiritual consciousness and ultimately lead the earthly man towards the supramental. So, the realisation of it is the first goal of man.

The Spiritual Consciousness: It is a part of our mind but superconscient to it. It has four mind planes: the higher mind, the illumined mind, the intuitive mind and the over-mind. All genuinely inspired writings come from this domain. When one rises into it, his spiritualization starts. All his consciousness becomes full of calm, anand, light, etc. But this consciousness cannot transform the man. For that he must rise to the supramental consciousness.

The Supramental Consciousness: It is entirely a different consciousness. And it has got the power to divinise the physical, the vital and the mental. Integral perfection of man — the mundane, psychic, spiritual and supramental perfection — is the goal of human life according to the integral psychology. The psychology has also given a method called *Purnayoga,* to realize the goal. The free progress system of education evolved at the S.A.I.C.E. endeavours to apply the integral psychology to the educational field and lead the student towards the psychic and ultimately to the supramental.

II. THE CONCLUSION

Sri Aurobindo's integral psychology gives a complete description of the consciousness-structure of the human being.

INDEX OF NAMES

INDEX OF SUBJECTS

Introduction of the Book

This book reports the first Ph.D. level study of Sri Auromere's Integral Psychology and the System of Integral Education being developed at Sri Aurobindo International Centre of Education and first report of application of Integral Psychology in the field of abnormal behaviours.

The book contains the description and evaluation of validity of evolutionary integral theory and praxis of Sri Aurobindo and The Mother's (Sri Auromere's) psychology in the background of the partial knowledge of scientific psychology, which, in fact deserves the name "mentology" and not the name "psychology", for, the scientific psychology studies only mental consciousness, rather only part of mind, with only rational methods of research, while integral psychology studies all parts of human being (mental-vital-physical, Psychic, spiritual, supramental and universal consciousness of man) and employs rational as well as super-rational methods of knowledge.

This study report describes the genesis of the universe, earth, living beings and the human species through the Natural (*Prakritik*) process of involution and evolution. Evolution has been explained in the light of phenomena of ten incarnations on earth.

It identifies three types of heredity and eleven types of environments that determine the evolutionary development of man in the universe. It delineates developmental goals, principles and processes of consciousness evolution of normal as well as abnormal behaviours of man and man's environmental worlds and describes (as models to be followed for integral studies in other fields of study) what type of organisational environment should be created in a school and a hotel to help man and the society to evolve into spiritual and supramental consciousness, the ultimate stage of evolution. It provides a complete description of the ongoing experiment of creation of educational environment in Sri Aurobindo International Centre of Education with evaluation of the success achieved. Likert-type rating scale had been constructed by the author for this evaluation. The author has also shown the paramount importance of integral psychology for individual, social, national, international and universal ultimate evolutionary transformation.

www.ingramcontent.com/pod-product-compliance
Lightning Source LLC
Chambersburg PA
CBHW041929260326
41914CB00009B/1225